CORRECTIVE EXERCISE

A Practical Approach

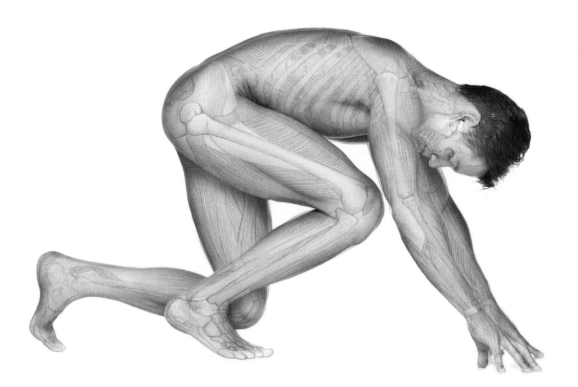

CORRECTIVE EXERCISE

A Practical Approach

Kesh Patel

Hodder Arnold

A MEMBER OF THE HODDER HEADLINE GROUP

Orders: please contact Bookpoint Ltd, 130 Milton Park, Abingdon, Oxon OX14 4SB. Telephone: (44) 01235 827720. Fax: (44) 01235 400454. Lines are open from 9.00–6.00, Monday to Saturday, with a 24 hour message answering service. You can also order through our website www.hoddereducation.co.uk

If you have any comments to make about this, or any of our other titles, please send them to educationenquiries@hodder.co.uk

British Library Cataloguing in Publication Data
A catalogue record for this title is available from the British Library

ISBN-10: 0 340 88932 2
ISBN-13: 978 0 340 88932 9

First Published 2005

Impression number   10 9 8 7 6 5 4 3 2 1
Year   2009 2008 2007 2006 2005

Hodder Headline's policy is to use papers that are natural, renewable and recyclable products and made fromwood grown in sustainable forests. The logging and manufacturing processes are expected to conform to the environmental regulations of the country of origin.

Cover photograph by Corbis. Artwork by Barking Dog Art. Internal photographs by James Newell. Internal artwork by Apple Agency. Typeset by Phoenix Photosetting, Chatham, Kent. Printed in Great Britain for Hodder Arnold, an imprint of Hodder Education, a member of the Hodder Headline Group, 338 Euston Road, London NW1 3BH by Arrowsmith, Bristol.

To my wife, Suzanne, and my daughter, Maya India, who continue to enlighten me, and have taught me to live in the moment and enjoy the sanctuary of unconditional love.

CONTENTS

ACKNOWLEDGEMENTS

It's impossible to adequately acknowledge and thank the many people who contributed to the development of this book.

I am especially indebted to Suzanne Patel, having been the lucky beneficiary of her wise editorial comments and relentless motivation in maintaining the books momentum.

A special acknowledgment goes to the team at Hodder Education, and in particular, Matthew Smith, for his guidance and support throughout the development of this book.

I would like to thank all the osteopaths, chiropractors, physiotherapists, sports therapists, personal trainers and massage therapists, that I have worked with, and who continue to keep me on my toes. To all the students I have taught over the years - the old dog has learned a few of your new tricks.

My heartfelt appreciation goes to all the wonderful clients that I have worked with over the years, who have opened up my understanding of the many facets of health. They have taught me that when you're headed in the right direction, you'll know it's right, because you're sure enough to be unsure, but never unsure enough to not do it.

I am especially thankful for the knowledge and wisdom of the many innovative health educators involved in the field of integrated health; in particular, the extraordinary Paul Chek whose work and philosophy continues to inspire me.

Finally, I would like to acknowledge the creative and inspiring work of Richard Bandler and the late Moshe Feldenkrais – who have taught me that in order to change the way we move, think and feel, we must first change the image of ourselves that we carry within us.

LIST OF FIGURES

LIST OF TABLES

PREFACE
A HISTORY OF CORRECTIVE EXERCISE

The concept of using exercise as a therapeutic tool is by no means a new one. As far back as the early nineteenth century, structured exercise was being used for the treatment of sedentary lifestyles, in the form of group gymnastics. By the turn of the twentieth century, the forward-thinking work of Eustace Miles and Eugene Sandow inspired many prominent physiologists and physicians to become interested in the use of exercise as a therapeutic modality. The extensive use of anthropometric measurements at the time introduced evaluation protocol into the exercise arena.

As the mid-twentieth century approached, the growing acceptance of the psychological benefits of exercise led to the introduction of mind-body exercise systems. The work of prominent physical educators, such as Frederick Mathias Alexander, Moshe Feldenkrais, Joseph Pilates and Milton Trager, was instrumental in this development. Largely provoked by their own personal experience of major illness or musculoskeletal impairment, they recognised the intimate relationship between physical fitness and pathology. Fundamental to their approach was an explicit understanding of human movement and how it relates to efficient functioning of the body. These concepts were further supported by the work of Rudolf Laban and Irmgard Bartenieff. Exercise was becoming recognised as a therapeutic tool within the context of physical rehabilitation and the foundations for the field of corrective exercise were being laid.

Today's modern and often sedentary lifestyle has reduced the need for spontaneous and functional movement, resulting in a multitude of musculoskeletal dysfunctions. The increased popularity and use of gyms has motivated many back into the exercise arena. Combined with the growing responsibility that individuals are taking for their own health, this has stimulated increased interest in exercise as a therapeutic tool. As a result there has been a merging of knowledge from the disciplines of rehabilitation and exercise. The field of corrective exercise bridges the gap between pure rehabilitation and exercise science.

1 An Introduction to Corrective Exercise

1
A PRACTICAL APPROACH TO CORRECTIVE EXERCISE

One of the most challenging areas of musculoskeletal rehabilitation is the identification of the weakest link: successful treatment of this link can have a wide-reaching effect throughout the whole body. The concept of using exercise as a therapeutic tool is by no means a new one. Musculoskeletal dysfunction is commonly caused by biomechanical weakness. With this in mind, the use of exercise to correct dysfunction is an interesting approach to rehabilitation. When exercise training is structured and integrated correctly, using a multifaceted approach, it can help the client to achieve, maintain and enhance their rehabilitative goals, often without the need for other intervention. A well-devised corrective exercise programme can enhance muscle performance, decrease the severity of injury, decrease the risk of re-injury and accelerate recovery and return to activity. Long-term solutions should focus not only on correcting the root cause of the problem, but also on teaching optimal movement patterns, for lifelong health and function.

Evaluation and programme design are at the heart of successful corrective exercise. This book presents a practical approach to corrective exercise in a systematic order, as illustrated in Figure 1.1.

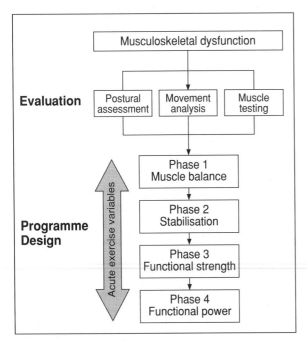

Figure 1.1. A systematic and practical approach to corrective exercise

Evaluation

The evaluation procedure seeks to uncover the root cause of dysfunction. This process requires an understanding of posture, movement and muscle testing, as well as a degree of therapeutic skill. Identifying the mechanical cause of musculoskeletal dysfunction is an important objective in correcting a problem and alleviating pain.

Failure to identify faulty postural alignment and muscle imbalance patterns often slows progression of an otherwise well-planned corrective exercise programme.

Although evaluation procedures may be performed in isolation, the full biomechanical status of an individual will be best determined by collation and interpretation of all data, while taking into account the unique individuality of the client.

Evaluation of the kinetic chain starts with an examination of static posture, with the aim of identifying any underlying muscle imbalances. This is a practical starting point for evaluation as it gives an overall idea of muscle function. The principles of overall postural assessment are outlined in Chapter 2, with more specific details of correct and faulty alignment being explored in the relevant sections.

The second step in evaluation involves movement analysis. This can offer the therapist a significant quantity of information relating to muscle recruitment and the presence of compensatory movement patterns. Knowledge of the building blocks of functional movement is crucial to interpreting the results of these tests and subsequent exercise prescription. Chapter 3 discusses the principles of movement and how these can be used to assess a client's lifestyle. Combining this knowledge with specific movement tests given later in the book will help to build a bespoke exercise programme.

Testing muscle function is the final step in the evaluation and adds to previous findings. The principles of muscle testing, as well as practical considerations, are outlined in Chapter 4. Specific tests for muscle length and strength are outlined in the relevant chapters.

Programme design

The importance of programme design cannot be overstated. Not all exercises can be recommended for everyone, and specific exercises are performed in different ways by different people. Exercises should always be adapted to the client's needs and performed correctly under good initial supervision.

It is necessary to design programmes that are flexible and progressive. An approach should be developed that will address the needs of the individual, yet also take into account the results of the evaluation. Exercise should also be functional to the client – that is, particular to the unique demands of their occupational, recreational or sporting environment.

Corrective exercise training should focus primarily on restoring muscle balance: if optimal balance is not achieved, any existing muscle imbalance may be increased further by exercise. Stability, functional strength and power development can then progress in accordance with the client's rehabilitation objectives.

The basis for exercise progression in this book focuses on the attainment of four specific objectives:

1 muscle balance
2 stability
3 functional strength
4 functional power.

These objectives are based on an understanding of exercise periodisation principles. As such, they will allow individuals of any ability to meet the objectives of rehabilitation and performance. Details of each of these phases are discussed in Chapter 5.

Successful exercise prescription is dependent on the manipulation of a number of acute exercise variables. It is necessary to select exercises that will be most beneficial to the client with regard to their needs and develop these exercises through effective management of load, repetitions, timing and recovery. This process should take place within a structured framework that involves systematic progression. As well as introducing the principles of programme design, Chapter 5 also discusses how exercise variables can be successfully managed to allow progression.

The body as an integrated system

The body is made up of a number of moving parts, or links, which are often referred to collectively as the kinetic chain. The kinetic chain is made up of three systems (see Figure 1.2):

1 the active (or muscular) system
2 the passive (or articular) system
3 the control (or neural) system.

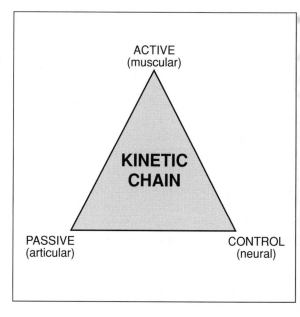

Figure 1.2. The kinetic chain

The optimal function of the kinetic chain is dependent on the integration of these mechanisms into an infinite number of reactions that produce movement. During movement there is distinct separation of the kinetic chain into three structural systems:

1 the shoulders
2 the trunk
3 the pelvis, hips and knees.

Dysfunction in any part of these structures can manifest as neuromuscular or musculoskeletal problems. Understanding the functional anatomy and biomechanics of these body systems is important. Parts 2, 3 and 4 provide an overview that will lay a foundation for effective exercise prescription.

Corrective Exercise: A Practical Approach offers all sports therapists, personal trainers and bodywork specialists a chance to build on and integrate their own knowledge and background into the context of corrective exercise, with the objective of achieving optimal neuromuscular and musculoskeletal health and performance. This book provides a unique perspective on the role of corrective exercise as an effective and practical therapeutic modality.

2
PRINCIPLES OF POSTURAL ASSESSMENT

Introduction

Optimal posture is part of habitual well-being, involving sound skeletal structure, soft-tissue integrity and proper neuromuscular control. The unique upright stance exhibited by humans creates specific functional demands on the musculoskeletal system during all daily activities. Even though the human body assumes many postures, it does not hold any of them for a significant amount of time, although certain characteristic and habitual postural patterns may become evident over a period of time.

Standing posture creates a closed kinetic chain, involving the body's three main support structures: the neck and shoulders; the trunk; and the pelvis, hips and knees. Forces are transmitted between the links of this chain in such a way that problems arising in one system can (and invariably do) affect other systems. With gravitational force being a significant factor in influencing human posture, any weight-bearing position in sitting, standing and gait can contribute to continuous stress and strain on the supporting structures. Changes in the length of muscles and/or connective tissue may subsequently result in diminished motion control, leading to faulty postural alignment and movement patterns. When this occurs, corrective exercise can be a useful tool in restoring muscle balance, via specific stretching and strengthening of the appropriate muscles.

Muscle recruitment in standing posture

Clinical evaluation of static posture requires the body to be in a standing, weight-bearing position. In optimal alignment the muscular effort required to hold this position is minimal, with most of the support coming from the body's ligamentous structures. The active muscles are generally anti-gravity muscles, which control postural sway in the sagittal and frontal planes within the three support systems. These are described below.

Neck and shoulders

There is slight activity in the neck flexors and extensors, depending on the degree of posterior and anterior postural sway, respectively. The upper trapezius, serratus anterior and supraspinatus also show some activity in supporting the shoulder girdle.

Trunk

During anterior postural sway, there is increased activity of the paraspinal muscles; during posterior sway, there is slight activity in the abdominals. Lateral sway may also produce some activity in the lateral trunk flexors.

Pelvis, hips and knees

The iliopsoas is continually active in standing posture to maintain pelvic and hip alignment. Postural sway produces phasic bursts of activity in the gluteus medius and tensor fasciae latae, as well as activity in the quadriceps and hamstrings. In the leg, the gastrocnemius and tibialis anterior are responsible for the control of sagittal plane postural sway.

Ideal alignment

Ideal skeletal alignment is a position in which there is minimal stress and strain on the body's support systems, and which is conducive to optimal movement and efficiency of the body. In reality, this alignment is represented by an erect and well-balanced head position, normal spinal curvatures, a neutral position of the pelvis and alignment of the lower extremities for weight bearing. It is important to note that optimal balance of the spine's normal curves contributes significantly to healthy posture.

Observation of posture

The common and most effective way to observe posture is from a lateral view. Figure 2.1 shows ideal alignment from a lateral view. When viewing posture laterally, the line of reference is located in the mid-frontal plane. Since the only fixed point in standing posture is where the feet make contact with the floor, the line of reference begins here, at a position slightly anterior to the lateral malleolus. There are a number of useful

surface and anatomical landmarks that coincide with the plumb line in the lateral view to assist in postural observation.

Posture should also be observed from an anterior and posterior view, with a plumb line being used as a fixed line of reference. When viewing posture anteriorly or posteriorly, the plumb line is positioned in the mid-sagittal plane, beginning midway between the heels and continuing through the middle of the pelvis, spine and skull. Table 2.1 gives details of optimal alignment of major landmarks in the sagittal and frontal planes.

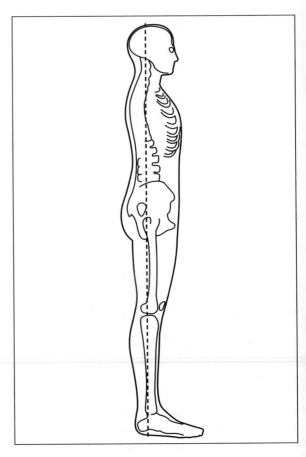

Figure 2.1. Ideal plumb alignment – lateral view

Table 2.1. Ideal standing alignment

Landmark(s)	Optimal alignment in standing
Feet	The longitudinal arch is dome-shaped and is not low or flat; the feet are toed out slightly (approximately 10°); in heeled shoes, the feet are parallel; weight should be central over arches and borne evenly between left and right feet.
Knees and legs	Legs are straight (not knock-kneed or bow-legged); forward-facing patella; laterally, the knees are not flexed or hyperextended.
Hips, pelvis and spine (posterior view)	Left and right posterior superior iliac spine are level (and anterior superior iliac spine, anteriorly); spine does not curve to the left or right; the hips are not rotated; shoulders are level (although the right shoulder may be slightly low and right hip slightly high in right-handed individuals, and vice versa for left-handed).
Hips, pelvis and spine (lateral view)	The buttocks are not prominent; abdomen should be flat in adults; the four natural curves of the spine should be evident (lordosis in the cervical and lumbar regions and kyphosis in the thoracic and sacral regions); there should not be any excessive curvatures present.
Chest, shoulders and arms	Chest should be positioned slightly upwards and forwards (halfway between full inspiration and full expiration); arms hanging relaxed by sides, with palms facing the body; elbows slightly bent with forearms facing forwards; shoulders are level and not in rotation; shoulder blades should lie flat against ribcage, with separation of about 4 inches.
Head	Head is in a position of optimal balance and is neither too far forwards nor too far back; cheekbones should be positioned in the same vertical line as the clavicles.

Interpretation and correction of faulty posture

The purpose of any postural correction is to restore muscle balance and normalise range of joint motion. It is also important that any patterns of faulty posture alignment be confirmed by muscle testing (length and strength); details of these tests for the shoulder, trunk, hip and knee are outlined in the appropriate chapters of this text.

Correction of faulty posture can involve several modalities, depending on the extent and aetiology of the dysfunction. Although correction may require use of special therapeutic techniques, such as soft-tissue manipulation and orthotic correction, corrective exercise can provide a long-term solution when combined with posture training. Posture training should be part of a preventative care programme and should become a habitual part of the client's lifestyle. Special attention should always be paid to observation and reinforcement of posture during execution of all exercises.

At times, there may be discrepancies between the results of postural assessment and muscle testing. In these instances, the differences may be due to a number of factors, such as the effects of an old injury, recent illness or specific 'guarding' patterns that have become habitual. These observations may require further historical investigation. When attempting to correct posture, the therapist must be realistic and accept the limits imposed by possible long-term structural variations.

In standing, faulty alignment will occur when a muscle fails to provide adequate support for weight bearing. If the fault has been long-standing, then further compensations may also be present further up or down the kinetic chain. Accurate assessment and observation of standing posture can thus provide valuable information on muscle balance to assist in corrective exercise prescription.

The following table outlines guidelines for postural correction, including exercise and overcoming habitual patterns. Details of specific alignment problems relating to the shoulder, trunk and hip, and corrective exercise, can be found in the relevant chapters.

Table 2.2.   Corrective exercise for common postural problems

Postural fault	Short muscles	Long muscles	Corrective exercise
Forward head carriage	Cervical extensors

Upper trapezius; levator scapulae | Cervical flexors | Stretch cervical extensors, if tight; strengthen cervical flexors; strengthen thoracic extensors; deep-breathing exercises, with arms overhead to stretch intercostals and upper abdominals; stretch pectoralis minor, shoulder adductors and internal rotators, if tight; strengthen middle and lower trapezius |
| **Thoracic kyphosis** | Shoulder adductors; pectoralis minor; intercostals

Internal oblique (upper lateral fibres) | Thoracic extensors

Middle and lower trapezius | |
| **Medially rotated shoulders** | Upper trapezius; serratus anterior; pectoralis minor | Middle and lower trapezius | |

Table 2.2.   Corrective exercise for common postural problems (continued)

Postural fault	Short muscles	Long muscles	Corrective exercise
Excessive lumbar lordosis	Lumbar erectors Hip flexors	Abdominals (external oblique) Hip extensors	Stretch low back, if tight; strengthen abdominals using posterior pelvic tilt exercises; stretch hip flexors, if short; strengthen hip extensors, if weak; educate proper postural alignment
Flat-back	Anterior abdominals Hip extensors	Lumbar erectors One-joint hip flexors	Strengthen low back muscles, if weak; strengthen hip flexors to aid in restoring anterior pelvic tilt; stretch hamstrings, if tight; educate proper postural alignment
Sway-back	Upper anterior abdominals (rectus abdominis and internal oblique) Hip extensors	Lower anterior abdominals (external oblique) One-joint hip flexors	Strengthen external oblique; stretch upper abdominals and intercostals by placing arms overhead and doing deep breathing (wall standing/sitting exercise); stretch hamstrings, if tight; strengthen hip flexors, if weak (standing hip flexion exercise or supine leg raise); educate proper postural alignment
High left hip (opposite for high right hip)	Left lateral trunk muscles Right hip abductors; right tensor fasciae latae; left hip adductors	Right lateral trunk muscles Left hip abductors (gluteus medius); right hip adductors	Stretch left lateral trunk and thigh muscles (including fascia); strengthen right lateral trunk muscles; strengthen left gluteus medius if weakness is pronounced; educate proper postural alignment

Table 2.2.   Corrective exercise for common postural problems (continued)

Postural fault	Short muscles	Long muscles	Corrective exercise
Knee flexion	Hamstrings; popliteus	Quadriceps; soleus	Stretch hamstrings and hip flexors, if tight; educate proper postural alignment
Knee hyperextension	Quadriceps; soleus	Hamstrings; popliteus	Stretch quadriceps, if tight; educate proper postural alignment, with emphasis on avoiding hyperextension
Medially rotated femur	Hip medial rotators	Hip lateral rotators	It is important to ascertain whether the rotation is acquired or structural; stretch medial rotators; strengthen lateral rotators; educate proper postural alignment
Knock knees	Iliotibial band; lateral knee muscles	Medial knee muscles	It is important to ascertain whether the problem is acquired or structural; stretch iliotibial band; educate proper postural alignment
Pronation	Peroneals	Tibialis posterior	Walking re-education exercises; educate proper postural alignment
Supination	Tibialis posterior	Peroneals	Walking re-education exercises; educate proper postural alignment

3
PRINCIPLES OF MOVEMENT

Introduction

All movement patterns can be considered functional if they fulfil the desired objective of movement. A number of different movements are possible for a given task, producing a number of desired outcomes. However, an outcome that is kinetic-chain-efficient, and thus biomechanically safe, is an important objective for the client. For effective corrective exercise prescription it is important to have an understanding of the basic building blocks of movement and how they fit together to create complex movement patterns. This information is a valuable tool that can be used to analyse faulty movements and correct them using exercise. Whereas postural assessment can help to identify underlying muscle imbalances, movement analysis will uncover how these imbalances contribute to movement impairment.

The prescription of exercise based on the building blocks of movement is known as functional training. In the framework of corrective exercise, the term suggests an approach to exercise that is centred on a client's occupational, recreational and sporting activities. For this reason, the concepts of functional training apply across a broad scope of exercises, involving different methodologies and rehabilitation tools.

This chapter aims to examine the building blocks of movement, and how this information can be used to support previous findings of muscle imbalance. The variables of human movement and their relevance to corrective exercise is also discussed.

Complex movement

The building blocks of movement

All complex movement can be broken down into basic building blocks; these base patterns are made up of six isolated joint actions in the sagittal, frontal and transverse planes: *flexion* and *extension* movements in the sagittal plane; *abduction, adduction* and *lateral flexion* movements in the frontal plane; and *rotational* movements in the transverse plane.

Primary movements consist of simultaneous joint actions to produce four important movement patterns: *lifting* (including squatting and lunging), *pulling*, *pushing* and *trunk rotation*. These patterns are useful in producing movement, generally in a straight line. This is the most advantageous method of overcoming external forces or objects, and when accuracy is needed in movement. Primary movements can be effectively trained with specific exercises and combined with other primary patterns to produce useful movement sequences. It is important to note that the coordinated sequencing of lifting, trunk rotation and pushing or pulling contributes significantly to the development of power during many activities of daily living. With this in mind it is important for the therapist to have a full understanding of the biomechanics of these four important patterns.

Complex or integrated movements consist of the sequential use of primary (and base) patterns to generate maximum force at the end of a movement. The precise sequencing of body parts occurs so that subsequent segments are accelerated with the appropriate timing, creating a speed that is functional to the movement. Many of these movements involve trunk rotation to assist in speed production. Although integrated movements are commonly seen in sports performance, such as a golf swing or kicking, there are many examples that occur in activities of daily living. These include swinging the legs out of bed in the morning, getting in and out of a car, or knocking in a fence post with a mallet.

Movement observation in corrective exercise

When a client demonstrates a faulty movement pattern, for example, an inability to squat correctly, the therapist must begin by breaking down that particular movement sequence into simple observable parts. This will help to identify dysfunction and can help to target corrective exercise. If the therapist understands the correct biomechanical sequence of the primary movement pattern, each individual part of the faulty movement can be observed in terms of joint and muscle action. If specific muscles are unable to perform their desired action, the overall movement will show decreased efficiency. Although pain may not always be present as a result of faulty movement, the faulty

movement should not be overlooked as a future source of pain. Any identified muscle dysfunctions should be confirmed via muscle testing, before exercise prescription begins. Failure to identify specific muscle dysfunction may lead to unnecessary exercise prescription.

The results of movement analysis should be used to build a programme that focuses on training movements, rather than muscles. If the objectives of rehabilitation include

Clinical perspective

Breaking down complex movements and re-educating the primary patterns may allow for correct execution of movements in an isolated way that is conducive to learning. Each individual pattern can then be built up progressively with the appropriate temporal and spatial control, to reproduce the complex pattern.

A performance-related example of this process is seen in the re-education of a forehand movement in tennis. The movement can be broken down into a modified squat (primary pattern), with hip medial/lateral rotation (base pattern) and a trunk rotation (primary pattern). Teaching proper squat mechanics (partial range of motion only) and integrating this movement with hip medial/lateral rotation will begin the facilitation of transfer of ground reaction forces through the lumbo-pelvic-hip complex.

The upper and lower body patterns can then be integrated, using cables or tubing, followed by medicine balls. The final step may include sports-specific drills, where the enhanced movement pattern is integrated into a coaching session, thus making the transition from the clinical to the performance environment.

performance-related goals, the programme can be developed further to include combinations of primary patterns with speed development (power-based exercise).

Variables of movement

Every movement has a set of six variables in differing proportions which make that particular movement unique. Understanding these variables is required so that they can be managed effectively during exercise to correct and enhance faulty movements. These six variables of movement are:

1 integration of muscle action

2 combination of biomotor skills

3 planes of motion

4 maintenance of centre of gravity over base of support

5 acceleration, deceleration and stabilisation

6 open and closed chain contribution.

This information is useful to the therapist because it will enable a client's daily activities to be profiled. Daily activities that combine all these variables to a high degree are considered to be complex or highly demanding movements; activities that use these to a lesser degree are simple or less demanding.

Assessment of movement in this way allows the therapist to select appropriate exercises that have the same profile as the client's daily activities. The resulting exercises will be tailor-made to the client's functional demands. Further manipulation of these variables in a corrective exercise programme will consequently lead to improved performance. The six variables of movement are summarised below.

1. Integration of muscle action

Movement begins with muscle recruitment, following the propagation of nerve impulses, in order to produce segmental motion of joints. Recruitment patterns involve the integration of a number of muscle actions sequentially or simultaneously: very rarely do muscles act in isolation. For a movement to be biomechanically correct and safe, there needs to be minimal joint stress, with maximal neuromuscular efficiency. For this to occur, muscle recruitment must involve the correct force couples and exhibit the correct firing sequence. The nervous system is organised in such a way as to optimise the selection of muscle synergies, rather than the selection of the individual muscles. In this way the nervous system 'thinks' in terms of movement patterns and not isolated muscle function. Training individual muscles over prolonged periods of time can create artificial feedback mechanisms, disrupted force couples and aberrant forces throughout the kinetic chain.

An understanding of agonistic/ antagonistic and synergistic muscle action during movement enables the therapist to prescribe individual exercises that demonstrate similar, if not identical, recruitment patterns. For example, when bending down to pick up a heavy object from the floor, the ascent should be initiated by a posterior pelvic tilt. This action is precipitated by contraction of the gluteals, a muscle group that is commonly weak. In the presence of gluteal weakness, the lumbar erectors will preferentially recruit, producing large and potentially damaging amounts of shear force through the lumbar vertebrae. Instructing clients in basic lifting patterns will facilitate optimal learning; if the client is particularly weak or shows signs of atrophy in the gluteals, isolation exercises could be prescribed to stimulate strength and hypertrophy as quickly as possible. However, once the goals of isolation have been attained, integration of the gluteals back into the lifting pattern should be prioritised.

2. Combination of biomotor skills

Biomotor skills can be described as the various abilities that are required to perform any given movement. All movement is made up of these skills in various amounts; the exact proportions will depend on the demands of a given task. The biomotor skills of a corrective exercise programme should closely match the abilities of the client and the demands of their lifestyle. The seven biomotor skills and their application in corrective exercise are shown in Table 3.1.

When injury or impairment occurs, one or more biomotor skills may be affected, resulting in a deficit. Because biomotor

Clinical perspective

When addressing biomotor deficits within a corrective exercise programme, it may seem beneficial to include exercises that train several skills at once within a training session. However, this may actually inhibit the development of specific skills at the expense of others. The exception to this rule is where time is limited, in which case this type of 'condensed' exercise may be productive. In this instance, single 'hybrid' exercises may be performed which address multiple biomotor skills, while simultaneously training a number of functional movement patterns. Examples of such exercises include the squat, the wood-chop and the supine lateral ball roll.

The subsequent restoration and further enhancement of biomotor skills can vastly improve and accelerate the therapeutic process, providing a range of challenging and interesting exercises.

Table 3.1.   Seven biomotor skills

Biomotor skill	Application in corrective exercise
Strength – the ability to apply force	Adding resistance to the body during exercise can develop strength and should be relevant to occupational or recreational demands. Care should be taken because loads that are too high can create a breakdown in neuromuscular stabilisation and cause the client to be susceptible to further injury or premature fatigue.
Power – force times velocity	Power can be increased by increasing the load (force) or increasing the speed (velocity) with which the load is moved. Power training provides the client with the ability to condition and restore movement patterns in a biomechanically correct manner and at a more functionally appropriate speed.
Muscular endurance – the ability of the muscles repeatedly to	Repetitive dynamic contraction allows for endurance gains that are based on high-repetition muscle contractions (usually 20 repetitions or more), while continuous tension produces

Table 3.1.   Seven biomotor skills (continued)

Biomotor skill	Application in corrective exercise
perform a sub-maximal task without fatigue	endurance gains based on sustained isometric muscle contractions. Muscular endurance is more important than strength development in certain rehabilitation protocols.
Coordination – the control over a series of muscular contractions, so as to create a desired motion	Corrective exercises that involve multiple joint actions can be used to improve coordination and can train clients to recruit muscles in the correct sequence. The development of coordination ranks high on the list of skills that can be acquired through classical movement-based systems such as Pilates and the Feldenkrais method.
Flexibility – the range of motion possible around a specific joint or series of articulations; specific to a given joint or movement	Most leisure or recreational activities require only normal amounts of flexibility, and functional range of movement may be more important for long-term injury prevention. Flexibility may be improved via a number of different techniques, such as static, active and PNF (proprioceptive neuromuscular facilitation) stretching; as well as through a number of popular flexibility-based disciplines, such as yoga or martial arts.
Balance – the ability to maintain a centre of gravity over a fixed base of support	Balance can be improved effectively by constantly stressing an individual's limits of stability in a proprioceptive and multi-planar environment, using balance-boards, stability balls, foam rollers and single-leg stances. The design and implementation of balance into a corrective exercise programme is critical for developing and improving the sequencing of muscle recruitment patterns required for joint stabilisation and optimal muscular control.
Agility – the ability to change direction of movement quickly	Many daily activities require a basic level of agility (e.g. walking); high levels of agility are generally reserved for high occupational demands or sports performance. Agility may be developed through the use of stability balls, wobble-boards or simple plyometric exercises, such as multi-planar hops.

abilities tend to exhibit codependency, a deficit in one can significantly influence another (for example, a loss of strength will affect an individual's ability to generate power and speed). Any biomotor deficits that have occurred as a result of injury should be corrected. Once restored, biomotor skills can be further improved for the purpose of performance enhancement, or as a preventative measure against further injury.

When qualifying the biomotor skills of a client, it is important to understand that the goal is to determine where to direct rehabilitative efforts: the primary objective is to restore deficits, rather than reinforcing competencies.

3. Planes of motion

Almost all activities of daily living involve movement in three planes of motion – sagittal, frontal and transverse planes. This characteristic is not exclusive just to complex movement patterns; for example, less complex activities, such as walking, involve sagittal plane movement, with smaller movements in the frontal and transverse planes. Walking also requires a large amount of stabilisation in all three planes for optimal movement.

Weakness in one plane during walking is exemplified in a client who has a weak gluteus medius. As the gluteus medius is one of the major frontal plane stabilisers of the hip joint, weakness can result in an altered gait pattern (Trendelenburg sign) that is characterised by a side-to-side 'wag' in the hips. Restoring strength to the gluteus medius is part of an overall corrective exercise programme that may also focus on gait re-education.

Multi-planar activities are best performed using free weights, body weight, cable machines, stability balls, balance-boards and plyometric training. Many traditional resistance machines work by placing the individual into a fixed plane of motion, thereby locking rotary joints into linear paths. This isolation significantly reduces the need for stabilisation in other planes, thus increasing the risk of wear and tear on joints and decreasing the functional carry-over into daily activities. For example, many exercises are often sagittal plane dominant. While flexion and extension are necessary to develop functional movement, there may be compromised stability of the frontal and transverse planes. If the client's occupational or recreational requirements are predominantly sagittal plane, there will still be an increased risk of injury due to the lack of stability in the other planes.

Clinical perspective

Integrated movements are essential to optimal physical function. These patterns are made up of multi-planar movement sequences, involving acceleration, deceleration and stabilisation mechanics, and the maintenance of balance over a base of support. Consideration of this plays an important part in equipment and exercise choice. The use of cables and pulleys has been shown to have greater functional carry-over to daily activities because of the greater freedom and variety of joint movement that they allow. In addition, the use of free weights or medicine balls may also provide similar functional joint and muscle loading. The overall effect of this type of training is to enhance significantly the ability to stabilise various joints, especially the spine, thus contributing to overall musculoskeletal health.

Many training machines found in gyms and health clubs offer only isolation of joint action in fixed planes of motion. For rehabilitation purposes, these types of motor patterns may not be sufficiently effective in meeting day-to-day demands. When an injured or painful body part needs to be less active, machines may be useful in isolating these parts, while simultaneously training other body parts. For example, when a client has low back pain, they can use machines that offer lumbar support, while still training the upper or lower extremities. Machines may also be used to regress an exercise if the client has muscle weakness. In this instance, the weak muscle can be strengthened in a machine prior to introducing more integrated exercises.

4. Maintenance of centre of gravity over base of support

Essentially, most functional movements occur from the standing position. From this position the body must overcome the effects of gravity while at the same time producing the desired movements. During these movements, muscle systems work to stabilise the upright posture in all three planes of motion.

This maintenance of upright posture relies heavily on the activation of *righting* and *equilibrium* reflexes to maintain balance. Righting reflexes tend to be dominant when an individual moves across stable surfaces, such as the pavement. They work by constantly adjusting body parts in relation to the head, and vice versa. Equilibrium reflexes are more dominant when moving across labile surfaces, such as sand and soft grass, or when the supportive surface is moving, such as on a bike or a train. In reality, many activities use a mixture of both reflex reactions, although one may dominate.

For general improvements in these reflexes the introduction of labile surfaces to a corrective exercise programme is sufficient. Exercise programmes that are based around fixed machines can be limiting, as the kinetic chain is being stimulated under an assisted pattern of stabilisation, thereby reducing the extent of muscle recruitment and balance requirement.

5. Acceleration, deceleration and stabilisation

Almost all movement occurs at varying speeds, involving acceleration and deceleration of intrinsic (body weight) and extrinsic (additional) loads. During these movements isometric muscle contraction

Clinical perspective

The demands placed on the kinetic chain during daily activities are numerous and often challenging. These include stabilisation during static postures; premeditated dynamic and ballistic movement; unpredictable loading; and maintenance of the centre of gravity over the base of support. For this reason, many therapists and trainers have been motivated to recommend exercise training on labile surfaces such as wobble-boards and stability balls. Although these devices can certainly challenge the motor system to meet the demands of particularly dynamic tasks, they may not be beneficial for some individuals in the first instance.

Regardless of injury status and training experience, all corrective exercise programmes should begin on stable surfaces to establish a positive slope of improvement. When there is sufficient qualification of static and dynamic stability, labile surfaces may be introduced slowly and progressively, until the specific goal of exercise is reached. Unnecessary use of this type of training may significantly develop certain biomotor skills at the expense of more important ones.

must occur to stabilise the loads. For example, lifting a weight from the floor involves acceleration of hip extension as a result of gluteal and hamstring contraction, followed by eccentric contraction of the abdominals and hip flexors to decelerate the movement. Isometric contraction must also occur in the trunk flexors and extensors, as well as the deeper abdominal muscles, to stabilise the spine, and in the knee extensors to stabilise the knee.

Movement at fixed speeds is rare, except in cases of heavy lifting that require optimal control and coordination. In the absence of adequate neuromuscular control, the body will move only within a range of speed that the nervous system has been programmed to allow, no matter how strong the muscles are.

When designing a corrective exercise programme it is important to account for the variations in performance speed that occur with daily tasks, as well as the significance of these speeds on the forces acting on the body. For example, lifting a 5 kg weight quickly may require more force generation than lifting a 10 kg weight slowly. The implications of this are often seen in clients who experience back pain while bending quickly to pick up light objects. Using a variety of lifting speeds and tempos, rather than fixed speeds, will enhance the development of functional movement.

6. Open- and closed-chain contribution

The kinetic chain refers to the link system of the body, in which the links are made up of a series of joints that connect bones to one another, with articulation of the joints provided by muscle action. The term *open-chain movement* is commonly applied to actions in which the distal end of a limb is free to move in space, whereas *closed-chain movement* refers to any exercise where the distal end of a limb meets with external resistance that prohibits or restrains its free motion. It is important to note that the muscle actions during open-chain movements are reversed during closed-chain movements. In reality, human movement is composed of a variety of open- and closed-chain movements. For example, picking up a shopping bag is a closed-chain movement with respect to the legs and an open-chain movement with respect to the trunk and upper body.

When designing a corrective exercise programme, it is important to prescribe compatible chain exercises, where possible. This will enhance the degree of functional carry-over to daily life. In some cases, compatible exercises may not be possible. For example, in the presence of closed-chain dysfunction, closed-chain exercise may result in compensatory muscle recruitment that may further hinder normal muscle activity. In this situation, the use of open-chain exercises that isolate specific joint movements may improve strength and range of motion significantly, prior to the reintroduction of closed-chain movements.

4
PRINCIPLES OF MANUAL MUSCLE TESTING

Introduction

Muscle weakness is a common characteristic of muscle performance, even in individuals who participate in regular physical activity. It is a misconception that participation in regular exercise or sport places adequate demands on all muscle groups, and precise muscle testing will often identify a number of weak muscles.

Muscle strength testing is used to determine the ability of muscles to provide stability and support as well as their capability to function during movement. Muscle length testing is used to determine whether muscle length is limited (too short to allow normal range of motion) or excessive (too long, allowing a larger range of motion).

Manual muscle testing is an integral part of the physical evaluation of a client. It provides the therapist with an important diagnostic tool for objective assessment of muscular weakness. Many neuromuscular and musculoskeletal impairments are characterised by muscle weakness, resulting in imbalance. Muscle weakness will result in loss of movement if the muscle cannot contract sufficiently to move the body part through a partial or complete range of motion; weakness allows a position of misalignment. It is important to understand that muscle shortness will also result in loss of motion if the muscle cannot be elongated through its full range of motion; shortness

causes a position of misalignment. A state of muscle imbalance exists when a muscle is weak and its antagonist is strong; the strong muscle tends to shorten and the weak muscle tends to lengthen.

Although shortness of muscles is commonplace, in many cases this is corrected most effectively by stretching the muscle and strengthening the antagonist. Where stretching is indicated, short muscles should be stretched in such a way as to prevent injury, with the end goal of permitting optimal joint function. The only exception is a restriction of motion for the sake of stability.

Imbalances may be the result of occupational or recreational activities in which there is repeated use of certain muscles, without adequate exercise of the opposing muscles. In any instance, imbalance may be symmetrical or asymmetrical, as revealed by accurate muscle testing. Muscle imbalances can also distort body alignment and are responsible for a number of faulty postures (see Chapter 2). These imbalances can contribute to unnecessary stress and strain on joints, ligaments and muscles. Manual testing of muscle strength and length is the therapist's tool of choice to determine the extent of an imbalance prior to corrective exercise prescription.

Identifying the changes that occur in muscle and the causes of these changes is the key to restoring optimal neuromuscular and musculoskeletal function. Changes in muscle are not limited to those who do exercise or have physically demanding jobs; even the most sedentary lifestyles are associated with repeated movements or postures that may cause functional changes in muscle. If these movements and postures are maintained in faulty alignment, there may be changes in muscle strength and length. Also, the role of the nervous system as a contributing factor to musculoskeletal pain is often underemphasised in rehabilitation. As commonly observed, many individuals with strong muscles develop pain syndromes. Often these syndromes need to be addressed by instructing the individual to control movements by conscious effort rather than by increasing muscle size.

Before designing an effective corrective exercise programme, it is important to understand that changes in recruitment patterns, as well as muscle length and muscle strength, are concurrent. The most effective approach should address all three issues: strength or stretching exercises alone are unlikely to affect muscle recruitment during functional activities. Because the maximal strength a muscle can develop is directly related to the initial length of its fibres, muscle strength and length testing provides the therapist with important information regarding muscle function. Knowledge of synergistic muscle action during functional movement, combined with accurate muscle testing, will give the therapist a valuable diagnostic tool when designing corrective exercise programmes.

Causes of muscle weakness

Many factors contribute to muscle weakness, including atrophy, stretch weakness and strain, often causing pain and fatigue as well as changes in muscle recruitment, such as substitution and altered (synergistic) dominance. Weakness should be addressed in accordance with the root cause – if due to disuse (atrophy), then corrective exercises; if due to overwork (strain), then rest; if due to overstretch (stretch weakness), then relief of the stretch.

Weakness resulting from muscle atrophy

Muscle weakness resulting from muscle atrophy is not normally associated with pain on contraction, but with an inability to hold the relevant limb in the test position or at any point against resistance in the test range. This type of weakness can affect both the active and passive tension of a muscle, subsequently influencing the static and dynamic stability of the joint it crosses: the result is a significantly reduced ability of the muscle to develop force, less stability of the joint and potentially faulty joint alignment. The decreased number of sarcomeres and connective tissue resulting from muscle atrophy means that muscle size and definition are often reduced.

The reversal of muscle atrophy is best achieved via corrective strengthening exercises that focus on specific muscles, particularly if there is an imbalance of synergists (as opposed to general atrophy). Exercises that emphasise major muscle groups may not necessarily correct atrophy of only one of the muscles within the group, but may contribute further to it.

Weakness resulting from muscle strain

Muscle weakness can also occur in the form of strain, resulting from excessive short-term stretching or excessive eccentric loading of muscle. Muscle strain is almost invariably associated with pain on contraction and palpation, and, as with atrophy, the muscle is unable to hold the limb in any position against resistance. Strained muscles should be rested at their ideal length to prevent further stretching.

Any exercise prescription should be relatively pain-free; once the muscle is no longer painful, any underlying weakness should be treated in the same way as atrophy.

Weakness due to overstretch

Muscles that are subject to prolonged periods of stretch may become weak and maintain a lengthened position. Characteristics that help to identify overstretch weakness are:

1 The muscle tests weak throughout its range of motion.
2 Postural alignment evaluation indicates an increased resting muscle length (for example, depressed shoulders or hip adduction/medial rotation).

Overstretch weakness may be reversed effectively via an exercise programme that strengthens the muscle and alleviates the stretch; concurrently, the client may also need to be instructed in correct postural habits, particularly during periods of inactivity (such as prolonged sitting or sleeping).

Overstretch can often progress to painful muscle strain if not corrected soon after the onset of the length change.

Practical considerations in muscle testing

Muscle testing requires a detailed knowledge of the agonistic and antagonistic actions of

Clinical perspective

It is important for the therapist to determine the cause of identified muscle weakness and be aware that weakness can result from all repeated movements or postures, even when asleep.

Three important examples exist of overstretch weakness during sleeping. The first is the development of elongated dorsiflexors (and shortened plantar flexors) in the supine position, caused by the downward force of the duvet on the feet.

Second, in the side-lying position, where the upper leg is in adduction, flexion and medial rotation, there will be prolonged stretching of the posterior gluteus medius. This condition is more prevalent in individuals who have a broad pelvis and is therefore more common in women. During manual muscle testing, these individuals will be unable to maintain the hip in abduction, extension and lateral rotation against resistance. This overstretch weakness can produce hip adduction or an apparent leg length discrepancy when standing.

Third, the side-lying position can also cause abduction and forward tilt of the lowermost scapula, particularly if the shoulder is pushed forwards during sleeping; this may result in overstretch of the lower trapezius and rhomboids. The top shoulder may also be subject to overstretch, via forward pull of the arm across the body.

muscles, as well as their role in stabilisation and substitution. The relationship between muscle imbalance and faulty movement offers a unique approach for treatment via corrective exercise. Specific exercises that are based on the results of the muscle tests offer the most effective treatment.

The order in which muscles are tested is generally a matter of preference; however, the tests should be ordered to avoid frequent and unnecessary changes in position for the client. Muscles that are closely related in action or position should be tested in sequence.

Length testing

Muscle length testing involves movements that increase the distance between the insertion and origin of a muscle, therefore elongating it in a direction opposite to the muscle action.

For muscles that pass over one joint only (for example, the iliopsoas), the range of joint motion and the range of muscle length will be the same. For muscles that pass over two or more joints, the range of muscle length will be less than the total range of motion of the joints over which the muscle passes. When measuring the range of motion of a two-joint muscle, it is necessary to allow the muscle to be slack over one joint in order to measure the range of motion in the other joint.

Precise testing requires that the bone of the origin of the muscle be in a fixed position, while the insertion moves in the direction of muscle elongation. Although mostly passive, length testing can involve active assisted movements on the client's part.

Strength testing

Muscle strength testing involves placing a body part in a position against gravity (where appropriate) and applying pressure directly opposite the line of pull of the muscle being tested; the body part proximal to the tested area is stabilised or fixated (if necessary) to ensure specificity of testing.

The placement, direction and amount of pressure applied to the body part are important (yet subjective) factors when testing for strength. As a general rule, pressure is applied gradually in order to

Clinical perspective

Limited joint range of motion caused by short muscles is an important contributor to musculoskeletal pain and is often treated by muscle stretching. Although vigorous passive stretching can yield significant improvements in joint range of motion within short time periods (10–20 minutes), these methods can disrupt muscle fibre alignment and damage the muscle. Stretching a markedly short muscle may be more effectively achieved by prolonged stretching at low loads over larger timescales, to produce more permanent structural changes in muscle.

Emphasis is often placed on stretching muscles that have shortened and not on correcting muscles that have lengthened. It is important to be aware that a lengthened muscle does not automatically shorten when its antagonist is stretched. The most effective treatment is to stretch the shortened muscle while simultaneously contracting the lengthened muscle. This approach is very successful as it addresses the length changes of all muscles involved and is particularly important in cases where the short muscle causes compensatory movement at a joint (or joints). For example, if short hamstrings cause compensatory lumbar flexion, the back extensors as well as the knee extensors should be contracted while stretching the hamstrings.

determine the degree of muscle strength. Sudden applied pressure can break the pull of an apparently 'strong' muscle.

When a muscle or muscle group attempts to compensate for a lack of function of a weak muscle, the result is a substitution movement. For accurate strength testing, substitution should be avoided by maintaining the correct test position and via assisted fixation. For example, during prone hip extension the lumbar erectors may cause anterior pelvic tilt (substitution), due to a weak gluteus maximus. This can be avoided by correct cuing of the movement by the therapist or by stabilisation of the pelvis.

In strength testing, grading is based on the ability of the client to hold the body part in a given position against gravity: in this instance, strength is graded as 'fair', because the pull of gravity is a constant factor. Grades above and below 'fair' involve a subjective evaluation based on the pressure applied.

Finally, it is important to note that muscle strength is not constant throughout the range of motion, and in testing it is not advisable to grade strength at various points in the range. The point in the range of motion that is used for grading is determined on the basis of whether the muscle is a one-joint or multi-joint muscle. The position for a one-joint muscle is at completion of range of joint motion; for a two-joint muscle, it is within the mid-range of the overall length of the muscle.

Altered dominance in muscle recruitment patterns

One of the most common contributors to muscle imbalance is *reciprocal inhibition*. An understanding of this concept, and the related phenomenon, *synergistic dominance*, is important during all stages of the evaluation process.

Reciprocal inhibition occurs when a tight muscle causes decreased neural input to its functional antagonist. When the neural drive of a muscle is reduced, it will no longer produce the same amount of force with proper timing. In order to maintain the same productivity of a given movement pattern, the synergists must take over the role of prime movers. The nervous system will respond by increasing the neural activity to the synergists: a concept known as synergistic dominance. Synergistic dominance produces a movement that occurs with altered neurological and mechanical control.

Reciprocal inhibition and synergistic dominance can lead to a decrease in the activity of the prime mover and can eventually result in atrophy and altered appearance of the muscle, and, consequently, pain and injury.

Alterations in the recruitment of synergists that can be clinically observed include repeated recruitment of only one muscle of a force couple or of one muscle of counterbalancing synergists. The result is a movement that is in the direction of the dominant synergist. With this in mind, any movement pattern repeated often enough has the potential to create imbalance within the tissues creating that movement.

The following examples highlight some of the more commonly observed synergistic dominance patterns that may be useful when considering corrective exercise prescription.

Dominance of the upper trapezius over the lower trapezius

Balance of the upper and lower trapezii is fundamental to optimal control of the scapular. Whereas the lower trapezius depresses the scapula, the upper portion elevates it and is often dominant. This commonly observed pattern of excessive elevation is generally a result of learned behaviour rather than an issue of muscle strength, and, as such, lower trapezius strengthening exercises alone may not be adequate; instruction in proper scapulohumeral rhythm has a greater likelihood of restoring balance and strength.

Dominance of the hamstrings over the abdominals

The hamstrings and abdominals combine to form a force couple for posterior pelvic tilt: the abdominals exert an upward pull on the pelvis, while the hamstrings exert a downward pull. When the abdominal muscles weaken, the hamstrings become the dominant driving force on posterior pelvic tilt, a pattern that becomes reinforced thereafter. The result is an imbalance in strength, with the abdominals testing weak and the hamstrings testing strong.

An observation of this imbalance can be made during straight leg-raising in a supine position. If the abdominals are weak, the contralateral hamstrings will stabilise the anterior pelvic tilt to a greater extent than the abdominals. Instruction in reducing the amount of hip extension via the hamstrings will help to increase activity of the abdominal muscles and restore optimal synergy between the two groups of muscles.

Dominance of the hamstrings over the gluteus maximus

The hamstrings and gluteus maximus also combine to form a force couple for hip extension. Where the gluteus maximus is the dominant muscle of hip extension, its attachments to the proximal and distal (via the ITB) femur reinforce the position of the femoral head in the acetabulum during hip extension, providing stability. Disruption of this synergy is commonly seen in sway-back postures, in which the hamstrings are dominant. During a prone hip extension movement, an individual with sway-back posture often recruits the hamstrings before the gluteus maximus; muscle testing of the gluteus maximus usually confirms weakness.

This hamstring dominance can predispose the individual to an overuse syndrome, such as muscle strain, and is a common occurrence in distance runners. Because the hamstrings (with the exception of the short head) do not attach on the femur, they do not offer precise control of the femoral head during hip extension; therefore, dominant activity of the hamstrings can also contribute to hip joint stress. This may be exacerbated further by the presence of weak hip flexors.

Dominance of the pectoralis major over the subscapularis

During the action of humeral medial rotation, the pectoralis major is often dominant over the subscapularis. Accurate observation and palpation of humeral movement during medial rotation will often support these findings in the first instance. If the pectoralis major is dominant, the humeral head will glide excessively in an anterior direction, unable to be counterbalanced by the action of the subscapularis (posterior glide of the humeral head). When the subscapularis is tested in the prone position, it usually tests weak, caused by excessive length.

Dominance of the rectus abdominis over the external obliques

The rectus abdominis and external oblique combine to form a force couple producing posterior pelvic tilt. Commonly, the rectus abdominis may be the more dominant muscle for this action, and is also visually observed by a depression of the chest. When instructed to perform lower abdominal exercises, the individual will have difficulty recruiting the external obliques, as indicated by palpation, instead preferring to engage the rectus abdominis. Assessment of the movement will reveal associated trunk flexion or chest depression.

5 PRINCIPLES OF PROGRAMME DESIGN

Introduction

Human movement is made up of integrated muscular performance, with muscles performing actions in a multi-planar environment, often at different speeds. For this reason the exercises presented in this book support an integrated approach to rehabilitation that can benefit many individuals. Approaches that focus solely on muscle strength at the expense of developing functional movement patterns are generally less effective.

Corrective exercise programmes should be designed in a structured yet purposeful manner. This concept is known as periodisation and is based on the correct manipulation of exercise variables over time, to ensure safe and effective progression.

The exercises presented in this book are ordered into four systematic and progressive phases, with each phase acting as a prerequisite to that which follows. The four phases are:

1 restoring muscle balance
2 restoring stabilisation
3 restoring functional strength
4 restoring functional power.

This chapter aims to discuss the rationale behind these progressions and highlight the adaptations that can be made during each phase. This is followed by a discussion of which exercise variables are needed for each specific adaptation, and how to manipulate these variables safely to achieve and maintain a positive slope of improvement for the client.

Phases of exercise progression

Undoubtedly, the most important outcome of any rehabilitation programme is improvement, as defined by the client's goals. Exercise progression is essential to achieve this outcome. Once a slope of improvement has been established, exercises may be progressed to increase functional performance, as well as general motivation.

The phases of exercise in this book are designed to follow a hierarchal structure in relation to the development of seven relevant biomotor skills: *flexibility, balance, muscular endurance, strength, coordination, agility* and *power/speed*. As the client moves through each phase, biomotor skill acquisition increases.

The therapist should aim to progress the client through the phases in the order described; however, all phases may not be necessary to restore optimal function. For example, the occupational and recreational demands of a specific client may be met through the exercises in phases 1 and 2 only.

Effective and appropriate periodisation of timescales is also important, and is dependent on the client's goals and their training experience/age. It is recommended that 4–6 weeks is spent in each phase before progression to the next phase; a frequency of exercise matching three times a week will be sufficient in achieving the required goals. If training experience and training age are high, the client may progress through each phase at a faster rate. However, it is the role of the therapist to determine accurately whether the client is ready for progression, by objective feedback (re-evaluation) and subjective feedback (observation and perceived exertion). Ultimately, the progress and success of any corrective exercise programme will be subject to individual compliance and the development of a practical home exercise programme.

The list of exercises contained in the later chapters are by no means exhaustive, although they do provide the therapist with a basic library from which to start prescription. Where possible, this library should be built upon in accordance with the four phases of progression to increase the number of options available.

Contraindications

Any contraindications to exercise should be fully understood by both therapist and client. If a particular movement pattern cannot be performed by the client, the therapist should explore variations of that movement before removing the exercise from the programme. In many cases, a good understanding of biomechanical principles will allow the therapist to reposition a client or regress an exercise to make it safer and eliminate risk of injury altogether.

Where the treatment of pain or impairment is beyond the level of competence of the therapist, referral may be necessary.

Clinical perspective

The use of soft-tissue treatment can often be combined with corrective exercise to assist progression in clients who present with local muscle ischaemia and abnormal muscle texture.

Ischaemia is often caused by muscle spasms, trigger points, poor posture or psychological stress, resulting in dysfunctions of agonist–antagonist relationships and/or imbalanced force couples. These dysfunctions may delay recovery as well as progression through exercise, unless alleviated at the outset. For this reason, appropriately qualified therapists can use a variety of soft-tissue treatments to remove muscle spasm and release the tissues that may otherwise impede normal muscular and joint function during exercise.

Phase 1 – Restoring muscle balance

Relevant biomotor development – flexibility, strength

The aim of phase 1 is to restore normal muscle length, in particular, of the muscles responsible for gross movement. This begins with a number of flexibility and strength exercises designed to restore range of motion and introduce postural awareness. The exercises should be based on functional movement patterns where possible – establishing familiarity of movement at an early stage will result in greater potential for application of movement post-rehabilitation. Range of motion should be developed in accordance with optimal joint and muscle function that is specific to the client. The client should be encouraged to play an active role in their treatment.

This phase is an essential first step in correcting any muscle imbalances, as identified by muscle testing. Before beginning this or any other phase, it is essential that acute pain and inflammation have been treated appropriately. Flexibility and mobility may also be enhanced through the use of additional approaches such as muscle energy technique (MET), active isolated stretching (AIS) or somatic education methods, such as the Feldenkrais method.

Phase 2 – Restoring stabilisation

Relevant biomotor development – flexibility, strength, muscular endurance, balance

The aim of phase 2 is to restore and enhance the joint stabilisation role of muscles by

retraining co-contraction force couples. This can be achieved using static, dynamic and reactive stabilisation exercises. Static stabilisation exercises activate agonist–antagonist force couples, with minimal joint movement, while dynamic stabilisation does so during a partial or full range of motion activities. Reactive stabilisation exercises focus on stimulating proprioceptive pathways that are the basis of more complex movements, and also help to condition balance and spatial awareness. All three mechanisms are essential for enhancing muscle activation awareness.

Exercises in this phase become progressively more complex by adding components of muscular endurance and balance (as well as continuing strength development). The range of stabilisation demands imposed on the body by the activities of daily living also requires training in a number of body positions in both open- and closed-chain settings. Muscular endurance is best conditioned through the use of positional holding patterns (up to 8 seconds) or higher repetition of movement; balance can be improved effectively via the introduction of the client to labile surfaces, such as a stability ball or balance-board, or by simply reducing the base of support, such as a single-leg stance.

The higher-repetition routines used in this phase help to increase vascularisation of tissues for better recovery, and prepare connective tissues for the higher demands of strength and power training in phases 3 and 4. Reactive movement patterns are selected where possible to increase the proprioceptive demands placed on the body: by performing exercises on labile surfaces (to a level that a client can control), the nervous system is forced to adapt by enhancing its central stabilisation mechanisms. This form of training can be extremely effective for

Clinical perspective

When muscles exhibit excessive length, stretching should be avoided, as well as postural positions that may further lengthen the already stretched muscles. For example, a low back that is excessively flexible will be stretched further during prolonged periods of slumped sitting. The objective in this situation is to correct posture during sitting. Although strengthening exercises can be used, for many active individuals strength will improve simply by avoiding overstretching.

Stretching exercises are encouraged where muscles are short. Exercises must be prescribed and administered correctly to avoid unnecessary stretching in other parts of the body.

increasing neuromuscular coordination and efficiency, and is an essential prerequisite for action-specific strength adaptations.

Selection of functional exercises will offer the client significantly more carry-over into daily life. These exercises are used as building blocks for the more advanced and complex movement patterns outlined in phases 3 and 4. Lack of the skills from this phase may result in deficits in movement pattern and movement response.

Clinical perspective

The use of visualisation and kinaesthetic awareness is an important teaching aid during the development of muscle balance and stabilisation in phases 1 and 2. This is particularly important when instructing on spinal alignment and muscle activation awareness.

The constituent movements of an exercise may be visualised in a slow-motion sequence prior to performance. This strategy is particularly useful for teaching integrated movement patterns, such as squatting or rotation. Sometimes use of a mirror can be beneficial in this process.

Alternatively, the practice of simple kinaesthetic techniques, such as progressive muscle relaxation (PMR), can help to establish control of joint stiffness. Instructing a client in self-palpation during muscle contraction may also help them to focus on the specific muscle or muscles involved.

Further information on the development of awareness for exercise can be gained from the work of Moshe Feldenkrais, F. Mathias Alexander and Thomas Hanna.

Phase 3 – Restoring functional strength

Relevant biomotor development – flexibility, strength, muscular endurance, balance, coordination

The aim of phase 3 is to restore functional strength and further develop coordination of movement, usually in a functional upright stance. This is achieved using combinations of primary movement patterns.

Strength training allows for increases in volume, intensity and force production to enhance the preparation of a client for the higher force demands of their daily or sporting activities. During exercise, concentric, eccentric and isometric muscle actions are emphasised, with progressing speeds of contraction to maximise better force production. Hypertrophy is often an adaptation in this phase of training.

Functional strength exercises are usually performed using resistance in the form of exercise bands or tubing, or free weights, although in many instances body weight is just as effective, particularly if the client is unaccustomed to resistance training. Many of these exercises can be modified to meet the requirements of functional activities, simply by manipulating body position or range of motion.

Strength training can also be modified effectively to increase 'stabilisation-endurance', essential for optimal joint stabilisation. This form of training entails the use of 'super-set' techniques, where a stable exercise, such as a floor bridge, is immediately followed with a stabilisation exercise that has a similar biomechanical motion, such as a supine hip extension (feet on a stability ball). High amounts of volume per unit time can be generated in this way.

The outcomes of this phase include

increased functional strength in both open- and closed-chain environments, as well as improved link-sequencing and force generation through the kinetic chain.

Phase 4 – Restoring functional power

Relevant biomotor development – flexibility, strength, muscular endurance, balance, coordination, speed, agility

The aim of phase 4 is to introduce speed of movement that has functional carry-over for daily living: a concept known as functional power. Movements in daily life are rarely performed at fixed speeds, but involve acceleration and deceleration, combined with stabilisation. For this reason, exercises that are performed with quick, powerful and explosive movements are used to improve functional power.

Many functional power exercises closely mimic common everyday movements and usually involve integration of the entire kinetic chain. Activities in the occupational and recreational environment do not typically require significant loading of muscles and joints; therefore exercises should focus on the control and stabilisation of movement under speed, rather than unnecessary amounts of resistance. Additional resistance may be applied where the functional demands of occupation or sport dictate.

Functional power training is achieved by either increasing the load (force), as in progressive strength training, or increasing the speed (velocity) with which the load is moved. Power training increases the rate of force production by increasing the number of motor units activated, the synchrony between them and the speed at which they are excited. By using either heavier weights (approximately 60 to 90 per cent, 1-repetition maximum) with explosive movement or low resistance with a high velocity, power output is significantly increased.

For power movements to occur safely, range of motion, stabilisation and functional strength must all be optimal. Particular emphasis should also be placed on optimal shoulder, trunk and hip integration, to ensure smooth coordination of ground reaction forces up through the body. This will result in coordination and control of movement, providing a high degree of functional carry-over into occupation, recreation and sport.

Clinical perspective

Plyometric training, originally known as jump training, is a form of power training that combines speed of movement with strength. The purpose of plyometrics is to heighten the excitability of the nervous system to help improve the reactive ability of the neuromuscular system.

Any movement that uses the stretch reflex to increase force production is plyometric in nature. During plyometric exercise, the eccentric pre-stretch of muscle places additional stress on the musculo-tendinous junction. This stretch-shortening cycle may be beneficial in the management of tendonitis, by increasing the tensile strength of the tendon.

Through a gradual and progressive eccentric-loading programme, the therapist can use plyometric exercise effectively to facilitate joint awareness, strengthen soft tissue during healing and increase functional strength and power in all three planes of movement.

Acute exercise variables

Progression through a corrective exercise programme requires the consideration and manipulation of specific acute exercise variables. These include:

- exercise selection
- number of exercises
- exercise sequence
- repetitions performed
- number of sets
- tempo of movement
- rest or recovery time
- load applied.

Manipulation of variables should be based on the current level of functional capacity of the client (that is, the volume and intensity of exercise they can currently tolerate). As the client improves during the exercise programme (observed or reported), functional capacity will increase. This positive slope of improvement can be maintained by further manipulation and management of acute exercise variables.

Exercise selection

Therapists and exercise professionals face the constant challenge of meeting a wide range of rehabilitation and performance objectives. No set of exercises is ideal for everyone and all corrective exercise programmes should consider the client's objectives, as well as their exercise history.

Exercise selection should be synonymous with the objective of achieving optimal movement capability for the client's demands. As such, the criteria for functional movement should be used as a guideline. Once exercises have been chosen, the therapist should consider how to progress as well as regress an exercise, while still training the required movement pattern. This is easily achieved by identifying the base and primary movements that the exercise is made of, and increasing the demands of those movements: for example, adding another plane of motion or challenging a particular biomotor ability.

Exercise selection should always be supported by the results of postural assessment, movement analysis and muscle testing. Given the individual nature and circumstances of each client, choosing the appropriate exercises should take into account the goals of the client, as well as other factors, including existing or past injury, training history and occupation.

Injury history

The effects of past injury often affect the individual's ability to perform exercises correctly, and the extent of this should be assessed carefully during the evaluation stages. Depending on the type of injury, exercises can be selected that work towards the goals of rehabilitation, while treating the injury itself.

Training history

Training history relates to training age and training experience. Training age signifies the amount of time spent doing exercise, whereas training experience is determined by biomotor development. Greater training age and experience allow for more advanced exercise selection.

Occupational history

Knowledge of the demands placed upon a client by their working environment is an essential requirement in successful exercise prescription, for two main reasons. First, occupational demands will determine the current level of functional capacity of the client (that is, the volume and intensity of exercise they can currently tolerate). Second, an understanding of the client's movement patterns in the workplace may suggest the mechanical cause of impairment or injury, which can then be corrected through exercise.

Number of exercises

The number of exercises selected for inclusion in a programme can mean the difference between success and continued improvement, or failure and non-adherence. If too many exercises are prescribed, the risk of injury increases, as the body can only recover from a certain level of physical stress. This is an important factor in clients with injury, as a significant number of resources will already be involved in combating pain or inflammation present.

Specificity is also reduced when too many exercises are used as the body has limited capacity to adapt to multiple stimuli.

Exercise sequence

The order in which exercises are performed is often overlooked, but it is an important factor that can contribute significantly to the success of an exercise programme. The following should all be considered when sequencing an exercise programme:

1 Highly integrated exercises should be performed before isolation exercises, to avoid fatigue of stabiliser muscles. Injury may result if stabiliser or smaller synergistic muscles are exercised in isolation first, and they may destabilise associated joints during the later execution of complex movement patterns.

2 Training should progress from the most important to the least important exercises, in relation to the objectives of exercise. This will prioritise specific skill and movement acquisition over those that are not as important.

3 Exercise should move from the most to the least neurologically demanding. The use of proprioceptive aids, such as stability balls and balance-boards, will significantly increase neural drive to muscles via further activation of righting and tilting reflexes. If placed at the start of a programme, these exercises will significantly challenge the client without too much risk of nervous fatigue.

Clinical perspective

Consideration of the spine is important in the sequencing of exercises within a single session. Prior activities and positions can affect the mechanics of the spine in ensuing activities. For example, the ligamentous and disc creep that occurs after prolonged sitting can result in ligament laxity and subsequent risk of injury. Although disc volume appears to redistribute evenly on standing, this can take time, sometimes up to half an hour. With this in mind, exercises involving loading under flexion should be avoided initially, before being sequenced alternately with exercises involving extension.

In order to reduce viscous friction within the spine, specific movement patterns should be performed as part of a warm-up. The most effective are those performed in a slow, continuous manner that emphasise precision and control of movement, for example, the cat-camel exercise or a sequence of Feldenkrais movements.

Repetitions

Corrective exercise programmes should generally begin with a 12–15 repetition range as this allows for a safe lifting load prior to progression. Further progression will then be dependent on the following factors:

1 Whether the client's rehabilitation objectives are power, strength, hypertrophy or muscular endurance/stabilisation

2 Biomotor ability – if the client does not have adequate biomotor skill to perform a prescribed exercise with good technique, a reduction in repetitions may be necessary to enhance motor development, before increasing repetitions

3 Available time – repetitions can be decreased if time is a factor.

Sets

The number of sets performed will depend on training experience and age, occupational and recreational demands and time availability. Performing more sets will greatly increase the volume and overall intensity of an exercise programme, thereby increasing recovery needs.

Tempo

Tempo refers to the speed at which repetitions are performed and is described in terms of concentric, isometric and eccentric movements. Therefore a '2-1-2' tempo would describe a movement which involves 2 seconds of concentric and eccentric movement, with a 1-second isometric pause (or hold) in the middle. Of the acute exercise variables, tempo is usually given the least consideration, but has an important role in rehabilitation. In the early phases of corrective exercise, where the development of new movement patterns is important, tempo should be slower and controlled to facilitate optimal muscle recruitment. Medicine balls and other plyometric exercises are favoured for task-specific high-speed movements.

Manipulation of the isometric component can produce holding patterns which can be used to improve muscular endurance. These patterns are integral to daily living where a number of isometric holds may be required, for example, gardening. To ensure optimal recovery of muscle, this duration should not exceed 8 seconds. When 8 seconds of isometric contraction can be achieved, an increase of repetitions and load should be prescribed. Corrective exercise programmes for endurance/stabilisation development should include both higher-repetition routines and holding patterns for optimal functional adaptation.

Rest

This refers to the rest period between sets of repetitions and is a crucial element in the client's recovery and consequent performance of an exercise. Too little rest may not provide adequate musculoskeletal and neuromuscular recovery, increasing the risk of immediate injury. Too much rest may reduce the overall intensity of exercise and may slow down or even prevent the desired adaptive response.

Load

The chosen load will be concurrent with repetitions performed and the expected adaptation. It is usually described as a percentage of the client's 1-repetition maximum, as determined objectively using resistance, or subjectively via perceived exertion.

A guide for how to manipulate sets, repetitions, load, tempo and rest for different objectives is given in Table 5.1.

Table 5.1. Manipulation of acute exercise variables for muscular endurance/stabilisation, strength, muscle hypertrophy and power

Adaptation	Sets	Repetitions	Load	Tempo	Rest
Muscular endurance	1–3	15–20	40–60%	1-2-4 1-8-4	0–60 seconds
Strength	2–4	4–6	80–90%	2-0-2	60–90 seconds
Hypertrophy	3–5	6–12	75–85%	1-2-3	30–60 seconds
Power	3–5	1–5 8–10	85–100% 30–45%	Explosive Explosive	2–4 minutes

2 The Shoulder

The shoulder is most appropriately referred to as the 'shoulder complex' and comprises a unique arrangement of bones, joints and muscles that allows the arm an incredibly large range of motion. It is considered one of the most complex musculoskeletal systems of the human body and serves as the functional link between the upper limb and the trunk. Consequently, the shoulder complex must provide mobility, combined with a stable base of support for the arm. While the absence of bony constraints offers this range of motion, stability is sacrificed, being provided by muscles and ligaments. Therefore, normal muscle balance and integration are essential for normal shoulder function, whether for everyday activities or for sport.

Movement of the shoulder and arm occurs through articulation of the shoulder girdle, consisting of the sternoclavicular and acromioclavicular joints, and the shoulder joint, also known as the glenohumeral joint. The dynamic and integrated movement of these joints is known as scapulohumeral rhythm, a phenomenon that requires the coordinated activity of up to 16 muscles. This intimate relationship between the scapula and the humerus results in greater mobility than any other single articulation in the body. Although, occasionally, movement of the scapula is deliberately restricted (as in some postural-based exercises), in all natural and functional movement, articulation of the scapula and the humerus is continuous.

Given the complexity of the shoulder, it is easy to see how a small imbalance in muscle action can lead to functional problems within the shoulder joint; in activities of daily living these often manifest as changes in scapulohumeral rhythm. These changes may cause, or be caused by, poor posture, muscle weakness and imbalance or altered muscle recruitment patterns, resulting in pain, injury and abnormal biomechanics of the shoulder. Effective treatment of these issues involves an understanding of normal shoulder movement, and the therapist must be able to assess correct alignment and movement of the shoulder girdle and shoulder joint, as well as muscle length and strength. Following this, corrective exercise can serve to address these biomechanical deficiencies and restore optimal function.

This section aims to discuss the functional anatomy and biomechanics of the shoulder complex and to relate these biomechanical principles to the accurate prescription of corrective exercise. A functional approach to clinical evaluation of the shoulder will also be presented, laying down an essential foundation to the understanding of exercise prescription. The final chapter provides the therapist with a number of corrective exercises for the shoulder within the context of an overall framework for functional progression. These exercises are designed to rehabilitate effectively and enhance the performance of the shoulder complex.

6 FUNCTIONAL SHOULDER ANATOMY

Overview of shoulder anatomy

The skeletal anatomy of the shoulder joint complex is shown in Figure 6.1. The large range of motion of the shoulder is achieved through the interaction of acromioclavicular and sternoclavicular joints of the shoulder girdle and the shoulder joint itself. This means that all scapula movement is

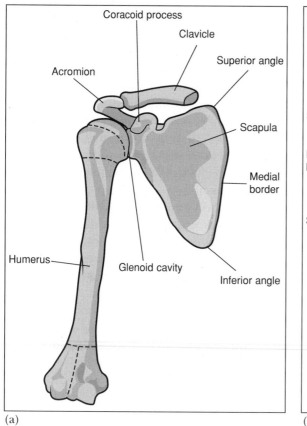

(a)

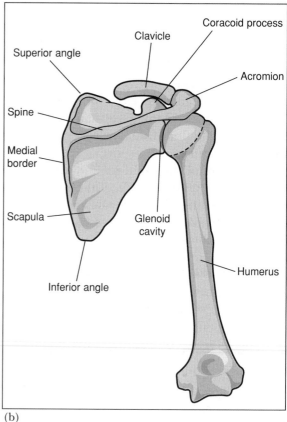

(b)

Figure 6.1. Skeletal anatomy of the shoulder complex – (a) anterior, (b) posterior views

accompanied by movement of the shoulder joint.

Structure and function of the shoulder girdle

The shoulder girdle is made up of the clavicles and the scapulae. The clavicle articulates at two points: laterally with the acromion, forming the acromioclavicular joint, and medially with the sternum, forming the sternoclavicular joint. The sternoclavicular joint provides the only point of articulation with the axial skeleton.

The sternoclavicular joint allows motion of the clavicle in all three planes of motion, producing the following observed movements:

❑ elevation and depression of the shoulder

❑ forward and backward movement of the shoulder

❑ circumduction of the shoulder, with the clavicle revolving forwards and downwards, or backwards and upwards.

Movement at the acromioclavicular joint is limited and involves a gliding motion of the clavicle on the sternum and rotation of the scapula. Movements at the sternoclavicular joint combine with movement at the acromioclavicular joint to produce the large range of movement observed with the scapula (see Figure 6.2).

The seven basic movements of the scapula are:

1   elevation – a movement in which the scapula moves in a superior or upward direction, such as that found in shrugging of the shoulders

2   depression – a movement in which the scapula moves in an inferior or downward direction, normally as a return from elevation or anterior tilt

3   abduction – a movement in which the scapula moves away from the vertebral column, following the line of the ribs

4   adduction – a movement in which the scapula moves towards the vertebral column

5   upward rotation – a movement in which the inferior angle of the scapula moves laterally and the glenoid cavity moves upwards

6   downward rotation – a movement in which the inferior angle of the scapula moves medially and the glenoid cavity moves downwards

7   anterior tilt – movement in which the coracoid process moves downwards and anteriorly, while the inferior angle moves upwards and posteriorly.

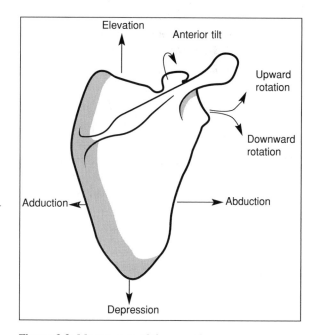

Figure 6.2. Movements of the scapula

During functional activities of daily living and sport, these individual scapula movements do not occur in isolation, and normally a degree of rotation or tilt accompanies abduction/adduction and elevation/depression.

Structure and function of the shoulder joint

The shoulder joint, also known as the glenohumeral joint, is a ball-and-socket joint formed by the articulation of the spherical humeral head with the glenoid fossa. The six basic movements of the shoulder joint are:

1 flexion – an anterior movement of the humerus in the sagittal plane, which may start from a position of 45° extension and ends in an overhead position of 180°. It is important to note that full flexion capability of the shoulder is the result of an integrated action of the shoulder girdle and shoulder joint, known as scapulohumeral rhythm; the first 120° of flexion from a neutral position are provided by the glenohumeral joint, with the remaining 60° of flexion occurring as a result of scapula abduction and upward rotation.

2 extension – a posterior movement of the humerus in the sagittal plane, which may start from a position of full flexion (180°) and end in a position of 45° extension (arm extended backwards). In the presence of elbow flexion, the range of motion for extension will be increased, due to a decrease in the pull of the biceps brachii.

3 abduction – a lateral movement of the humerus in the frontal plane, starting from a neutral position (arm by the side of body) and ending in a position of 180° vertically overhead. This end position is the same as that attained in flexion and is

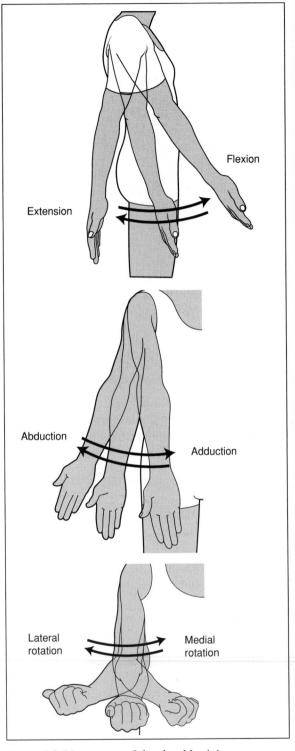

Figure 6.3. Movements of the shoulder joint

the result of coordinated shoulder girdle and shoulder joint movements (scapulohumeral rhythm).

4 adduction – a medial movement of the humerus in the frontal plane, often as a return to the neutral position (arm by the side of body) from full abduction (180°). Adduction also accounts for up to 10° of motion in a direction that is obliquely upwards and in front of the body.

5 lateral rotation – a movement in which the humerus turns about its longitudinal axis, resulting in the anterior surface of the humerus facing away from the mid-sagittal plane (arm turned outwards). The starting point is where the shoulder is in 90° abduction and the elbow flexed to 90°; the end position is where the forearm is parallel to the head at 90° lateral rotation.

6 medial rotation – a movement in which the humerus turns about its longitudinal axis, resulting in the anterior surface of the humerus facing towards the mid-sagittal plane (arm turned inwards). The starting point is where the shoulder is in 90° abduction and the elbow flexed to 90°; the end position is 70° medial rotation, if no shoulder girdle movement is allowed.

Three additional functional movements of the shoulder joint occur as a combination of the above motions:

1 horizontal adduction – a forward movement of the flexed arm in the horizontal plane

2 horizontal abduction – a backward movement of the flexed arm in the horizontal plane

3 circumduction – a sequential combination of flexion, abduction, extension and adduction of an extended arm, so that the arm draws a cone shape with its apex at the glenohumeral joint.

Muscles of the shoulder

During movement of the shoulder complex the synergistic action of up to 16 muscles acts to mobilise and stabilise the scapula and shoulder joint (see Figure 6.4). These muscles have attachments on the scapula, the thorax, the vertebral column and the humerus. The majority are obliquely oriented to provide rotatory as well as linear motion of the shoulder complex.

Clinical perspective

Shoulder pain is commonly associated with medial rotation, which can make the shoulders appear rounded forwards at rest. This will prevent the arm being lifted to a full overhead position (that is, the ability to achieve full flexion or abduction).

When lifting the arm to a full overhead position, a degree of lateral rotation is needed. Medial rotation of the shoulder at rest prevents the natural lateral rotation of the arm as it is lifted. This results in a reduced ability to lift the arm overhead without compensatory movement or pain.

Therefore, a primary objective in corrective exercise would be to restore a functional degree of lateral rotation.

Understanding how these muscles work together to provide stability and movement will enable the therapist to prescribe corrective exercise, restoring muscle balance, range of motion and functional strength.

Pectoralis major

A large fan-shaped muscle consisting of an upper (clavicular) and a lower (sternal) portion. The clavicular portion primarily adducts the arm horizontally and is also

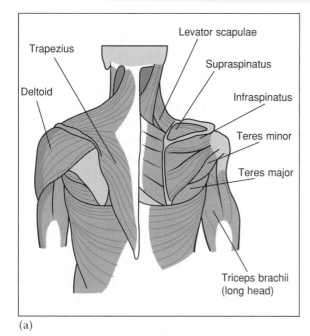

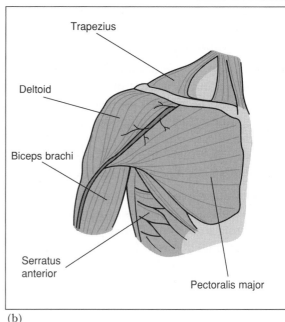

(a)   (b)

Figure 6.4. Muscles of the shoulder – (a) posterior, (b) anterior views

responsible for medial (inward) rotation. Above the horizontal plane the clavicular portion aids further abduction. The sternal portion has an opposite action and produces a downward and forward movement of the arm.

The pectoralis major works synergistically with the serratus anterior and is important in all pushing, throwing and punching movement patterns in the sagittal plane.

Pectoralis minor

A small muscle lying beneath the pectoralis major, involved in anterior tilt of the scapula as well as in downward rotation, depression, abduction and lateral tilt.

When the scapula is stabilised by the middle trapezius and rhomboids, such as during pulling or rowing actions, the pectoralis minor exerts an upward pull on ribs three to five, thus contributing to good thoracic posture. In this way it is regarded as an important postural muscle.

Subclavius

A thin muscle that depresses the clavical, draws the shoulder forwards and downwards and helps to stabilise the sternoclavicular joint during all shoulder movements.

Coracobrachialis

A muscle that acts to adduct the arm weakly and stabilise the humerus during shoulder movement. During adduction it works synergistically with the clavicular portion of the pectoralis major; during stabilisation it works with the middle deltoid and the long head of the triceps.

During multi-planar movement it contributes to global stabilisation of the glenohumeral joint.

Trapezius

A large scapula muscle consisting of three parts (upper, middle and lower fibres), involved in four major movement patterns of the scapula: elevation, upward rotation, adduction and depression.

The upper fibres elevate the scapula during movement and stabilise the scapula during load-bearing activities. The middle fibres adduct the scapula (with the rhomboids) and the lower fibres depress the scapula (along with the pectoralis minor). The upper and lower fibres combine to form a force couple, producing upward rotation of the scapula.

Latissimus dorsi

A broad sheet of muscle that extends, adducts and medially rotates the arm. It also draws the shoulder downwards and backwards. Through its attachment to the inferior angle of the scapula it keeps the scapula positioned against the thoracic wall.

Levator scapulae

A muscle that elevates the medial border of the scapula in conjunction with the upper portion of the trapezius. With the rhomboids and pectoralis minor it acts to produce a downward rotation of the scapula.

Rhomboids (major and minor)

From a functional perspective, the rhomboids act as a single muscle. Their primary action is to adduct and stabilise the scapula in conjunction with the middle fibres of the trapezius. This force couple is important in both static and dynamic shoulder posture.

The secondary action of the rhomboids is downward rotation of the scapula.

Serratus anterior

This muscle works to abduct the scapula, an action that is antagonistic to the action of the rhomboids. It also combines with the upper trapezius to form a force couple that rotates the scapula during abduction and flexion of the arm.

Deltoid

A large muscle of the shoulder consisting of three parts: anterior, middle and posterior portions. The anterior portion acts to flex and medially rotate the arm and is active during all forward movements, such as throwing and punching. The middle portion acts to abduct the arm and the posterior portion extends and laterally rotates the arm.

The rotator cuff group

As a group the rotator cuff muscles act to draw the humerus towards the glenoid fossa and subsequently prevent the larger muscles from dislocating the humerus during movement.

Supraspinatus

Aids the deltoid in abduction of the arm as well as weakly flexing the arm.

Infraspinatus

The main action of this muscle is to rotate laterally and abduct the arm. In particular, this muscle prevents posterior dislocation of the arm during crawling movements.

Teres minor

This muscle contributes to a force couple with the infraspinatus, producing lateral

Clinical perspective – Comparative anatomy of the shoulder and hip joint

The shoulder girdle and joint are dependent upon functional stability of the whole kinetic chain; shoulder instability may be a common manifestation of instability within the hip.

Many approaches to rehabilitation and conditioning of the shoulder and hip joints have been derived from the study of primary reflexes that emerge shortly after birth, such as cross-crawl patterns, where there is smooth integration of the shoulder and hip complexes. Cross-crawl movements, such as four-point kneeling exercises, have been successful in many therapeutic settings. These are based on a number of biomechanical principles, for example, the glenohumeral joint becomes more stable under load, in a closed-chain environment.

Interestingly, there are a number of structural similarities between the shoulder and hip joints. Both joints exhibit a high degree of mobility as ball-and-socket joints, and serve as foundations for the more flexible spinal segments of the cervical and lumbar spine, respectively.

rotation of the arm. It also weakly adducts the arm.

Subscapularis

This muscle's main action is medially to rotate the arm. It specifically contributes to anterior stabilisation of the glenohumeral joint.

Teres major

A small muscle that medially rotates, adducts and extends the arm. During these actions it works with the latissimus dorsi.

Biceps brachii

A large muscle of the arm, which crosses the shoulder joint to flex weakly and adduct the arm.

Triceps brachii (long head)

This muscle aids in extension of the arm as well as adduction of the arm from an abducted position.

Table 6.1.   Summary of muscles involved in shoulder movements

Movement	Prime mover	Synergist
Scapula elevation	Upper trapezius Levator scapulae	Rhomboids Serratus anterior (upper fibres)
Scapula depression	Pectoralis minor Latissimus dorsi	Pectoralis major Lower trapezius
Scapula adduction	Rhomboids Trapezius (middle/lower)	Latissimus dorsi
Scapula abduction	Serratus anterior	Pectoralis minor
Upward rotation of scapula	Trapezius (upper/lower)	Serratus anterior (lower fibres)
Downward rotation of scapula	Rhomboids Pectoralis minor Levator scapulae	Latissimus dorsi Pectoralis major
Flexion	Anterior deltoid Coracobrachialis	Pectoralis major (clavicular portion)
Extension	Latissimus dorsi Teres major Posterior deltoid	Teres minor Triceps brachii (long head)
Abduction	Middle deltoid Supraspinatus	Anterior/posterior deltoid Serratus anterior
Adduction	Pectoralis major Latissimus dorsi	Teres major Anterior deltoid
Medial rotation	Subscapularis Pectoralis major Latissimus dorsi Teres major	Anterior deltoid
Lateral rotation	Infraspinatus Teres minor	Posterior deltoid

7
EVALUATION OF THE SHOULDER

Shoulder evaluation is an important prerequisite to corrective exercise prescription as it helps to identify muscle and movement imbalances of the shoulder complex. This is done using evaluation techniques that draw on an understanding of the functional anatomy of the shoulder in the context of static and dynamic shoulder posture.

This section outlines evaluation of shoulder alignment, scapulohumeral rhythm and muscle length and strength. Combining the results of these assessments will help build a progressive corrective exercise programme.

Alignment analysis

Overall shoulder alignment is a good indicator of changes in muscle length and of joint alignment that may need to be corrected to allow for optimal motion, during exercise or daily activities. Observed muscle tightness or weakness can then be determined by testing for length and strength. Deviations in alignment are those that differ from the ideal postural standard.

Normal scapula alignment

In ideal postural alignment, the scapulae lie parallel to one another against the thorax, with the medial border of each positioned about two inches from the thoracic spine; superiorly and inferiorly, the scapulae are positioned between ribs two and seven (see Figure 7.1). The scapulae are tilted approximately 30° anterior to the frontal plane.

Common alignment problems

Common scapula misalignments to look for when assessing static shoulder posture include the following.

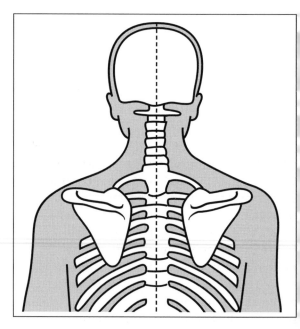

Figure 7.1. Normal scapula alignment – posterior view

Scapula elevation

Elevation of the scapula causes the shoulders to appear closer to the ears, making the neck appear short.

Elevation of the entire scapula suggests shortness of the upper trapezius; if scapula adduction is also observed, rhomboid and levator scapulae shortness may also be present.

Elevation of the superior angle suggests shortness of the levator scapulae.

Excessive scapula depression

Depression of scapulae causes the clavicles to appear horizontal; in excessive depression, the acromioclavicular joint is lower than the sternoclavicular joint.

Depression suggests upper trapezius weakness, and the pectoralis major and latissimus dorsi may be short. During flexion/abduction, this can result in excessive stress at the acromioclavicular and glenohumeral joints.

Scapula adduction

Adduction is observed when the medial border of the scapula is less than 2 inches from the spine; the rhomboid and middle trapezius may be short, while the serratus anterior is weak.

Scapula abduction

Abduction is observed when the medial border is more than 3 inches away from the spine and the scapula is positioned more than 30° anterior to the frontal plane. In this case, the glenoid is positioned further forwards and the humerus will appear medially rotated. Exercise prescription should focus on corrective scapula adduction as, more often than not, adduction of the scapula will also correct the apparent rotation in the humerus.

The short muscles in abduction-rotation are the serratus anterior and pectoralis major.

Anterior tilting

Anterior tilting causes the inferior angle of the scapula to protrude away from the thorax. This is often associated with shortness of the pectoralis minor and/or shortness of the biceps brachii and anterior deltoid. If the biceps brachii is short, correct scapula repositioning will cause the elbow to flex.

Downward rotation

Downward rotation occurs when the inferior angle of the scapula is closer to the spine and the medial border is not parallel. In most cases, the rhomboids and levator scapulae are short, and the upper trapezius and serratus anterior are weak. This is a common deviation in those with shoulder pain.

Scapular winging

Winging of the scapula is observed when the medial border protrudes away from the thorax and is associated with weakness of the serratus anterior. Winged scapulae may also

Clinical perspective

Clients with scoliosis often have kyphosis and rotation of the spine, which forms a rib 'hump', resulting in misalignment of the scapula on one side of the body. If the rib 'hump' causes the scapula to wing, the client should not be encouraged to correct the alignment by contraction of the scapula adductors. Shortness of these muscles restricts abduction and upward rotation of the scapula, leading to possible rotator cuff tears, impingement and neck pain, caused by excessive tension in the upper trapezius.

be due to a flat thoracic spine, a rounded back or even scoliosis.

In clients who perform chin-ups or climbing activities, there may be hypertrophy of the subscapularis, which gives rise to the appearance of winged scapula; in this case, the scapulae are no longer flat on the thorax.

Movement analysis

Overall shoulder movement is best observed by looking at the integrated relationship of the shoulder girdle and shoulder joint – a phenomenon known as *scapulohumeral rhythm*. For every 3° of shoulder movement, the glenohumeral joint contributes 2° of movement and the scapula contributes 1° of movement. This timing is considered to be the normal standard for shoulder movement.

Scapulohumeral rhythm is seen in all movements of the shoulder, especially during the later stages of flexion and abduction. Assessment of these movements can be made by visual means and can be assisted using palpation of the inferior angle of the scapula during movement. It is important to note that if the scapula and humerus are not correctly aligned at the start of movement, compensation will occur *during* movement, giving rise to potential joint and muscle stress.

By instructing the client to perform flexion and abduction (and rotation) movements (as outlined below), the therapist can identify deviations in scapulohumeral timing and subsequent muscle imbalances.

Upward rotation

During full flexion, the scapula will stop moving when the shoulder is flexed to 140°, with the remaining movement occurring at the glenohumeral joint. At 180° of flexion, the inferior angle should be close to the midline of the thorax in the frontal plane, and the medial border should be upwardly rotated to 60°. At this point, the scapula should slightly depress, posterior tilt and adduct. Excessive kyphosis and/or a short pectoralis minor can inhibit this end range movement.

Movement of the inferior angle beyond the midline indicates excessive scapula abduction, suggesting rhomboid weakness. This test can be administered in both standing and supine positions.

Scapula winging

The scapula should not wing during flexion/abduction movements or during the return. Winging indicates weakness of the serratus anterior muscle.

Scapula elevation

There should be some elevation (shrugging) of the shoulder during flexion/abduction, especially during the later stages (greater than 90°).

If there is excessive depression at rest, elevation of the scapula during these movements must be restored, usually by strengthening the upper trapezius.

Position of the humerus

The head of the humerus should stay centred throughout flexion/abduction. For this to occur, the rotator cuff musculature must offset the upward pull of the deltoid by laterally rotating the humerus, to prevent impingement at the acromion.

In clients with rotator cuff weakness, the pectoralis major and latissimus dorsi may act instead to force the humeral head into the glenoid fossa. Because both these muscles medially rotate the humerus, lexion/abduction movements will alter the position of the humeral head in the glenoid, causing impingement and pain.

Spine

There should be minimal movement of the spine during full flexion/abduction movements. A thoracic kyphosis will cause an anterior tilt of the scapula, thereby limiting full flexion capability. This is a movement impairment commonly seen in those whose occupations involve prolonged seated postures.

Scapula adduction

When the elbow is flexed to 90°, lateral rotation of the shoulder should not cause scapula adduction during the first 35° motion. Adduction of the scapula is a sign of rhomboid dominance and/or poor control of shoulder rotation.

If there is an accompanied posterior movement of the humeral head, this may indicate dominance of the posterior deltoid over the teres minor and infraspinatus.

Muscle length

Muscle length testing will determine whether the range of muscle length is normal, limited or excessive. For full range of motion in the

Table 7.1. Muscles whose adequate length is important for full shoulder movement

Movement	Muscles
Scapulohumeral flexion or abduction	Pectorales major and minor Latissimus dorsi Teres major Subscapularis Rhomboids
Lateral rotation	Pectoralis major Latissimus dorsi Teres major Subscapularis
Medial rotation	Teres minor Infraspinatus Posterior deltoid

shoulder there are a number of muscles that must have adequate length. Muscles important in scapulohumeral movement during flexion or abduction and lateral and medial rotation that should be tested are listed in Table 7.1.

The lengths of these muscles can be assessed using the tests outlined below. To eliminate trunk movement during testing, these tests should be administered with the client supine, knees bent and low back flat on the couch.

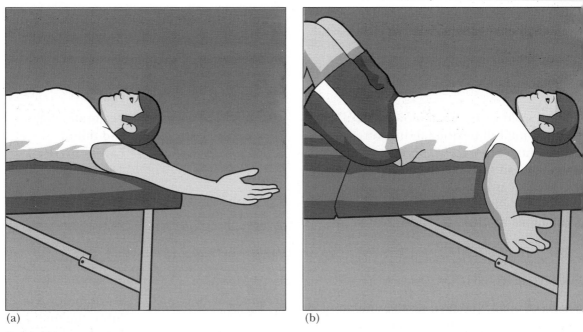

(a)   (b)

Figure 7.2. Test for length of pectoralis major – (a) normal length of lower fibres, (b) normal length of upper fibres

Muscle(s): Pectoralis major.
Starting position: Client is supine, with knees bent, low back flat, arms by sides.
Test: Clavicular portion – the shoulder is laterally rotated (palm up) and arm is abducted to 90°; sternal portion (lower fibres) – as above, except that the arm is abducted to 135°.

Normal length: The arm rests at table level, with low back remaining flat.
Shortness: Shortness is observed when the arm does not drop down to the level of the table.
Excessive length: The arm drops below the level of the table if the client is positioned at the edge of the couch.

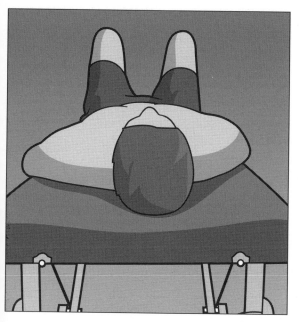

Figure 7.3. Test for length of pectoralis minor – left, normal length; right, short

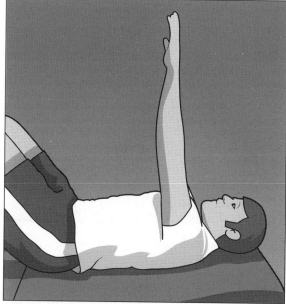

(a)

Muscle(s): Pectoralis minor.
Starting position: Client is supine, with knees bent, low back flat, arms by sides.
Test: Therapist looks down at the client's shoulders from the head of the couch.
Normal length: The back of the shoulder is in contact with the couch.
Shortness: The shoulder is raised above the level of the couch.

Muscle(s): Teres major, latissimus dorsi, rhomboids.
Starting position: Client is supine, with knees bent, low back flat, arms by sides.
Test: Client raises both arms in flexion overhead, keeping arms close to the head.
Normal length: Arms are brought down to table level, while maintaining a flat low back.
Shortness: Inability to get arms to table level. If the client has tightness of the upper abdominals, this will give a false test reading in favour of shortness.

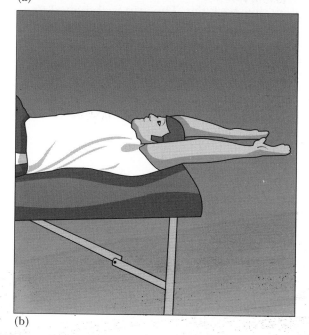

(b)

Figure 7.4. Test for length of teres major, latissimus dorsi, rhomboids – (a) start position, (b) end position

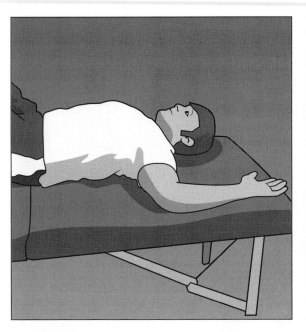

Figure 7.5. Test for length of medial rotators

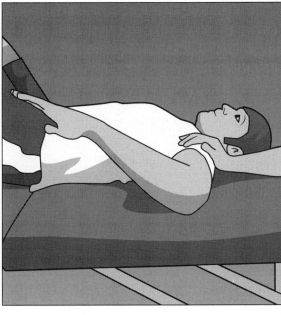

Figure 7.6. Test for length of lateral rotators

Muscle(s): Medial rotators.
Starting position: Client is supine, with knees bent, low back flat. The arm is abducted to 90° and the elbow is flexed to 90°, with the forearm perpendicular to the table.
Test: Lateral rotation of shoulder, bringing forearm down towards the table, parallel with head.
Normal length: Forearm flat on table (90°), with low back flat.

Muscle(s): Lateral rotators.
Starting position: Client is supine, with knees bent, low back flat. The arm is abducted to 90° and the elbow is flexed to 90°, with the forearm perpendicular to the table.
Test: Medial rotation of shoulder, bringing forearm down towards the table (palm down), while therapist holds the shoulder down. This will prevent compensatory movement of the shoulder girdle.
Normal length: Forearm almost flat on table (70° of motion).

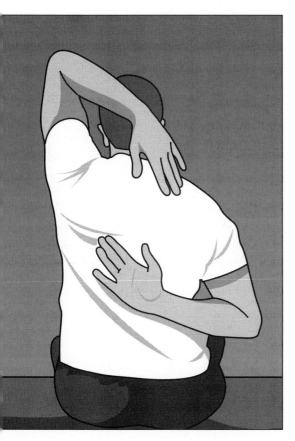

Figure 7.7. Test for length of medial and lateral rotators

Muscle(s): Medial and lateral rotators.
Starting position: Client is standing, with arms by sides.

Test: Client reaches one hand behind back to touch the inferior angle of the opposite scapula (medial rotation), and reaches the other hand over the shoulder on the same side to touch the superior angle of the scapula (lateral rotation).
Normal length: No excessive movement substitution by the shoulder girdle.
Shortness: Substitution of the shoulder girdle when reaching behind the back indicates functional shortness of the lateral rotators. Substitution of the shoulder girdle when reaching over the shoulder indicates functional shortness of the medial rotators. Excessive substitution of the shoulder girdle may result in overdevelopment of the pectoralis minor.

Muscle strength

Muscle strength testing in the shoulder will determine the ability of muscles to provide stability and movement. As shoulder muscle weakness can be caused by disuse as well as overuse, it is essential for the therapist to collate these results with those of alignment and movement analysis and muscle length testing.

The major shoulder muscles that contribute to movement and stability which should be tested are outlined below.

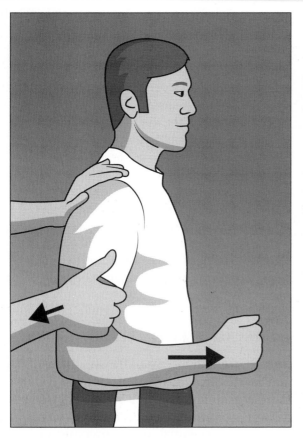

Figure 7.8. Anterior deltoid strength test

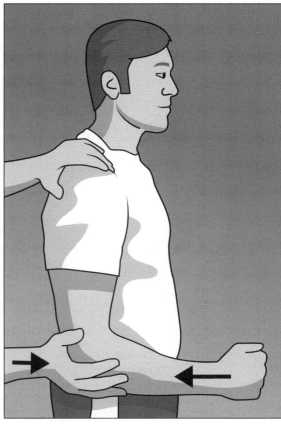

Figure 7.9. Posterior deltoid strength test

Muscle(s)/movement: Anterior deltoid/flexion.
Starting position: Sitting with elbow flexed to 90°.
Test: Place palm down on acromion to stabilise scapula and palpate anterior deltoid. Client resists posterior palmar pressure applied on the anterior arm around lower bicep.
Weakness: Decreased ability to push arm forwards-upwards.
Shortness: Decreased range of motion in extension.

Muscle(s)/movement: Posterior deltoid/extension.
Starting position: Sitting with elbow flexed to 90°.
Test: Place palm down on acromion to stabilise scapula and palpate long head of triceps with thumb, and posterior deltoid with palm. Pressure is now applied with other hand on the distal humerus in an anterior direction.
Weakness: Decreased ability to push arm backwards-upwards.
Shortness: Decreased range of motion in flexion.

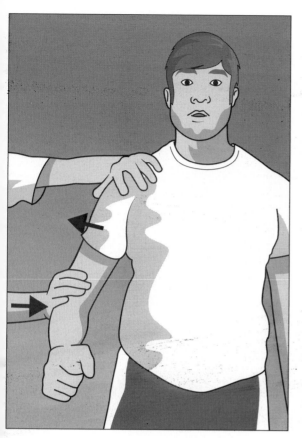

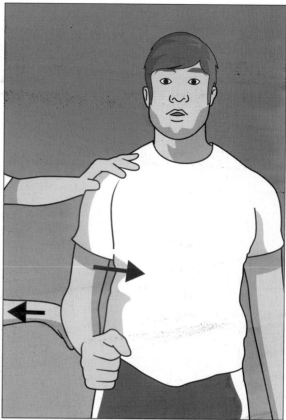

Figure 7.10. Middle deltoid strength test

Figure 7.11. Pectoralis major/latissimus dorsi strength test

Muscle(s)/movement: Middle deltoid/abduction.
Starting position: Sitting with elbow flexed to 90°.
Test: Stabilise the acromion with palm on middle deltoid. Other palm applies pressure on lateral epicondyle of humerus, as client abducts arm.
Weakness: Decreased ability to lift arm in abduction; downward translation of humeral head.
Shortness: Decreased range of motion in adduction.

Muscle(s)/movement: Pectoralis major/adduction.
Starting position: Sitting with elbow flexed to 90°.
Test: Stabilise acromion with palm on middle deltoid. Other palm applies pressure on medial epicondyle of humerus, as client adducts arm. Palpate pectoralis major during movement.
Weakness: Decreased ability to adduct arm.
Shortness: Decreased range of movement in abduction.

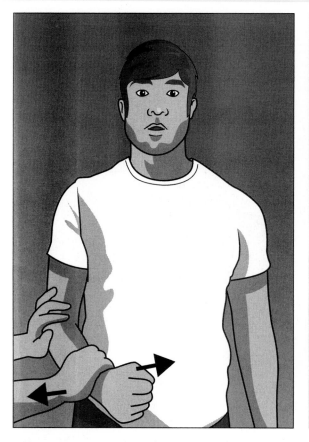

Figure 7.12. Internal rotator strength test

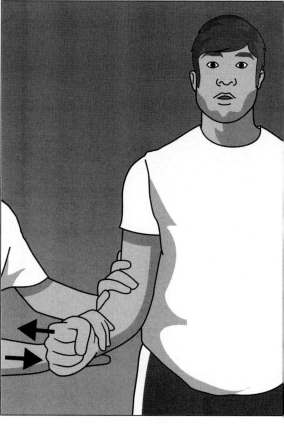

Figure 7.13. External rotator strength test

Muscle(s)/movement: Subscapularis, pectoralis major/internal rotation.
Starting position: Sitting with elbow flexed to 90°.
Test: Stabilise humerus by holding elbow joint by waist. Place other hand on wrist and instruct client to rotate arm inwards against resistance.
Weakness: Decreased ability medially to rotate humerus; humerus assumes position of lateral rotation.
Shortness: Range of motion limited in lateral rotation and overhead flexion.

Muscle(s)/movement: Infraspinatus, teres minor/external rotation.
Starting position: Sitting with elbow flexed to 90°.
Test: Stabilise humerus by holding elbow joint by waist. Place other hand on wrist and instruct client to rotate arm outwards.
Weakness: Decreased ability laterally to rotate humerus; humerus assumes position of medial rotation.
Shortness: Range of motion limited in medial rotation.

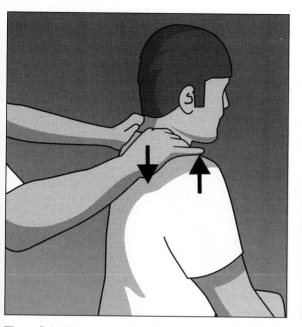
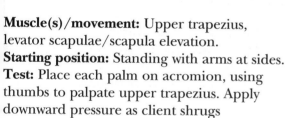

Figure 7.14. Upper trapezius/levator scapulae strength test

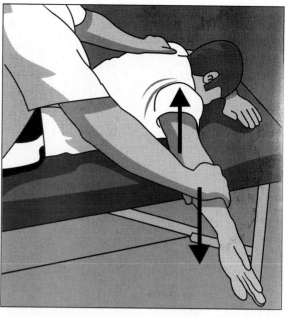

Figure 7.15. Rhomboid strength test

Muscle(s)/movement: Upper trapezius, levator scapulae/scapula elevation.
Starting position: Standing with arms at sides.
Test: Place each palm on acromion, using thumbs to palpate upper trapezius. Apply downward pressure as client shrugs shoulders.
Weakness: Decreased ability to elevate scapulae and extend cervical spine; the presence of scapula abduction as rhomboid stabilisation is lost; medial rotation.
Shortness: Scapula starts movement from a position of adduction and elevation; shortness accompanies serratus weakness (rhomboid dominance).

Muscle(s)/movement: Rhomboid/scapula retraction.
Starting position: Prone, lying with test arm held away from table in medial rotation and 90° abduction. The scapula should be slightly elevated.
Test: One hand is placed on the opposite scapula to fixate it. Pressure is applied against the forearm in a downward direction, and client resists.
Weakness: Decreased ability to retract scapulae; abduction of scapula and forward shoulder position in static posture.
Shortness: Scapula starts movement from a position of adduction and elevation; weak serratus.

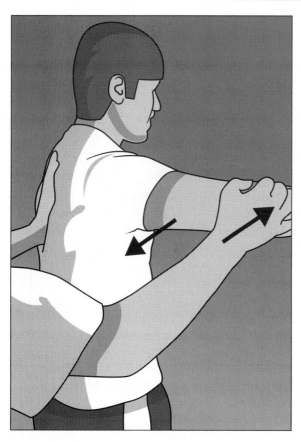

Figure 7.16. Serratus anterior strength test

Muscle(s)/movement: Serratus anterior/scapula protraction.
Starting position: Standing with arm flexed to 90° and elbow flexed to approximately 90°.
Test: Stand behind client and place palm on thoracic spine to stabilise trunk. Cup the other hand around the flexed elbow and apply resistance posteriorly. Client to resist motion by pushing the elbow forwards.
Weakness: Winging of scapula; difficulty in flexing arm.
Shortness: Abduction of scapula during static alignment, often accompanied by weak rhomboids; forward shoulder position.

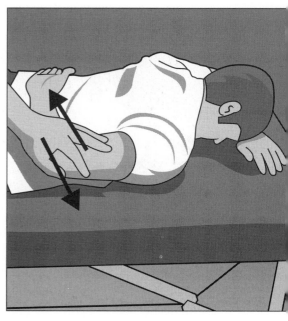

Figure 7.17. Teres major strength test

Muscle(s)/movement: Teres major/extension, adduction.
Starting position: Prone, lying with arm in extension and adduction; elbow is flexed to allow hand to rest on lower back.
Test: Pressure is applied against arm, just above elbow, in the direction of abduction and flexion.
Weakness: Decreased ability to hold extension/abduction.
Shortness: Full range of motion limited in lateral rotation and abduction; scapula will begin to rotate simultaneously with flexion/abduction.

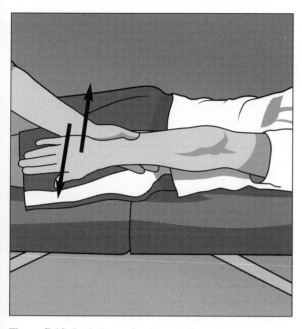

Figure 7.18. Latissimus dorsi strength test

Muscle(s)/movement: Latissimus dorsi.
Starting position: Prone, lying with arm straight by the sides, in medial rotation.
Test: Pressure against forearm in direction of abduction and slight flexion. Client tries to adduct and extend arm.
Weakness: Inability to adduct arm towards body. Lateral trunk flexion is reduced.
Shortness: Limitation in flexion/abduction. Depression of shoulder girdle downwards. Seen in long-term crutch-walking patients.

8
CORRECTIVE EXERCISE FOR THE SHOULDER

Corrective exercise progression

The goals of corrective exercise for the shoulder are twofold: to re-establish muscle balance and neuromuscular control and to provide adequate functional progression for reintegration into activities of daily living and/or sport.

Stability of both the scapula and shoulder joint is desirable before functional strength can be introduced; but at the same time, the complex mobility that the shoulder affords must not be overlooked. Therefore, an effective rehabilitation programme should include stability and mobility exercises.

The client may then progress to functional strength exercises that condition the shoulder complex for load-bearing and load-transferring activities once mobility and stability have been restored. Many of these movement patterns fall into the three main categories of pushing, pulling and rotation. During each of these movements, the shoulder is intimate with the back and contralateral hip musculature.

With this in mind, the final stages of corrective exercise should focus on whole-body power movements that enable the lower extremities to coordinate and transfer ground reaction forces through the torso and up to the shoulder, for example, during lifting, throwing and chopping actions.

The following exercises are divided into four progressive phases.

Phase 1 – Muscle balance

These exercises are aimed at restoring normal muscle length, in particular, the muscles responsible for gross shoulder movement. Many of the exercises can be started during the acute stages of injury and progressed by adding resistance, either manually by the therapist or with weights. As a result, pain-free and compensation-free range of motion will be re-established within the shoulder joint and shoulder girdle.

Phase 2 – Static, dynamic and reactive stabilisation

These exercises aim to match the functional stabilisation demands of the shoulder, by emphasising co-contraction force couples at the shoulder girdle and shoulder joint. Static stabilisation exercises activate the rotator cuff musculature, with minimal joint movement, while dynamic stabilisation requires activation of agonist–antagonist force couples during range-of-motion activities. Reactive stabilisation exercises focus on stimulating proprioceptive pathways that exist in functional shoulder movements and help to condition feedback and feed-forward mechanisms.

These exercises will re-establish scapular control and rotator cuff strength in both open- and closed-chain settings.

Phase 3 – Functional strength

The goal during this phase is to reintegrate shoulder stabilisation into activities of daily living and/or sports performance; in order to prescribe exercise accurately, it is important for the therapist to understand the functional demands of the patient, including occupational, recreational and sporting factors. These movements can then be restored to integrate pain-free shoulder strength and function. Before reintegration it is important to address deficiencies elsewhere in the kinetic chain.

The outcomes of this phase include increased functional strength in both open- and closed-chain environments, as well as improved link-sequencing and force generation from the lower extremities through to the shoulder complex.

Phase 4 – Functional power

These exercises address the specific demands imposed on the shoulder by activities seen in both occupation and sport. Almost all shoulder joint and shoulder girdle movements involve acceleration and deceleration mechanics, and are rarely performed at fixed speeds, for example, picking up a child from the floor or pushing a car door shut.

The preferred method of conditioning during this phase is plyometric exercise, requiring quick, powerful and explosive movements of the shoulder, often in conjunction with the entire kinetic chain. For this to occur safely, range of motion, stabilisation and functional strength must all

be optimal. Particular emphasis should also be placed on optimal hip and trunk rotation, to ensure smooth coordination of ground reaction forces up through the body.

This will result in coordination and control of movement, providing a high degree of functional carry-over into occupation, recreation and sport.

Corrective exercises for the shoulder

Phase 1 exercises – Restoring muscle balance and flexibility

Scapulohumeral muscle stretch
Muscle group(s): Latissimus dorsi, teres major/minor, pectoralis major
Phase/modality: Flexibility, muscle balance
Equipment: None

Purpose
- ❏ To stretch the latissimus dorsi, pectoralis major and teres major/minor.
- ❏ To increase range of motion of shoulder flexion.
- ❏ To decrease upper back curve.
- ❏ To increase performance of abdominal muscles.

Prerequisites
- ❏ Pain-free range of motion in shoulder flexion.
- ❏ Adequate pelvic control to maintain flat lumbar spine.
- ❏ Clients with kyphosis may need to place a pillow under thoracic spine and head.

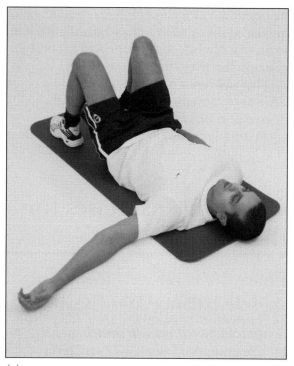

(a)

(c)

(b)

Figure 8.1. Scapulohumeral muscle stretch – (a) pectoralis major upper fibres, (b) pectoralis major lower fibres, (c) latissimus dorsi/teres major/teres minor

Starting position

Client is supine, with hips and knees flexed, low back flat, arms at sides.

Correct performance

❑ To stretch the pectoralis major, the client keeps elbows extended and abducts the arms to 90°. In this position, they are instructed to pull back the scapula with the middle trapezii to stretch the pectoralis major. Stretch is held for 5–10 seconds before resting and repeating for a total of 10 repetitions. To stretch the lower fibres of the pectoralis major, the stretch is performed in a position of 130°

abduction. Here, the client is instructed to depress the scapula using the lower trapezius.

❑ To stretch the latissimus dorsi, the client keeps the elbows extended while flexing both shoulders. Arms should be kept close to ears and the shoulder should be maintained in lateral rotation. The lower back must remain flat against the table/floor. The client holds the end range for 5–10 seconds and then returns arms to the sides, performing 10 repetitions.

❑ To stretch the teres major/minor, the client performs the above, except that once shoulder flexion reaches 90°, the client uses the opposite hand to hold the inferior angle of the scapula against the chest wall and completes the movement. The client holds the end range for 5–10 seconds, alternating arms after 10 repetitions.

Medial rotation
Muscle group(s): Lateral rotators
Phase/modality: Flexibility, mobility, strength
Equipment: None

Purpose
❑ To stretch lateral rotators of shoulder.
❑ To eliminate anterior tilt of scapula with rotation.
❑ To eliminate anterior glide of humeral head during medial rotation.
❑ To improve performance of lateral rotators.

Prerequisites
❑ Pain-free range of motion in abduction.
❑ If range of motion is limited in rotation, a small weight can be added to assist the stretch. The weight should be heavy enough to exert a rotational effect, but not so heavy as to stimulate lateral rotation.
❑ Optimal flexibility of scapular motion.

(a)

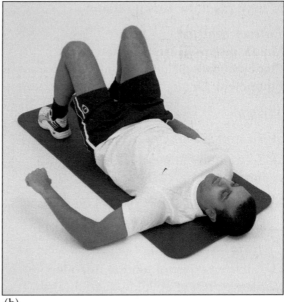
(b)

Figure 8.2. Medial rotation – (a) before, (b) after

Starting position

Client is supine, with hips and knees flexed, shoulder abducted to 90° (neutral rotation), elbow flexed to 90°. A small towel may be placed under the arm to align humerus in the scapula plane. The client holds down the shoulder with the opposite hand to prevent anterior motion of the humeral head or anterior tilt of the scapula.

Correct performance

❑ The client medially rotates the humerus, allowing the forearm to drop to the table, without lifting the shoulder girdle.

❑ The arm is returned and the movement is repeated slowly and continuously 5–10 times until full range of motion is achieved, without compensation or pain.

❑ The exercise is repeated with the other arm.

Progressions

After client is able to perform the movement correctly, the addition of weights can be used to strengthen the lateral rotators.

Lateral rotation

Muscle group(s): Medial rotators
Phase/modality: Flexibility, mobility, strength
Equipment: None

Purpose

❑ To stretch shoulder medial rotators.

❑ To train the humerus to move independently of the scapula.

❑ To improve performance of medial rotators.

Prerequisites

❑ Pain-free range of motion in abduction. If pain is present at 90° abduction, the degree of abduction should be reduced, by supporting arm on a towel to position

shoulder in mild flexion (plane of scapula).

❑ Optimal flexibility of scapular motion.

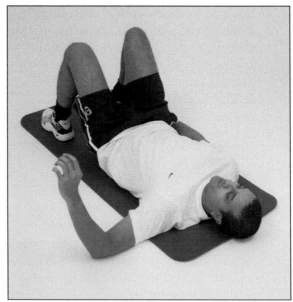

(a)

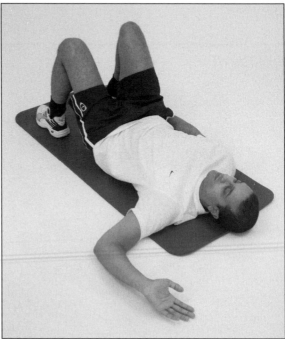

(b)

Figure 8.3. Lateral rotation – (a) before, (b) after

Starting position

Client is supine, with hips and knees flexed, shoulder abducted to 90° (neutral rotation) and elbow flexed to 90°, as in the previous exercise.

Correct performance

❑ Client laterally rotates humerus while maintaining a constant position of the scapula and no humeral head movement.

❑ The arm is returned and the movement is repeated slowly and continuously 5–10 times until full range of motion is achieved, without compensation or pain.

❑ The exercise is repeated with the other arm.

Progressions

After client is able to perform the movement correctly, the addition of weights can be used to strengthen the medial rotators.

Side-lying circumduction and thoracic integration

Muscle group(s): Shoulder, arm, chest back

Phase/modality: Flexibility, mobility, strength
Equipment: None

Purpose

❑ To enhance awareness and performance of scapulohumeral rhythm.

❑ To integrate range of motion of the shoulder/arm into gentle thoracic and trunk movements.

Prerequisites

❑ Pain-free range of motion at the shoulder and elbow.

❑ A good degree of flexibility in the trunk rotators.

Starting position

Client is side-lying, with hip and knee flexion to approximately 90°. The spine should be in a neutral position, with the head resting comfortably on the straight flexed arm. The topmost arm should be positioned in 90° abduction and 90° elbow flexion, and in horizontal adduction, so that the palm rests on the floor, about 12 inches in front of the client's chest. The elbow should be positioned above the wrist.

(a)   (b)

Figure 8.4. Side-lying circumduction and thoracic integration – (a) before, (b) after

Correct performance

❑ Keeping the palm in position (some movement at the wrist is allowed), the client begins to move the elbow in a circular motion, moving it forwards, down, back and up, as if drawing a circle.

❑ To integrate the movement with the trunk, the client is instructed to allow the head and trunk to rotate inwards as the elbow moves away from the body – as if they are about to kiss the floor; as the elbow moves down towards the feet, the client should move the trunk back to the centre and gently depress the scapula; as the elbow moves towards the body, the client should gently retract the scapula while rotating the torso outwards; and finally, when the elbow moves upwards, the client should elevate the scapula (shrugging).

❑ The movement should be continued smoothly for 5–10 repetitions, before changing direction. The exercise is repeated on the other side.

❑ Particular awareness should be placed on smooth integration of the scapulohumeral rhythm with torso rotation.

Progressions

Surgical tubing may be tied around the client's arm, just above the elbow, to provide gentle multidirectional resistance.

Trapezius activation
Muscle group(s): Middle and lower trapezius
Phase/modality: Muscle balance, flexibility, endurance, stabilisation
Equipment: None

Purpose

❑ To improve performance of the middle and lower trapezius muscles.

❑ To integrate trapezius action into lateral rotation of the shoulder.

(a)

(b)

(c)

Figure 8.5. Trapezius activation – (a) level 1, (b) level 2, (c) level 3

Prerequisites

❑ Optimal scapular control and flexibility.

❑ Optimal range of motion in shoulder lateral rotation.

❑ Ability to maintain a neutral lumbar curvature, with adequate abdominal strength.

Starting position

Client is lying prone, with legs straight. Shoulders and elbows are flexed, with fingers interlaced behind head. Towels may be placed under each shoulder to correct any anterior tilt of the scapulae.

Correct performance

❑ LEVEL 1 – the client lifts the arms by adducting the scapulae. The client should visualise a diagonal downward movement of the scapulae and should not allow the shoulders to shrug – this would suggest upper trapezius and rhomboid action. The position should be held for up to 8 seconds, before relaxing and repeating 5–10 times. (Special attention should be paid to depressing the shoulder girdle using the lower trapezius, rather than the latissimus dorsi.)

❑ LEVEL 2 – the client assumes the same position as above, except that the hands are now resting by the sides of the head on the ulnar borders (thumbs pointing upwards). The client adducts the scapula as before, by bringing the shoulder blades towards and down the spine. The client should lift the arm and hand while contracting the trapezius. The hand should remain slightly higher than the elbow to emphasise lateral rotation. This position is held for up to 8 seconds, before relaxing and repeating 5–10 times.

❑ LEVEL 3 – the client is positioned as above, except that the elbows are now extended with the shoulders in 120° abduction. The client adducts the scapula as before, by bringing the shoulder blades towards and down the spine, lifting the arms 1–2 inches off the table/floor. This position is held for up to 8 seconds, before relaxing and repeating 5–10 times.

Progressions

❑ This exercise may be performed using alternate arms, with an opposite glute contraction to re-educate a cross-crawl pattern.

❑ Small weights may be added to each hand.

Prone serratus pull
Muscle group(s): Serratus anterior, shoulder/arm
Phase/modality: Muscle balance, strength
Equipment: None

Purpose

❑ To re-establish neuromuscular control of the scapula protractors.

❑ To restore balance between the scapula retractors and protractors.

❑ To improve performance of the serratus anterior muscle.

Prerequisites

❑ Pain-free extension of lumbar spine. If the client has an excessive lumbar lordosis, this exercise should not be used.

❑ Optimal scapular control.

Starting position

The client is prone, lying with the upper body supported on both elbows. The elbows should be positioned under the shoulders and the scapulae should assume a neutral position of retraction/protraction.

 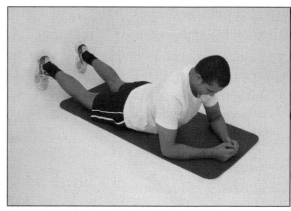

(a)   (b)

Figure 8.6. Prone serratus pull – (a) before, (b) after

Correct performance

❑ The client begins by allowing the thorax to drop down towards the floor, by controlling scapula retraction under gravity. Using equal pressure applied through both elbows, the client then pushes the thorax upwards (as if trying to push the floor away from the body). This action will contract the serratus anterior.

❑ The client should aim to increase awareness of the movement, as well as scapula control, through protraction.

Progressions

The therapist may apply pressure to the upper back to increase strength of the serratus anterior.

Standing shoulder flexion
Muscle group(s): Shoulder flexors, serratus anterior, rotator cuff
Phase/modality: Flexibility, muscle balance, strength, stabilisation
Equipment: None

Purpose

❑ To increase range of shoulder flexion.

❑ To improve performance of serratus anterior and shoulder flexors.

❑ To reduce compensatory elevation of shoulder girdle during flexion.

❑ To encourage depression of the humeral head during flexion.

Prerequisites

❑ Some pain-free range of motion in flexion.

❑ Adequate abdominal control to stabilise lumbar spine.

Starting position

Client stands close to and facing the wall, with feet comfortably apart. The shoulders and elbows are flexed to 90°, with the ulnar surface of the forearms and hands resting on the wall. The client should exert some pressure against the wall, to create a depression force of the humeral heads.

Correct performance

❑ The client flexes the shoulders by sliding the hands up the wall. The humerus should not medially rotate during flexion.

(a)   (b)

Figure 8.7. Standing shoulder flexion – (a) before, (b) after

The movement is stopped when the client reaches a comfortable range of flexion or when pain occurs in the region of the acromion.

❏ The end position is held for up to 8 seconds, before returning to the start and repeating 5–10 times.

❏ If the rotator cuff is particularly weak, the client can use one hand to assist shoulder flexion.

❏ The therapist can also assist in scapula upward rotation, particularly if the rhomboids are dominant.

Progressions

❏ If complete range of motion can be achieved, the client can lift the hands away from the wall at end range and hold, before allowing the arms to slide back down to the start position.

❏ To enhance performance of this exercise, the client should be instructed to think about scapula abduction and upward rotation.

Standing shoulder abduction

Muscle group(s): Shoulder abductors, trapezius
Phase/modality: Flexibility, muscle balance, strength, stabilisation
Equipment: None

Purpose

❏ To improve performance of the trapezius.

❏ To increase range of scapula upward rotation.

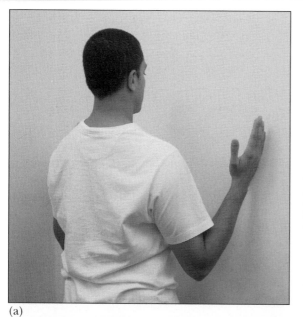

(a)

(b)

(c)

Figure 8.8. Standing shoulder abduction – (a) start position, (b) upper trapezius activation, (c) lower trapezius activation

❑ To improve control of humeral lateral rotation.

Prerequisites
❑ Pain-free range of motion in shoulder abduction (up to 140°).

❑ Adequate abdominal control to stabilise lumbar spine.

Starting position
Client stands close to and facing the wall, with feet comfortably apart. The elbows are

flexed, with the arms at the sides of the body, in slight abduction, and the ulnar surface of the forearms and hands resting on the wall – this position requires lateral rotation of the humerus and adduction of the scapulae. The client should exert some pressure against the wall, to create a depression force of the humeral heads.

Correct performance

❏ UPPER TRAPEZIUS – the client is instructed to abduct the shoulders by sliding the forearms up the wall, in a diagonal pattern. When abduction reaches 90°, the client should shrug the shoulders while continuing abduction/elevation. This will activate the upper trapezius. At completion of motion, the client should lift the arms away from the wall by adducting the scapula and hold this position for up to 8 seconds.

❏ LOWER TRAPEZIUS – the client should abduct the shoulders as before, continuing to end range. At completion,

they are instructed to lift the arms away from the wall by adducting and depressing the scapula. This position is held for up to 8 seconds, before reversing the motion back to the start position.

❏ The therapist should ensure that the client is adducting the scapula and not just moving the glenohumeral joint or depressing the scapula using the latissimus dorsi.

Progressions

Holding times should be increased progressively, up to 8 seconds.

Wall climbing
Muscle group(s): Shoulder flexors, shoulder abductors
Phase/modality: Flexibility
Equipment: None

Purpose

To restore active full range of motion in flexion and abduction.

(a)

(b)

Figure 8.9. Wall climbing – (a) before, (b) after

Prerequisites

Pain-free active range of motion.

Starting position

Client stands close to and facing wall, with elbow flexed, shoulder in slight extension and palm on wall.

Correct performance

❑ Client begins by slowly walking the hand up the wall, into shoulder flexion, extending the elbow as the hand gets higher. Range of motion should be restricted to a pain-free arc.

❑ The client should be instructed to be aware of scapulohumeral rhythm during the movement.

❑ The hand is walked back down and the movement repeated 5–10 times, before changing hands.

Progressions

The exercise can also be performed as an abduction movement, with the client standing side-on to the wall.

Wall corner stretch

Muscle group(s): Pectoralis major, pectoralis minor, anterior deltoid
Phase/modality: Flexibility
Equipment: None

Purpose

❑ To stretch the anterior musculature of the shoulder.

❑ To stretch the anterior joint capsule.

Prerequisites

Pain-free range of motion in shoulder abduction (90°) and extension.

Starting position

Client is standing, facing the corner of the wall, with arms abducted to approximately 90°, elbows flexed to 90° and palms on both walls.

Correct performance

❑ Client begins by gently leaning their body weight forwards to stretch the anterior shoulder musculature.

❑ The stretch is held for 10–15 seconds, before resting and repeating 5 times.

Standing circumduction

Muscle group(s): Posterior shoulder

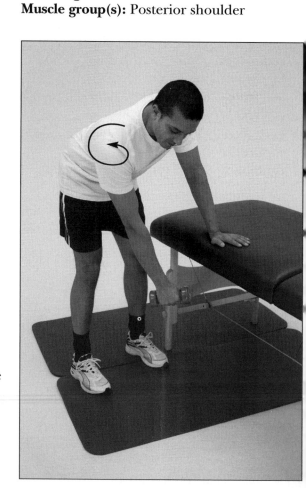

Figure 8.10. Standing circumduction

Phase/modality: Flexibility
Equipment: Couch

Purpose

❏ To stretch the posterior shoulder musculature, particularly when flexion abduction is restricted in the early stages of rehabilitation.

❏ To stretch the posterior joint capsule.

Prerequisites

Pain-free range of motion.

Starting position

Client is standing and leaning over a table/couch, with one hand supporting upper body. The other hand is allowed to drop down towards the floor.

Correct performance

❏ The client begins by allowing the arm to move in a circular pattern, as if drawing a circle with the hand.

❏ The movement is repeated for 5–10 circles, before changing direction. The exercise is repeated with the other arm.

Progressions

❏ Increase size of circle.

❏ Addition of weight, by holding a dumb-bell, to increase the stretch.

Assisted shoulder flexor/abductor stretch

Muscle group(s): Latissimus dorsi, teres major
Phase/modality: Flexibility
Equipment: None

Purpose

To stretch the latissimus dorsi and teres major.

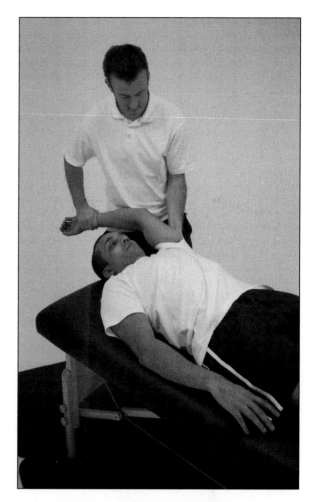

Figure 8.11. Assisted shoulder flexor/abductor stretch

Prerequisites

Pain-free range of motion in flexion/abduction.

Starting position

❏ Client is lying supine, with knees bent and low back flat.

❏ The shoulder to be stretched is in a maximum flexion/abduction position and in slight medial rotation.

Correct performance

❏ The therapist holds the arm just above the elbow and applies traction in an overhead direction, while gently pulling the arm down towards the couch. The other hand is used to stabilise the scapula, to prevent excessive abduction.

❏ The stretch is held for up to 20 seconds.

❏ Muscle energy techniques may be used if the muscle is particularly tight.

Assisted pectoralis minor stretch

Muscle group(s): Pectoralis minor
Phase/modality: Flexibility
Equipment: None

Purpose

To stretch the pectoralis minor.

Prerequisites

Pain-free range of motion of the scapula.

Starting position

Client is seated, with arms by sides.

Figure 8.12. Assisted pectoralis minor stretch

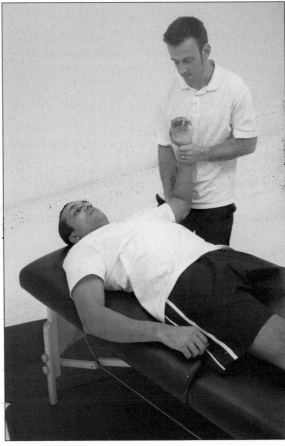

(a)

Figure 8.13. Assisted medial/lateral rotator stretch – (a) start position, (b) medial rotator stretch, (c) lateral rotator stretch

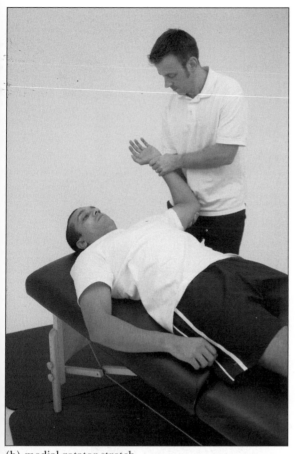

(b) medial rotator stretch

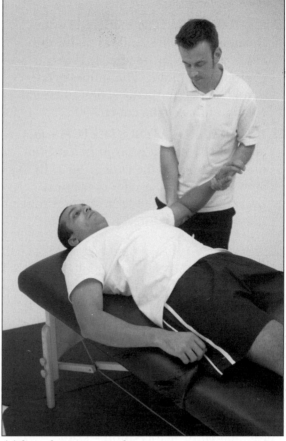

(c) lateral rotator stretch

Correct performance

❏ Therapist stands behind patient and pulls the shoulders back and down, holding for up to 20 seconds.

❏ If the pectoralis minor is particularly tight, muscle energy techniques may be used.

❏ This stretch may also be performed with the client supine.

Assisted medial/lateral rotator stretch
Muscle group(s): Rotator cuff, pectoralis major, latissimus dorsi, deltoid
Phase/modality: Flexibility
Equipment: None

Purpose

To stretch the medial and lateral rotators of the shoulder.

Prerequisites

Pain-free range of motion in abduction/rotation.

Starting position

❏ Client is supine, with knees bent and low back flat.

❏ The shoulder to be stretched is in 90° abduction, with elbow flexed to 90°.

Correct performance

❑ MEDIAL ROTATOR STRETCH – the therapist holds the arm just above the elbow and applies traction to the glenohumeral joint. The humerus is gently rotated in the direction of lateral rotation towards the couch (90°).

❑ LATERAL ROTATOR STRETCH – as above, but rotation is taken in a medial direction towards the couch (90°). In this stretch, the client applies downward pressure to the shoulder with their other hand, to prevent anterior translation.

(a)

Phase 2 exercises – Restoring static, dynamic and reactive stabilisation

Four-point kneeling cross-crawl

Muscle group(s): Shoulders, back, abdominals

Phase/modality: Stabilisation – static, dynamic, reactive; strength

Equipment: None

Purpose

❑ To integrate scapulohumeral movement and stability with opposite hip movement.

❑ To strengthen the shoulder flexors/abductors.

❑ To condition the spinal rotators.

Prerequisites

❑ The client must be able to hold and maintain a neutral spine, prior to the movement.

❑ The client must be able to stabilise the spine through abdominal bracing.

(b)

Figure 8.14. Four-point kneeling cross-crawl – (a) before, (b) after

Starting position

Client begins on all fours with a neutral spine alignment.

Correct performance

❑ Client slowly raises one arm (thumb up) to shoulder height, holding for 3 seconds before returning, maintaining optimal alignment. Repeat for the other side.

❏ Perform 6 repetitions, alternating each side.

❏ As a variation, perform the movement laterally, by taking the arm out to the side. This will place more emphasis on shoulder abductors/extensors.

Progressions

❏ Once good control and alignment are achieved, the client can progress to raising alternate arm and alternate leg. As the leg is raised to hip height, ensure that the toe is pointed away (triple extension). Particular attention should be focused on smooth coordination of the arm and leg, ensuring that optimal stability and alignment are maintained throughout.

❏ The duration of the hold can also be increased to a maximum of 8 seconds.

❏ Increase repetitions to a maximum of 15 each side.

❏ Perform with eyes closed.

❏ For increased strength through the shoulder musculature, the client can hold a small dumb-bell. Alternatively, the therapist can apply gentle pressure along the arm, thereby changing the perceived resistance.

❏ Perform the exercise unilaterally holding an oscillating Bodyblade®, before repeating on the other side.

Ball circumduction

Muscle group(s): Shoulders, rotator cuff, abdominals
Phase/modality: Stabilisation – static, dynamic, reactive; strength
Equipment: Stability ball, small medicine ball

Purpose

❏ Strengthens rotator cuff group.

❏ Increases proprioception within the glenohumeral joint.

❏ Increases upper body strength.

Prerequisites

❏ Adequate functional flexibility in the anterior shoulder musculature.

❏ If client has an upper-crossed posture, the stretching of the pectorales major and minor, latissimus dorsi, upper trapezii and levator scapulae must precede loading of the glenohumeral joint, to ensure optimal scapular retraction and depression.

Starting position

Client begins by placing a stability ball against the wall at shoulder height. Client stands in front of it, with arm fully extended, palm in the centre of the ball. Maintain good posture, with neutral spine and some abdominal bracing.

Correct performance

❏ Client performs circumduction at the glenohumeral joint so that the ball rolls round in a circular pattern.

❏ Complete 10 circles before changing direction. Repeat with the other arm.

❏ Focus on the scapulohumeral rhythm during the entire movement.

Progressions

❏ Increase the size of the circle.

❏ Put more body weight into the movement by standing further back from the ball. Ensure that optimal alignment is still maintained.

❏ The exercise may be performed kneeling upright, with one hand on the ball,

Figure 8.15. Ball circumduction

progressively putting more body weight into the ball. This position will engage the abdominal musculature to a greater degree.

❑ The exercise can be progressed finally to a four-point kneeling position, with one hand on a small medicine ball. In this position, there will be a larger involvement of the rotator cuff, as there is more body weight through the shoulder/arm complex.

Closed-chain weight shifts
Muscle group(s): Shoulders, rotator cuff, chest, abdominals
Phase/modality: Stabilisation – static, reactive; strength

Equipment: Rocker-board, balance-board, Vew-Do™ board

Purpose
❑ Lateral rhythmic stabilisation during flexion.
❑ Strengthens rotator cuff group.
❑ Increases proprioception within the glenohumeral joint.
❑ Increases upper body strength.

Prerequisites
❑ Adequate functional flexibility in the anterior shoulder musculature.
❑ Optimal scapular control.

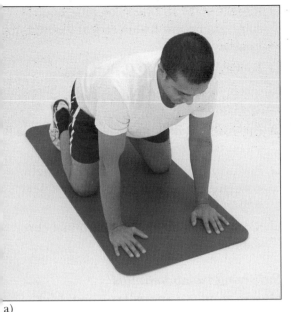

a)   (b)

Figure 8.16. Closed-chain weight shifts – (a) before, (b) after

❑ Good control of neutral spine alignment.

Starting position
Client begins in a four-point kneeling position, with neutral spine.

Correct performance
❑ While holding neutral alignment, client starts shifting weight from left to right hand, in a rocking motion, gradually increasing range of motion.

❑ Repeat up to 10 times each side.

Progressions
❑ Place both hands on a rocker-board, positioned for frontal plane movement (rocking side to side).

❑ Place both hands on a balance-board and try to maintain a pure frontal plane movement, from side to side.

❑ Place both hands on a Vew-Do™ board and try to keep the board horizontal while shifting it side to side.

Prone iso-abdominals
Muscle group(s): Shoulders, chest, back, abdominals
Phase/modality: Stabilisation – static, dynamic; strength
Equipment: None

Purpose
❑ Strengthens rotator cuff group in flexion.

❑ Increases proprioception within the glenohumeral joint.

❑ Increases upper body strength and core stabilisation.

❑ Functionally integrates upper and lower body stability.

Prerequisites
❑ Client must be instructed in diaphragmatic breathing.

(a)

(b)

Figure 8.17. Prone iso-abdominals – (a) before, (b) after

- ❑ Adequate abdominal bracing.
- ❑ Neutral spine alignment.

Starting position

Client assumes a prone position, with elbows and shoulders flexed to 90°. The elbows should be positioned under the shoulders.

Correct performance

- ❑ Client begins by bracing the abdominals and lifting the body up onto the forearms.
- ❑ Hold body position and optimal spinal alignment for 3 seconds, before returning and resting.

- ❑ Repeat up to 10 times, keeping neutral spine alignment from cervical through to lumbar spine.
- ❑ Focus on quality, NOT duration.

Progressions

- ❑ Increase holding time to a maximum of 8 seconds.
- ❑ Perform weight shifts from left to right arm (rocking) for additional shoulder stability.
- ❑ Raise alternate legs, for additional core stabilisation.

Side-lying iso-abdominals

Muscle group(s): Shoulders, chest, back, abdominals
Phase/modality: Stabilisation – static, dynamic; strength
Equipment: None

Purpose

- ❑ Strengthens rotator cuff group in abduction.
- ❑ Increases proprioception within the glenohumeral joint.
- ❑ Increases upper body strength and core stabilisation.
- ❑ Functionally integrates upper and lower body stability.
- ❑ Conditions the oblique musculature.

Prerequisites

- ❑ Client must be instructed in diaphragmatic breathing.
- ❑ Adequate abdominal bracing.
- ❑ Neutral spine alignment.
- ❑ Functional flexibility in the lumbo-pelvic-hip complex.

a)

b)

Figure 8.18. Side-lying iso-abdominals – (a) before, (b) after

Starting position

Client is lying on the right side with legs bent. Optimal postural alignment must be maintained throughout movement. Place right elbow directly under right shoulder.

Correct performance

❏ Client begins by bracing the abdominals and lifting body up onto right forearm.

❏ Hold body position and optimal spinal alignment for 3 seconds, before returning and resting.

❏ Repeat up to 10 times, keeping neutral spine alignment from cervical through to lumbar spine. Repeat on the left side.

❏ Focus on quality, NOT duration.

Progressions

Increase holding time to a maximum of 8 seconds.

Wall push-up

Muscle group(s): Anterior shoulder, rotator cuff, serratus anterior
Phase/modality: Stabilisation – dynamic, reactive; strength
Equipment: None

Purpose

To strengthen the anterior shoulder musculature in a close chain.

❏ To strengthen the rotator cuff in flexion/abduction.

❏ To increase proprioception in the glenohumeral joint.

❏ To activate the scapula protraction mechanism.

Prerequisites

❏ Optimal scapular control.

❏ Pain-free range of motion in flexion and abduction.

❏ Good control of neutral alignment and abdominal brace.

Starting position

Client stands facing a wall, with elbows extended, both palms on the wall, about shoulder-width apart.

Correct performance

❏ Client performs a push-up against the wall, by flexing elbows and allowing scapula to retract.

(a)

(b)

Figure 8.19. Wall push-up – (a) before, (b) after

❑ For additional multi-planar stabilisation, the push-up may be performed against a stability ball on the wall. Ensure that the movement is performed with minimal ball wobble.

❑ The client may progress to performing a box push-up (four-point kneel position). This position will provide further integration of the abdominal musculature

❑ The box push-up can be progressed further by placing the hands on a rocker-board or Vew-Do™ board. This will serve to enhance proprioception within the glenohumeral joint.

❑ Full push-up.

❑ Push-up with legs on stability ball.

Seated push-up
Muscle group(s): Shoulder/arm
Phase/modality: Stabilisation – static, dynamic; strength
Equipment: Bench/couch

Purpose
❑ To strengthen shoulder musculature in a closed chain.

❑ To strengthen the rotator cuff.

❑ To strengthen the scapular depressors and adductors.

Prerequisites
❑ Optimal scapular control.

❑ Pain-free range of motion in elevation, depression and extension.

❑ Good control of neutral alignment.

Starting position
Client is seated at the end of a bench or couch, with hands gripping the edges, feet on floor.

❑ Pushing body away from wall, client allows the scapula to protract fully as end range of elbow extension approaches. This will engage the serratus anterior.

❑ Repeat 10 times, maintaining good spinal alignment throughout the movement.

Progressions
❑ The therapist may increase resistance by applying pressure to the upper back.

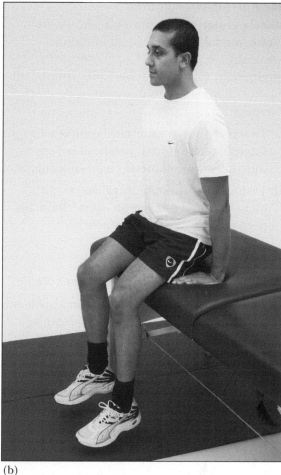

(a)   (b)

Figure 8.20. Seated push-up – (a) before, (b) after

Correct performance

❑ Client begins the movement by bracing the abdominals and lifting body weight off the bench. The body should rise no more than 4 inches (depending on arm length).

❑ Slowly return and repeat up to 10 times.

❑ The client should be instructed to focus on depressing and adducting the scapula (visualise a diagonal movement downwards), while simultaneously lifting the sternum vertically upwards.

Progressions

❑ Seated on a stability ball. This will add a multi-planar dimension to the exercise, as well as providing a key progression from a closed-chain to an open-chain environment.

❑ Feet off the floor. This progression requires the client to lift the whole body.

❑ Full dip movement, where the body is allowed to drop further to the floor, before pushing upwards. This progression activates the triceps to a greater degree.

Medial/lateral rotation

Muscle group(s): Rotator cuff, shoulders
Phase/modality: Dynamic stabilisation, strength
Equipment: Cable, exercise band, dumb-bell

Purpose

❏ To strengthen rotator cuff complex in internal and external rotation, before integration into kinetic chain movement.

❏ To increase the stability of the glenohumeral joint in an open chain (in preparation for throwing activities).

Prerequisites

❏ Functional flexibility in shoulder rotation.

❏ If the client has an upper-crossed posture, this must be corrected prior to loading (stretch pectorales major and minor, latissimus dorsi, upper trapezius, levator scapulae).

Starting position

❏ Client is standing with a square stance, side-on to the line of resistance (cable or exercise band). The elbow is flexed to 90° and the client is holding the band or cable handle. The elbow is held close to the side of the body.

❏ For medial rotation, the hand nearest the cable should be holding the handle. For lateral rotation, the opposite hand should be holding the handle.

Correct performance

❏ MEDIAL ROTATION – standing in good alignment, with abdominals braced, client slowly rotates the forearm inwards, keeping the elbow by the side of the body.

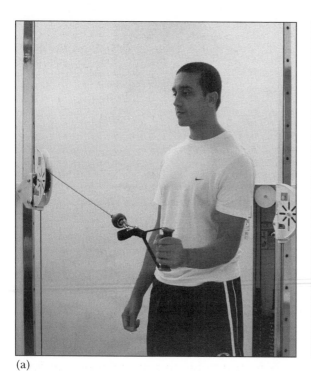
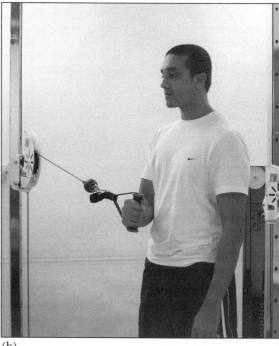

(a)   (b)

Figure 8.21. Medial/lateral rotation – (a) lateral rotation end position, (b) medial rotation end position

❏ It is important that the upper arm does not move during the rotation (except around a vertical axis). Repeat 10 times before changing arms.

❏ LATERAL ROTATION – client slowly rotates the forearm outwards. Repeat 10 times before changing arms.

❏ Emphasise movement from the glenohumeral joint.

❏ As a variation, lateral rotation may be performed in a side-lying position, using a dumb-bell. As above, the client keeps the elbow close to the body and rotates the forearm outwards (or upwards, in this case).

Progressions

❏ Increase the resistance of the band or use a heavier dumb-bell.

❏ Perform the exercise with a dumb-bell in a supine position, with arm abducted to 90°. This progression allows for medial and lateral rotation within the same exercise and is particularly useful for rotator cuff strength during throwing actions.

Shoulder PNF patterns

Muscle group(s): Shoulder/arm, rotator cuff, abdominals, back
Phase/modality: Dynamic stabilisation, strength
Equipment: Cable, band, dumb-bell

Purpose

❏ To condition the shoulder/arm complex through the common 'chopping' and 'lifting' diagonal movement patterns, seen in daily living and sport.

❏ To integrate the rotator cuff back into 'chopping' and 'lifting' patterns.

Prerequisites

❏ Pain-free functional range of motion in abduction.

❏ Optimal rotator cuff function.

Starting position

❏ Client is standing side-on to an adjustable cable/band system (high and low settings).

❏ 'REACHING FOR SEATBELT' – client holds a low cable next to the body.

❏ 'PUTTING ON SEATBELT' – client holds a high cable across the body.

❏ 'DRAWING THE SWORD' – client holds a low cable across the body.

❏ 'REPLACING THE SWORD' – client holds a high cable next to the body.

❏ Hold good postural alignment, with abdominals braced.

Correct performance

❏ 'REACHING FOR SEATBELT' – client moves the arm from a low position next to the body to a high position on the opposite side of the body. The elbow should start in extension and move to flexion at the end of the movement. The shoulder starts in neutral and moves through flexion-horizontal adduction-medial rotation. The hand starts by the side of the body and ends in a position over the opposite shoulder. Repeat slowly 10 times.

❏ 'PUTTING ON SEATBELT' – client moves the arm from a high position on the opposite side of the body to a low position on the same side of the body. The elbow should start in flexion and move to extension at the end of the movement. The shoulder starts in flexion-horizontal adduction-medial rotation and

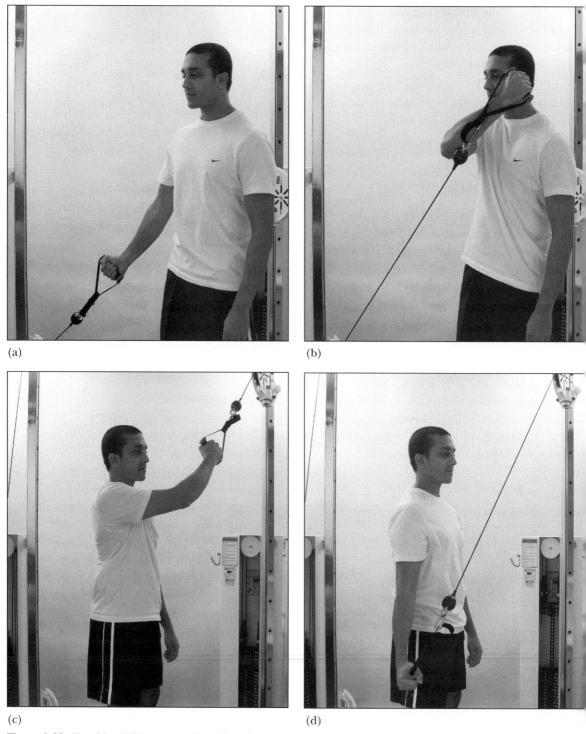

(a)

(b)

(c)

(d)

Figure 8.22. Shoulder PNF patterns: 'Reaching for seatbelt' – (a) start, (b) end positions; 'Putting on seatbelt' – (c) start, (d) end positions;

(e)

(f)

(g)

(h)

Figure 8.22. (contd) 'Drawing the sword' – (e) start, (f) end positions; 'Replacing the sword' – (g) start, (h) end positions.

ends in neutral. The hand starts in a position over the opposite shoulder and ends at the side of the body. The client should be instructed to visualise putting on a seatbelt. Repeat slowly 10 times.

❑ 'DRAWING THE SWORD' – client moves the arm from a low position on the opposite side of the body to a high position on the same side of the body. The elbow should start in slight flexion and move to full extension at the end of the movement. The shoulder starts in slight flexion-horizontal adduction-medial rotation and ends in 110–130° abduction. The hand starts in a position over the opposite hip and ends in a position just above the head. The client should be instructed to visualise drawing a sword. Repeat slowly 10 times.

❑ 'REPLACING THE SWORD' – client moves the arm from a high position on the same side of the body to a low position on the opposite side of the body. The elbow should start in full extension and move to slight flexion at the end of the movement. The shoulder starts in 110–130° abduction and ends in slight flexion-horizontal adduction-medial rotation. The hand starts in a position just above the head and ends in a position over the opposite hip. Repeat slowly 10 times.

❑ Particular attention should be focused on scapulohumeral rhythm throughout the movement, as well as maintaining neutral spinal alignment.

❑ There should be no rotation in the torso during the movement.

❑ The flexion patterns may be performed with a dumb-bell for variation.

Progressions
❑ Increase weight or resistance of band.

❑ Perform the exercise in a single-leg stance

❑ These patterns may be performed using an oscillating Bodyblade®.

❑ This exercise can be progressed further into a full 'wood-chop' movement, by slowly introducing torso rotation and, finally, a lateral weight shift. For further details of the wood-chop exercise, please refer to phase 3.

Scaption
Muscle group(s): Shoulders, rotator cuff
Phase/modality: Dynamic stabilisation, strength
Equipment: Dumb-bell, exercise band

Purpose
❑ To strengthen the shoulder abductors/flexors.

❑ To maximise stability of the glenohumeral joint.

❑ To increase scapular control.

Prerequisites
❑ Pain-free range of motion in abduction.

❑ Functional rotator cuff.

❑ Optimal core strength.

Starting position
Client is standing in good postural alignment, with dumb-bells in each hand, in slight medial rotation.

Correct performance
❑ Brace the abdominals and raise arms, keeping thumbs at 45° angle. The arms should be raised at an angle of 30° forwards of the frontal plane (the plane of the scapula).

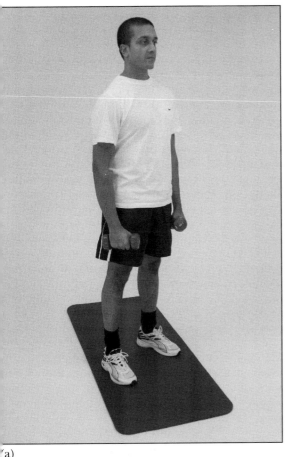

(a)   (b)

Figure 8.23. Scaption – (a) before, (b) after

❏ Do not allow the head to jut forwards
  (sternocleidomastoid activation).

❏ Lower and repeat 10 times.

Progressions

❏ Increase weight.

❏ Alternate arms.

❏ Single-leg stance.

Phase 3 exercises – Restoring functional strength

Standing push pattern (cable)
Muscle group(s): Shoulder/arm, chest,
abdominals
Phase/modality: Strength, stabilisation,
balance
Equipment: Cable, exercise bands

Purpose

❏ To integrate the shoulder musculature
  into the 'push' movement pattern.

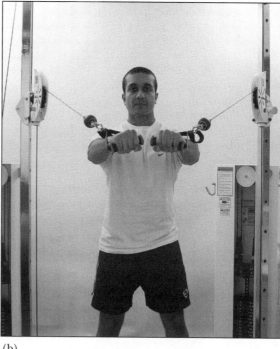

(a)   (b)

Figure 8.24. Standing push pattern (cable) – (a) before, (b) after

❑ To strengthen the pectoralis major and triceps brachii.

❑ To increase force generation through the entire kinetic chain.

Prerequisites

❑ Functional flexibility and range of motion of the shoulder/arm complex.

❑ Good level of core strength.

❑ Upper extremity muscle balance. Clients with upper-crossed posture should undergo a flexibility programme before attempting these movement patterns.

Starting position

❑ Client is standing with a square stance, facing away from the cable machine.

Handles are held, with elbows flexed to 90° and arms abducted to 90°, in a position where the elbows are in line with the shoulders.

❑ Abdominals should be braced prior to movement.

❑ It is important that the arms do not start from a position of horizontal abduction (elbows behind shoulders). This will avoid unnecessary stress on the anterior joint capsule.

❑ Ensure that weight distribution is even between both feet and central from heel to toe. Allow the knees to bend slightly and do not lean into the movement. In this position, the core musculature will activate to keep the body upright.

Correct performance

❏ While holding good postural alignment and a strong abdominal brace, slowly push the handles out in front of the body.

❏ During the movement, allow a small amount of horizontal adduction at both shoulders, so that the handles meet in the centre, in front of the body.

❏ Slowly return both arms to the start position, before completing 10 repetitions.

❏ It is important to avoid 'swaying' during the movement. This can be minimised by choosing a light enough weight and activating an abdominal brace just before the movement begins.

Progressions

❏ Increase weight (gradually).

❏ Alternate arms – increases core activation.

❏ Split stance – this position will increase the stabilisation requirement in the frontal plane, thereby recruiting the torso rotators to a greater degree.

❏ Single-leg stance – increases the reactive component, as well as the multi-planar stabilisation requirement.

❏ Sitting on a stability ball (with both feet/one foot in contact with floor) – conditions and trains reactive stabilisation (especially within the core musculature).

❏ Kneeling on a stability ball.

❏ Standing on a balance-board/rocker-board.

Variations

There are two main open- and closed-chain variations within the 'push' pattern that can be used as exercises within their own right, as progressions to the above or simply to add variety to an existing rehabilitation programme. These include the following:

❏ PUSH-UP (closed chain) – please refer to phase 2 for a complete description of this exercise and progressions.

❏ BENCH PRESS (open chain) – this exercise involves lying on a bench and 'pushing' a barbell or dumb-bells above the body in the same motion as described above. The limiting factor of this exercise is that when lying on a bench, the scapulae are somewhat restricted in adduction, thereby putting excessive stress through the anterior joint capsule of the glenohumeral joint. This can be overcome by performing the exercise supine on a stability ball, using dumb-bells rather than a barbell. This position will allow the scapula to retract freely around the curvature of the ball. This exercise will increase the reactive stabilisation requirement of the core, as well as increasing proprioceptive input to the shoulder musculature.

Standing pull pattern (cable)

Muscle group(s): Shoulder/arm, back, abdominals
Phase/modality: Strength, stabilisation, balance
Equipment: Cable, exercise bands

Purpose

❏ To integrate the shoulder musculature into the 'pull' movement pattern.

❏ To strengthen the upper back musculature and the biceps brachii.

❏ To increase force generation through the entire kinetic chain.

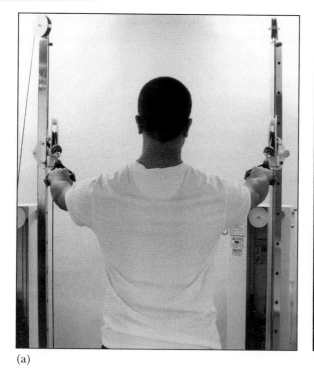

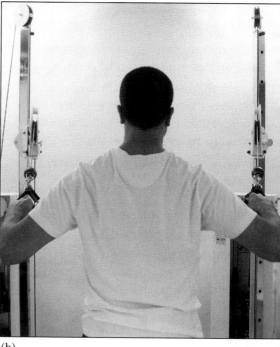

(a)   (b)

Figure 8.25. Standing pull pattern (cable) – (a) before, (b) after

Prerequisites

❏ Functional flexibility and range of motion of the shoulder/arm complex.

❏ Good level of core strength.

❏ Upper extremity muscle balance. Clients with upper-crossed posture should undergo a flexibility programme before attempting these movement patterns.

Starting position

❏ Client is standing with a square stance, facing the cable machine. Handles are held, with elbows extended and arms flexed to 90°.

❏ Abdominals should be braced prior to movement.

❏ Ensure that weight distribution is even between both feet and central from heel to toe. Allow the knees to bend slightly and do not lean backwards. In this position, the core musculature will activate to keep the body upright.

Correct performance

❏ While holding good postural alignment and a strong abdominal brace, slowly pull the handles towards the body, maintaining elbows at shoulder level.

❏ The handles should be pulled inwards until the elbows line up with the shoulders.

❏ Slowly return both arms to the start position, before completing 10 repetitions.

❏ It is important to avoid 'swaying' during the movement. This can be minimised by choosing a light enough weight and activating an abdominal brace just before the movement begins.

Progressions

❏ Increase weight (gradually).

❏ Alternate arms – increases core activation.

❏ Split stance – this position will increase the stabilisation requirement in the frontal plane, thereby recruiting the torso rotators to a greater degree.

❏ Single-leg stance – increases the reactive component, as well as the multi-planar stabilisation requirement.

❏ Sitting on a stability ball (with both feet/one foot in contact with floor) – conditions and trains reactive stabilisation (especially within the core musculature).

❏ Kneeling on a stability ball.

❏ Standing on a balance-board/rocker-board.

Variations

❏ There is a useful functional variation of the pull pattern that is worth mentioning here. It is called the bent-over row and is a common movement pattern found in many gyms and rehabilitation centres worldwide.

❏ In this exercise, the client picks up a barbell or a pair of dumb-bells and assumes a square stance. From here they should bend the knees slightly and flex the hips to approximately 60°, so that the hands are positioned just above the knees. The spine should remain in neutral throughout the movement; therefore, good levels of torso stability are required for this exercise.

❏ The client then begins to 'row' (pull) the bar towards the lower chest region, before lowering.

❏ This exercise can be progressed by adding more weight.

Clinical perspective

The human body is regularly subjected to the push/pull pattern in both open- and closed-chain daily activities, for example, opening/closing doors, pushing a child in a buggy, pushing a lawnmower, sawing wood; it is also a vital movement pattern in many sports, including boxing, rowing and windsurfing.

Shoulder press

Muscle group(s): Shoulder/arm, trapezius, abdominals
Phase/modality: Strength, stabilisation, balance
Equipment: Barbell, dumb-bells, exercise band

Purpose

❏ To strengthen the shoulder musculature (deltoid, upper trapezius).

❏ To integrate the kinetic chain into overhead movements of daily living and sport.

Prerequisites

❏ Pain-free range of motion in flexion/abduction.

❏ Adequate levels of core strength.

❏ Optimal postural control and alignment.

Starting position

❏ Client is standing holding a barbell (slightly wider than shoulder-width grip) in front of the body. Alternatively, a pair of dumb-bells can be held by the sides of the body.

(a)   (b)

Figure 8.26. Shoulder press – (a) before, (b) after

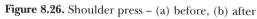

❏ The barbell is lifted into a position just below the chin (start position). In this position the elbows are fully flexed.

❏ The abdominals are braced and the body and spine are in good alignment.

Correct performance

❏ Push the barbell (or dumb-bells) upwards, extending the elbows, until arms are maximally abducted. Maintain optimal body alignment and do not allow the spine to overextend. This can be achieved by holding an abdominal brace throughout the movement.

❏ Slowly return the bar to the start position and repeat 10 times.

❏ Aim to use equal force through both shoulders and arms to push the bar upwards.

Progressions

❏ Increase weight.

❏ Single-arm dumb-bell shoulder press/alternate dumb-bell shoulder press – this exercise will increase activation of the core musculature (especially the contralateral obliques); in an attempt to stabilise the body, integrate the frontal plane.

❏ Sitting on a stability ball.

❏ Standing on a rocker-board.

Pull-down

Muscle group(s): Scapular
depressors/adductors, back, biceps
Phase/modality: Strength, stabilisation
Equipment: Cable, exercise band

Purpose

❏ To strengthen the latissimus dorsi and
lower trapezius.

❏ To aid balance between the scapula
elevators and depressors, for injury
prevention.

Prerequisites

❏ Pain-free range of motion in
adduction/abduction.

❏ Adequate levels of core strength.

❏ Optimal postural control and alignment.

Starting position

❏ Client is seated in front of a cable
machine, holding the handles, with elbows
extended and hands wider than shoulder-
width apart. The arms are in almost full
abduction, forming a V-shape. Palms are
facing towards each other (neutral grip).

❏ The spine should be held in neutral
alignment and the abdominals braced,
ready for movement. In this position, the
scapulae should be elevated, under the
pull of the cables.

Correct performance

❏ The movement consists of two parts,
which take place in the frontal plane and
should be integrated together to produce
a smooth continuous motion: (1) the
elbows are flexed, as they are brought

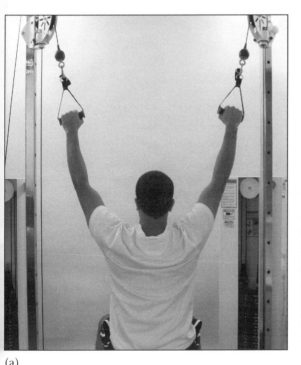
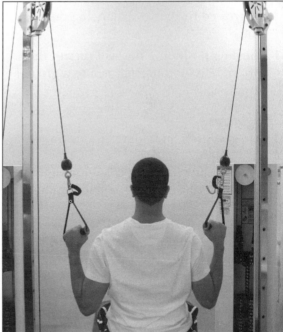

(a)   (b)

Figure 8.27. Pull-down – (a) before, (b) after

down towards the side of the hips; (2) the scapulae are depressed and adducted.

❏ Return to the start position, by extending the elbows and allowing the scapulae to elevate, against the upward pull of the cable. Do not allow the arms to 'jerk' back.

❏ Perform 10 repetitions.

Progressions

❏ Increase the weight – it is important not to compromise weight for good technique in this exercise. If the weight is too heavy, the latissimus dorsi may end up doing all the work, because it has a larger mechanical advantage, and it may be difficult to depress the scapulae; in this situation, the scapula adduction/elevation mechanism will take over, resulting in the facilitation of the rhomboid/upper trapezius force couple.

❏ Seated on a stability ball. This may be progressed further by balancing on one foot.

❏ Kneeling position – this will recruit the core stabilisation mechanism to a greater extent.

Upright row
Muscle group(s): Shoulders, upper trapezius, biceps
Phase/modality: Strength, stabilisation
Equipment: Cable, band, barbell, dumb-bells

Purpose

❏ To strengthen the shoulder and upper back musculature.

❏ To integrate the kinetic chain in an upward 'pull' pattern.

Prerequisites

❏ Pain-free range of motion in adduction/abduction.

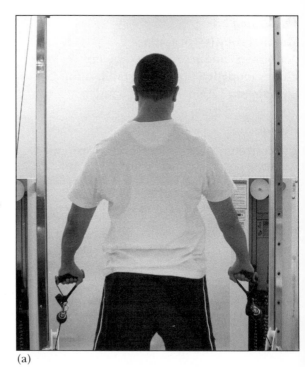

(a)

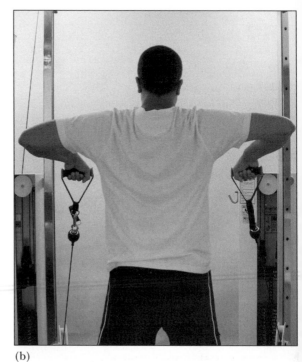

(b)

Figure 8.28. Upright row – (a) before, (b) after

- Adequate levels of core strength.
- Optimal postural control and alignment.

Starting position

- Client is standing in front of a low cable machine, holding the handles in front of the body. Alternatively, a barbell can be held. The hands should be no wider than shoulder-width apart, with a pronated grip. The elbows are extended (arms straight).
- The spine should be held in neutral alignment and the abdominals braced, ready for movement.

Correct performance

- Begin the movement by flexing the elbows and abducting the arms in a smooth, continuous manner, so that the handles (or barbell) are 'rowed' upwards towards the chin.
- The movement is completed at 90° of humeral abduction and slight horizontal abduction (elbows pulled slightly posteriorly – this activates the scapula adduction mechanism).
- Slowly return to the start position and perform 10 repetitions.

Progressions

- Increase weight.
- Standing on a balance-board.
- Where possible, practise this exercise using all available equipment, including cables, bands, barbells and dumb-bells. Using free weights will condition the body in a more functional way.

Dips

Muscle group(s): Shoulders/arms, scapula depressors
Phase/modality: Strength, stabilisation

Equipment: Bench, chair

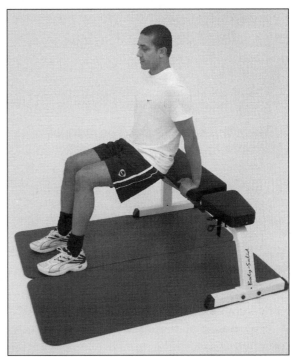

(a)

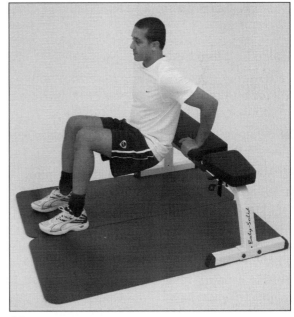

(b)

Figure 8.29. Dips – (a) before, (b) after

Purpose
- ❑ To increase strength of the chest and triceps.
- ❑ To enhance shoulder stabilisation.

Prerequisites
- ❑ The client should have a functional need for loading the shoulder in this position.
- ❑ The client must have 45° or more of active, compensation-free shoulder extension to perform this exercise safely.
- ❑ This exercise is not vital for developing maximal strength of the arms or chest.

Starting position
- ❑ Client has hands placed on the edge of a bench or heavy chair, so that the shoulder is in comfortable extension. Glutes must be kept as close to the bench as possible. Feet should be together and knees slightly bent.
- ❑ Hands should be close to the sides of the body, with arms straight and scapulae retracted.

Correct performance
- ❑ Bending the arms, slowly lower the body down until the shoulders are just above elbow height (elbows flexed to 90°).
- ❑ Straighten the arms to return the body to the starting position.
- ❑ Maintain good form and alignment and perform 10 repetitions.
- ❑ Only lower the body to a comfortable point.

Pull-over

Muscle group(s): Latissimus dorsi, pectoralis major, triceps brachii
Phase/modality: Strength, stabilisation
Equipment: Dumb-bell, medicine ball, exercise band

(a)

(b)

Figure 8.30. Pull-over – (a) before, (b) after

Purpose
- ❑ To strengthen latissimus dorsi, pectoralis major and triceps brachii, in a functional movement pattern.

❏ This pattern may be particularly useful for those involved in overhead activities that involve double extension, for example, painting/decorating or throwing actions.

Prerequisites

The client must demonstrate good functional flexibility (specifically the latissimus dorsi and pectorales major and minor) throughout the shoulder girdle to perform this exercise without compensation in the spine.

Starting position

Client is lying supine on a bench, or the end of a couch, holding a medicine ball/dumb-bell vertically overhead, with elbows extended.

Correct performance

❏ Lower the weight backwards slowly, while flexing the elbows and shoulders, so that the elbows end up slightly higher than the shoulders and the elbows are flexed to 90°.

❏ Brace the abdominals and extend the shoulders and elbows to bring the weight back to the start position (arms straight).

❏ Range of motion should be limited to that specified by assessment.

Progressions

❏ Lying supine on a stability ball.

❏ This exercise can be progressed to a functional power movement by slowly lowering the weight and then accelerating through the upward movement, in a smooth manner. Alternatively, the arms can be kept straight throughout the movement, effectively lengthening the lever arm and making the exercise harder. Adding speed in this way requires a high level of core strength and stabilisation,

combined with perfect movement technique, and is only suitable for high-performance conditioning programmes (sport-specific throwing actions).

High-low wood-chop
Muscle group(s): Shoulders, arms, torso rotators, total body
Phase/modality: Strength, stabilisation, balance
Equipment: Cable, exercise band

Purpose

❏ To integrate the shoulder musculature into a total body movement that requires core stabilisation.

❏ To re-educate the torso rotation mechanism and strengthen the oblique musculature.

Prerequisites

❏ Functional flexibility of the shoulder/arm, without compensation in the spine.

❏ Adequate strength and flexibility in the oblique musculature and lumbar spine.

❏ Adequate leg strength.

Starting position

❏ Client is standing in a shoulder-width stance, facing away from the cable machine, holding the handle with both hands above the right shoulder. In this position, the left hand should grip the handle first, with the right hand over the top of the left hand.

❏ Good spinal alignment should be maintained, with a strong abdominal brace, prior to the movement.

Correct performance

❏ Starting from optimal posture, initiate a rotational movement, from the trunk

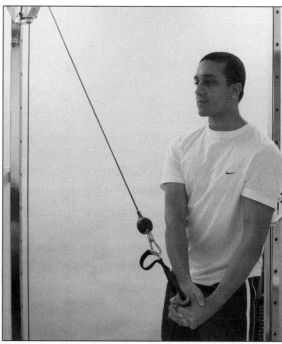

(a)   (b)

Figure 8.31. High-low wood-chop – (a) before, (b) after

outwards, towards the left. Do not pull with the shoulders or arms. Pull the cable handle downwards and across the body.

❑ Use a slow tempo to start with. Avoid beginning the movement from a forward flexed position.

❑ Do not push so quickly that the shoulders round forwards; generate movement from the core instead of the arms.

❑ Allow the torso and arms to move back to the start position and repeat up to 10 times.

Progressions

❑ As stability is developed, progress to lateral weight shifting (moving weight from right to left leg and vice versa), so that the movement resembles a wood-chopping motion.

❑ The wood-chop may also be progressed by performing the exercise seated on a stability ball. This will increase awareness of the obliques to a greater extent, providing the ball is kept still throughout the movement.

❑ LOW-HIGH WOOD-CHOP – cable is adjusted so that the line of resistance starts low and moves high.

❑ LATERAL WOOD-CHOP – cable is adjusted so that the line of resistance is horizontal.

❑ This exercise can also be progressed to a functional power movement by accelerating through the chop downwards and slowly returning to the start. Adding speed in this way requires a high level of core strength and stabilisation, combined with perfect movement technique, and is only suitable for high-performance conditioning programmes (sport-specific).

Clinical perspective

The wood-chop movement patterns provide a foundation to many rotational activities, both occupational and sport-specific, and are based on PNF (proprioceptive neuromuscular facilitation) flexion/extension patterns. When progressed to involve weight shifting, the movement presents a more efficient way of generating force from the ground up and transferring these ground forces across the lumbo-pelvic-hip complex and out through the shoulder and arm. In this way, the shoulder/arm musculature will not compensate and overwork at the expense of the spine and lower extremities.

The movement can be modified very successfully to rehabilitate, condition and enhance many occupational and sporting actions, including manual labouring, tennis and golf.

All of the above movement patterns are functional in nature, requiring static, dynamic and reactive stabilisation in open- and closed-chain situations; the exercises resemble many occupational, recreational and sporting actions. Muscles do not work in isolation, but combine to form important force couples, which then integrate with parts (or the whole) of the kinetic chain, resulting in force generation. With this in mind, it is crucial to *train the movement, not the muscle*; this means strengthening and stabilising the shoulder girdle and shoulder joint throughout ranges of motion that are functional for that person. In order to achieve this goal, it is important for the therapist to assess the load-bearing capabilities of the shoulder in a functional setting. This will involve knowing what the functional demands of the client's job/sport are, and testing the client with loads that are relevant to the activities they perform. For example, a mother who has a two-year-old child would benefit from a shoulder conditioning programme that progresses her towards handling around 10 kg (approximate weight of a two-year-old child), in various lifting and carrying activities – for example, squatting to pick up a child, lifting a child to a carrying position, and so on. By considering the daily routine of the mother, the number of load-bearing activities she performs and the different positions she puts her body into, the therapist can begin to put together a well-structured rehabilitation and conditioning programme, tailored to her needs.

Phase 4 exercises – Restoring functional power

Medicine ball chest pass
Muscle group(s): Chest, shoulders, core
Phase/modality: Power, stabilisation
Equipment: Medicine ball

Purpose
❑ Improves concentric acceleration, dynamic stabilisation and eccentric deceleration of the shoulder joint and girdle.
❑ Enhances the body's ability to transfer force along the kinetic chain.

Prerequisites
❑ If a lower- or upper-crossed posture is noted, a proper stretching programme must be completed before attempting this exercise to ensure ideal lumbar alignment and stability.

(a)   (b)

Figure 8.32. Medicine ball chest pass – (a) before, (b) during

❑ The client must exhibit good core strength and stabilisation.

Starting position

❑ Ensure that the client completes a thorough neuromuscular warm-up, to engage the nervous system prior to the exercise.

❑ The client should stand in optimal alignment, holding a medicine ball in front of the chest, with feet pointing straight ahead.

❑ Abdominals should be braced, in preparation for the movement.

Correct performance

❑ Start by standing tall, with shoulder blades depressed and retracted. Hold medicine ball close to chest.

❑ Movement is the summation of the shoulder protraction, elbow extension and wrist flexion as the ball is accelerated horizontally away from the body.

❑ Therapist catches the ball and throws it back. The client should try to catch the ball, decelerating through the shoulder/arm complex, bringing the ball back into the chest.

❑ Maintain a solid foundation through the

(c)

Figure 8.32. *(contd)* Medicine ball chest pass – (c) after

lower extremities by maintaining an abdominal brace throughout the movement.

❑ Repeat continuously until power begins to diminish (that is, throwing speed slows down) or when 12 repetitions have been completed.

❑ The therapist should look for any compensations through the kinetic chain.

Progressions
❑ Standing on a balance-board.
❑ Standing on one leg.

❑ A rotational component can be added to this exercise to increase power in the transverse plane. The client starts in the same position as above, but instead of passing the ball in front of the body, they can rotate the torso 45° and then pass the ball. It is important to ensure that the force generation begins with a slight weight shift to one leg; this is followed by activation of the oblique musculature to rotate the body in the same direction; finally, the shoulder/chest musculature is engaged to pass the ball away at a 45° angle. The ball is thrown back and the client has to decelerate the kinetic chain and return to the start. This variation requires a high degree of coordination and is only suitable when the client is able to demonstrate good link sequencing from the ground up.

Squat raise
Muscle group(s): Legs, back, shoulders, arms, core
Phase/modality: Power, stabilisation, balance
Equipment: Medicine ball, dumb-bell

Purpose
❑ Improves concentric acceleration, dynamic stabilisation and eccentric deceleration of the entire kinetic chain.
❑ Enhances the body's ability to transfer force along the kinetic chain, during extension and flexion.
❑ Particularly useful for activities and sports where force is generated from the ground up, towards the upper extremities (for example, tennis, basketball, golf, boxing).

Prerequisites
❑ Client must demonstrate a good squat/lift pattern.

(a)

(b)

Figure 8.33. Squat raise – (a) before, (b) after

❏ Pain-free range of motion in shoulder flexion.

❏ If a lower- or upper-crossed posture is noted, a proper stretching programme must be completed before attempting this exercise to ensure ideal lumbar alignment and stability.

❏ The client must exhibit good core strength and stabilisation.

Starting position

Client is standing in a square stance, holding the weight with both hands in front of the body. The arms are straight and the hands are positioned at waist/hip level (slight shoulder flexion).

Correct performance

❏ Begin the movement by squatting down to a point where the weight is just above the floor. Brace the abdominals, ready for acceleration.

❏ Accelerate the weight upwards by focusing on the smooth integration of ankle dorsiflexion, knee and hip extension and shoulder flexion. The end position is where the arms are extended overhead and the body is in optimal postural alignment.

❏ Slowly return to the bottom position and repeat until the speed cannot be maintained or when 12 repetitions have been completed.

❑ It is important to brace the abdominals just before the point of acceleration, to protect from spine from overextension at the top of the movement.

(a)

(b)

Progressions
Increase the weight.

Barbell clean and press
Muscle group(s): Shoulders, total body, core
Phase/modality: Power, stabilisation, balance
Equipment: Barbell

Purpose
❑ Increases total body strength and power. It is important to remember that the strength and power developed here are completely relative to the posture of the client during the exercise and the range of motion the client moves through.

❑ Enhances the body's ability to transfer force along the kinetic chain.

(c)

Figure 8.34. Barbell clean and press – (a) before, (b) during, (c) after

Prerequisites

❏ The client must exhibit good lifting/squatting technique and be able to perform the upright row and shoulder press exercises.

❏ If a lower- or upper-crossed posture is noted, a proper stretching programme must be completed before attempting this exercise, to ensure ideal lumbar alignment and stability.

❏ The client must exhibit good core strength and stabilisation.

❏ The client must be properly progressed through stability and strength phases, in order to ensure that there is adequate flexibility, core strength and time for adaptation, thereby reducing chance of injury.

❏ The therapist must have a justifiable reason and system of programme progression to implement this advanced exercise. This exercise is useful in activities where there are distinct stages of link sequencing/power transfer – for example, lifting a child and placing them into a high chair, or during a tennis serve.

Starting position

❏ Begin with feet shoulder-width apart and toes pointing forwards.

❏ Bend the knees slightly and bend at the waist, grasping the barbell with both hands slightly wider than shoulder-width apart (palms facing body).

❏ Brace the abdominals.

Correct performance

❏ Perform an explosive triple extension movement in the lower extremities –

ankle, knee and hip extension, and drive the elbows high. Make sure the barbell travels in a vertical, linear fashion (close to body).

❏ As bar reaches shoulder height, externally rotate the arms and 'catch' the weight in front of the shoulders, simultaneously dropping into a half-squat position, to get under the weight. From here, contract the glutes to stand into a full upright position, with bar resting on your chest.

❏ Brace the abdominals, sink into a half-squat position to pre-stretch the glutes and quickly follow this with another explosive movement, pushing the barbell up into a shoulder press. This movement should start from a glute contraction, as if pushing the floor away and, at the same time, pushing the bar upwards. Stand tall at the top, with good posture and a strong abdominal brace.

❏ Carefully lower the barbell back to the ground. Reset posture and perform 6–8 repetitions.

Progressions

❏ Increase the weight gradually, while maintaining good technique.

❏ This advanced exercise should be performed in 'chunks' before attempting the whole sequence. The client should be competent in performing a dead lift, upright row and shoulder press; these movements can then be combined successively. For example, once the dead lift can be performed, the client can attempt a dead lift with the upright row (also known as the 'clean'); once this double sequence is perfected, the final pressing movement can be added, to complete the entire motion.

3 The Trunk and Spine

The human spine is a remarkable structure of mobility and stability, characterised by an inherent S-shaped curvature. The integrity is preserved by the unique and functional arrangement of the anterior and posterior trunk musculature. The balance between mobility and stability is under the close control of the central nervous system; the large muscles of the trunk provide mobility, with the smaller, deeper muscles controlling stability. The dynamic interaction of the anterior and posterior trunk muscles provides specific co-contraction patterns, designed to stabilise and mobilise the spine during activities of daily living. Because the structure of the spine is inherently unstable, activation of the trunk musculature is essential for the maintenance of trunk position and control during static and dynamic postures.

As the functional link between the shoulder and pelvis, the spine is able to accommodate the many movement patterns seen in daily activities. These movements are almost always continuous with movement at the shoulder or pelvis: the thoracic spine rotates with the shoulders and the lumbar spine rotates with the pelvis. The trunk musculature plays a crucial role in the efficient transfer of ground reaction forces from the lower body through to the upper body, which in turn creates movement at the upper limbs; with optimal force transfer comes optimal power, which is necessary for all human movement.

The specific functional loads and complexity of movement patterns imposed on the trunk musculature by almost all daily activities often predispose the spine to aberrant forces, which, if left unchecked, may lead to acute and chronic spine dysfunction. Poor posture, muscle weakness or imbalance and faulty muscle recruitment may be contributing factors to spinal problems and may result in a lack of spinal stability and/or control, loss of coordinated movement, asymmetry of weight distribution and back pain. Effective treatment of these problems involves an understanding of spine biomechanics, and the therapist must be able to assess correct posture and movement of the spine as well as trunk muscle function. Following this, corrective exercise can serve to address any biomechanical deficiencies and restore optimal function.

This section aims to discuss the functional anatomy and biomechanics of the spine and trunk, with particular emphasis on the role of the trunk musculature in producing movement. A functional approach to clinical evaluation of the spine and trunk is discussed to provide an essential foundation for the understanding of exercise prescription. The final chapter provides the therapist with a number of corrective exercises for the trunk within the context of an overall framework for functional progression. These exercises are designed to rebalance the trunk musculature effectively to function optimally within everyday activities.

9
FUNCTIONAL TRUNK AND SPINE ANATOMY

Overview of spine anatomy

The spinal column forms the basic structure of the trunk and plays an important role in the maintenance of both static and dynamic posture. It allows individual as well as integrated movement of the head, neck and trunk. Structurally, it is able to do this via its division into the cervical, thoracic and lumbar regions, each giving rise to a distinct set of vertebral movements; functionally, a system of local and global muscles acts to mobilise and stabilise the spine. The skeletal anatomy of the spine is shown in Figure 9.1.

Structure and function of the spine

The spine, also known as the vertebral column, consists of 33 vertebrae. There are 7 cervical (neck) vertebrae, named C1–7; 12 thoracic (chest and rib) vertebrae, named T1–12; and 5 lumbar vertebrae, named L1–5. The sacrum is made up of 5 fused vertebrae (S1–5) and the coccyx, or tailbone, consists of 4 small fused vertebrae. The unique 'wedge' shape of the sacrum allows it effectively to absorb ground reaction forces from the lower extremities, as well as body weight forces from above.

Each vertebra consists of an anterior and posterior part, linked to one another via intervertebral discs. When two vertebrae are joined together by a disc, along with ligamentous support, this functional unit is known as a 'motion segment' (see Figure 9.2).

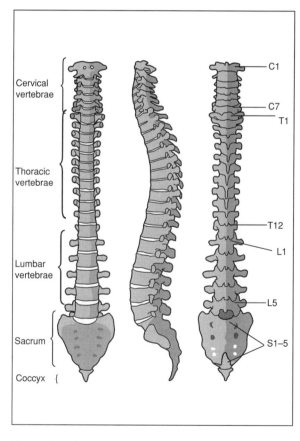

Figure 9.1. Skeletal anatomy of the spine

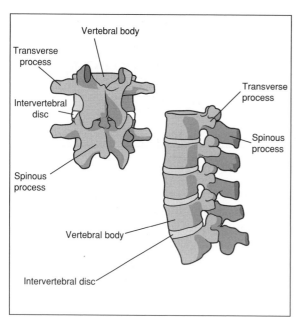

The intervertebral disc comprises a fibrous outer layer (annulus fibrosus) and a soft, jelly-like nucleus (nucleus pulposus). The annulus fibrosus consists of concentrically arranged rings of collagen fibres, as well as fibrocartilage; this structure helps to keep the nucleus pulposus under tension, thus contributing to shock absorption and maintaining the shape of the disc.

The range of motion of the spine as an integrated column is considerable; the movements allowed are flexion, extension, lateral flexion and rotation (see Figure 9.3).

Figure 9.2. A motion segment of the spine

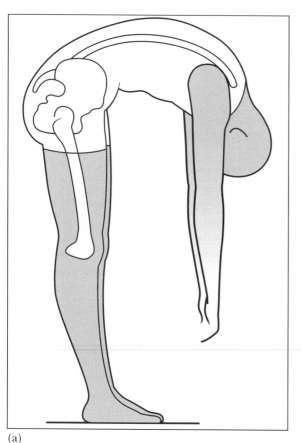

(a)

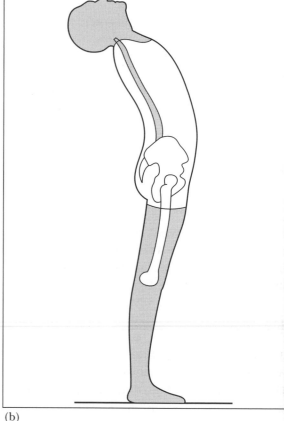

(b)

Figure 9.3. Movements of the spine – (a) flexion, (b) extension, (c) lateral flexion, (d) rotation

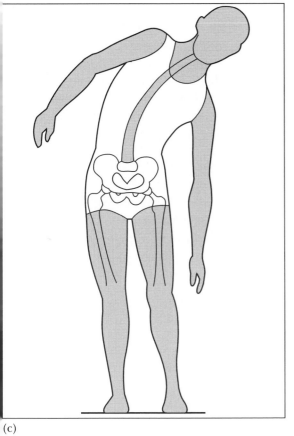

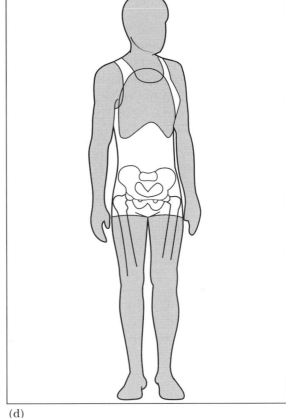

(c)

(d)

Figure 9.3. (contd) Movements of the spine

Flexion

Forward bending in the sagittal plane, with greatest movement occurring at the lumbosacral junction. This results in compression of the anterior portion of the intervertebral discs, causing a posterior (and lateral) migration of the annulus.

Extension

The return from flexion, with greatest movement in the cervical and lumbar spine. Hyperextension is backward bending in the sagittal plane from a neutral position. The thoracic spine has limited extension

capabilities due to the overlapping of the spinous processes.

Lateral flexion

Side bending in the frontal plane. Greatest motion occurs in the cervical and lumbar spine, but is limited in the thoracic spine, as the ribs act as splints for the vertebrae.

If lateral flexion in the lumbar spine occurs to the right, there is rotation of the lumbar vertebrae to the left. When lateral flexion occurs in a forward flexed position, the opposite occurs: the vertebrae turn right, with most of this coupled movement taking place in the thoracic spine.

Rotation

Rotary movement of the spine in the transverse plane. Rotation is classified according to movement of the upper spine in reference to the lower spine. Greatest movement occurs in the cervical spine, becoming increasingly limited towards the lumbar spine. As posture becomes more hyperextended, rotation occurs further down the spine. In forward flexion, rotation occurs higher up the spine.

Whenever rotation occurs in the spine, it is accompanied by a slight degree of lateral flexion to the same side.

Muscles of the trunk

The trunk is made up of several groups of muscles that extend, laterally flex, rotate and flex the trunk (see Figure 9.4). All these

Clinical perspective

During functional activities of daily living and sport, these individual movements of the spine may not necessarily occur in isolation, but as combined movements, for example, flexion accompanied by slight rotation during asymmetrical bending (picking up a shopping bag). When these combined movements occur, there may be aberrant forces exerted on the spine that can result in acute and chronic pain. It is therefore important for the therapist to be aware of the specific functional movements performed by each client, in order to condition the trunk muscles appropriately for the level of demand required.

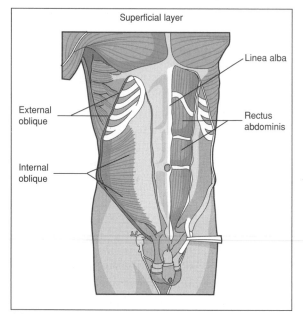
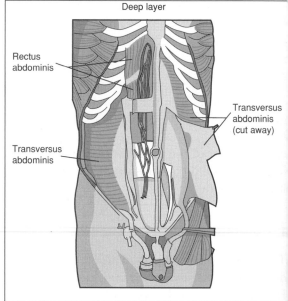

(a)

Figure 9.4. Muscles of the trunk – (a) anterior, (b) posterior

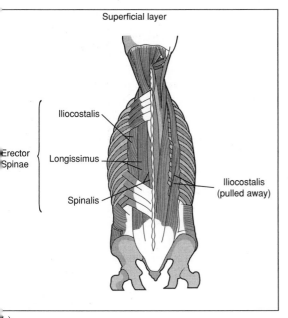

Superficial layer

Iliocostalis

Erector Spinae

Longissimus

Spinalis

Iliocostalis (pulled away)

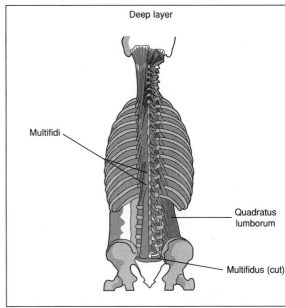

Deep layer

Multifidi

Quadratus lumborum

Multifidus (cut)

b)

Figure 9.4. (contd)

muscles play an important role in stabilising the trunk, but under the influence of gravity, it is the back extensors that contribute significantly to this cause.

This section focuses on some of the important back extensor muscles, as well as on the deep and superficial abdominal musculature, both of which are effective

Clinical perspective

Weakness of the back extensors results in a distinct loss of spinal stability; however, functional weakness of these muscles is rare and is a common misdiagnosis in low back pain. In fact, one of the underlying reasons for this feeling of weakness is faulty postural alignment – something that is commonplace in low back pain patients and often caused by weakness of the abdominal musculature.

movers and stabilisers of the spine. Understanding the roles of these muscles in movement of the trunk is a prerequisite to effective corrective exercise prescription.

Obliquus externus abdominis (external oblique)

A large, flat muscle, the fibres of which originate on the lower 8 ribs and run diagonally downwards and inwards, to insert laterally on the anterior iliac crest and medially on the rectus sheath.

When the external obliques act bilaterally, their action is to flex the lumbar and thoracic spine against resistance. Unilateral contraction in conjunction with other posterior-lateral muscles results in lateral flexion of the spine to the same side; however, unilateral contraction with the opposite internal oblique (and other spinal rotators) produces rotation to the opposite side. The external oblique shows greatest activity during trunk flexion activities from a supine position.

Obliquus internus abdominis (internal oblique)

A smaller, fan-shaped muscle that lies beneath the external oblique. Its fibres originate from the iliac crest and thoracolumbar fascia, running diagonally upwards to insert on the cartilage of the lower four ribs, and medially to the rectus sheath.

Bilateral contraction of the internal oblique causes flexion of the lumbar and thoracic spine; unilaterally, it acts to flex laterally and rotate the spine to the same side.

The internal oblique shows greatest activity during trunk rotation and hip flexion and extension movements.

Rectus abdominis

A long, flat muscle originating on the pubic crest, with fibres extending upwards to insert on the xiphoid process and ribs 5–7. The rectus is normally divided into three or four bellies of tendinous bands. Each part of the rectus is enclosed within a sheath of connective tissue (rectus sheath) that is continuous with the lateral abdominals and thoracolumbar fascia. These fibres meet centrally to form the linea alba.

Bilateral contraction of the rectus abdominis causes flexion of the lumbar and thoracic spine, and unilateral contraction causes lateral flexion.

The upper portion of the rectus shows greatest activity during spine flexion activities initiated from the upper body. The lower portion shows greater activity during

movements that decrease pelvic tilt (flattening the low back). The lower portion of the rectus abdominis is an important postural muscle and often needs conditioning to restore muscle balance and normal lumbar curvature.

Transversus abdominis

A broad sheet of muscle whose fibres run horizontally from the thoracolumbar fascia and lower 6 ribs to the linea alba.

Its main action is to compress the abdominal viscera by 'narrowing' the waist, and, as such, is a muscle used in forced exhalation. Unlike the other abdominal muscles, it is not a mover of the spine, but aids in stabilising the trunk, especially when integrated with the entire abdominal wall.

Erector spinae

A complex group of muscles consisting of three longitudinal columns: iliocostalis, longissimus and spinalis. The erector spinae forms the largest muscle mass of the back. It contributes little to the maintenance of upright posture and engages most during actions of extension, hyperextension and lateral flexion, when performed against gravity or resistance.

The iliocostalis muscle runs from the iliac crest to the ribs. The iliocostalis is the most lateral of the three parts of the erector spinae. In concert with the other erector spinae muscles, its unilateral action is to flex the spine laterally; bilaterally, it extends the spine.

The longissimus is the longest of the three groups and runs between the transverse processes of the vertebrae. In concert with the other erector spinae muscles, its unilateral action is to flex the spine laterally; bilaterally, it extends the spine.

The spinalis is the least prominent and most medial of the three groups. Together with the other erector spinae muscles, its unilateral action is to flex the spine laterally; bilaterally, it extends the spine.

Multifidus (deep posterior spine)

As part of the deep posterior spinal muscles (and the transversospinalis group), this group of small muscles originates from the transverse process of one vertebra, running obliquely and medially upwards and inserting on the vertebra above, or often onto the second or third vertebra above. Collectively, the multifidi are thought to be responsible for localised movements, contributing to segmental stability of the spine.

Psoas major

A long muscle that is located at the back of the abdominal wall, the fibres of which originate from the bodies of the twelfth thoracic and all lumbar vertebrae, and insert onto the lesser trochanter. As a muscle of the lower spine, it acts to flex the vertebral column; as a muscle of the pelvis, it flexes the thigh.

Quadratus lumborum

A flat muscle extending from the iliac crest to the lowest rib and upper four lumbar vertebrae. It causes lateral flexion of the

Clinical perspective

The functional division of the abdominal muscles necessitates a truly integrated approach to rehabilitation and conditioning, often employing exercises that incorporate larger movement patterns under load.

It is important to understand that there does not appear to be a functional separation of the upper and lower rectus abdominis, although the upper and lower portions can be emphasised preferentially in certain activities. However, any exercise that recruits the rectus abdominis will still activate upper and lower portions, as during a trunk curl exercise, for example.

On the other hand, the upper and lower portions of the obliques can be recruited separately to produce the many movements of torso twisting and side bending, as seen in many daily activities and sport. Due to their criss-crossing fibre alignment, the obliques also play a crucial role in enhancing spine stability.

One of the main roles of the transversus abdominis during movement is in the maintenance of intra-abdominal pressure, especially during heavy load bearing. Due to a similar fibre orientation, it almost always co-contracts with the internal oblique to contribute to spinal stability.

lumbar spine when acting unilaterally, and stabilises the pelvis and lumbar spine bilaterally.

Table 9.1.   Summary of the major muscles involved in trunk movements (thoracic and lumbar spine)

Movement	Prime mover	Synergist
Flexion	Rectus abdominis Internal oblique External oblique	Quadratus lumborum (towards end range of flexion)
Extension	Erector spinae Quadratus lumborum Multifidus	Trapezius (lower fibres) Internal oblique
Lateral flexion	Quadratus lumborum Rectus abdominis Erector spinae Internal oblique External oblique	Psoas Multifidus
Rotation	Internal oblique External oblique Multifidus	Psoas Erector spinae Rectus abdominis Quadratus lumborum

10
EVALUATION OF THE TRUNK

Evaluation of the flexors, extensors and rotators of the trunk holds the key to successful exercise prescription, for both prevention and alleviation of spinal dysfunction.

This chapter outlines evaluation of the trunk in relation to alignment of the spine, movement and muscular strength. With regard to the spine, particular attention will be paid to the thoracic and lumbar regions, as it is these areas that rely heavily on the balanced support and control provided by the trunk muscles. Combining the results of these assessments will help to build a progressive corrective exercise programme.

Alignment analysis

Optimal alignment of the spine and pelvis is conducive to good alignment of the trunk, as well as alignment of the upper and lower extremities. This position minimises joint stresses during weight bearing in almost all daily activities.

For the purpose of gaining information about trunk muscle balance, spinal alignment is best observed in the standing lateral view. The client stands with feet apart in a comfortable and normal posture, and is lined up with a suspended plumb line. The fixed point of reference is slightly anterior to the lateral malleolus, a base point which represents the mid-frontal plane in ideal alignment. Deviations from the ideal standard are noted by the therapist. Plumb-line testing in the anterior and posterior views can also be employed to provide information regarding lateral curvatures of the spine.

Normal lateral alignment of the spine

The normal curves of the spine are labelled according to their direction of convexity in the sagittal plane: anterior in the cervical region (lordosis), posterior in the thoracic region (kyphosis) and anterior in the lumbar region (lordosis). In the same way, lateral curvature is also named in the direction of convexity, such as that present in scoliosis.

In ideal lateral alignment, the plumb line should run through the following points of reference, as outlined in Figure 10.1:

❏ mastoid process
❏ bodies of cervical vertebrae
❏ axis of shoulder joint
❏ approximately midway through trunk
❏ bodies of lumbar vertebrae.

Deviations of the points of reference from the ideal plumb line highlight the degree of faulty alignment. It is useful to describe these deviations as slight, moderate or severe, rather than by quantitative means. Restoration of trunk muscle balance is a key

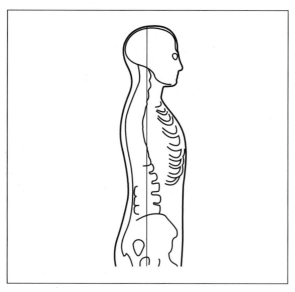

Figure 10.1. Normal alignment of the spine

factor in re-establishing optimal alignment of the spine.

Common alignment problems

Acquired misalignments occur when weak trunk muscles cannot provide adequate support for the spine. In contrast, short trunk muscles may limit range of motion of the spine, thus contributing to overall muscle imbalance. It is important to note that if correction of spinal alignment causes undesirable changes in the alignment of other joints, then the impairment is probably structural, not acquired.

Common misalignments to look for when assessing static spinal alignment include the following, and are often associated with low back pain.

Lumbar lordosis

Lumbar lordosis is observed as hyperextension of the lumbar spine, with the pelvis in anterior tilt. A degree of hip flexion will also be observed.

Lordosis suggests weakness of the abdominals, in particular, the external oblique, and also the hip extensors, namely the gluteus maximus. The muscles that are short are the lumbar erectors and the hip flexors.

Flat-back posture

Characteristics of a flat-back posture include lumbar spine flexion (flattened low back), posterior pelvic tilt and hip extension. It is the opposite observation of lordosis.

This posture suggests weakness of the lumbar erectors and one-joint hip flexors. The muscles that are short include the anterior abdominals and the hip extensors.

Sway-back posture

Sway-back posture is characterised by a forward-displaced pelvis and a backward-displaced upper trunk. As a result, the pelvis is posteriorly tilted, with a degree of hip extension.

Weak muscles include the lower abdominals (especially the external oblique) and one-joint hip flexors. Short muscles include the upper portion of the rectus abdominis and internal oblique, as well as the hip extensors.

Scoliosis

Scoliosis is characterised by a lateral curvature of the spine. Since the vertebral column cannot bend laterally without rotating, scoliosis involves both lateral flexion and rotation. The cause of scoliosis can be acquired (functional), often relating to neuromuscular problems affecting the muscles of the trunk, or structural (idiopathic), involving changes in the bony structure of the spine or unilateral extremity impairment.

In both functional and idiopathic scoliosis, muscle weakness and tightness still exist and unilateral corrective exercise can provide significant benefits in many patients. Common weak muscles often include the abdominals (rectus abdominis and internal oblique) and paraspinal muscles on the side of convexity, as well as the external oblique on the side of the concavity. Muscle testing should also include: back extensors; lateral trunk; hip adductors/abductors/flexors/extensors; middle and lower trapezius; latissimus dorsi; and iliotibial band/tensor fasciae latae.

Movement analysis

Many tests exist for observing movements of the trunk in a number of positions. However, those performed in the standing position will provide an adequate foundation from which the therapist can build.

The results of these tests are not necessarily intended for end range of motion assessment, but rather to observe important functional movements that highlight muscle recruitment patterns and subsequent imbalance.

From a standing position, the client is asked to perform four standard movements:

❏ forward bending (flexion)

❏ backward bending (extension)

❏ side bending (lateral flexion)

❏ rotation.

The therapist observes the shape of the spine and trunk during movement; any deviations should be noted as excessive movement, limited movement or timing impairments.

Forward bending: Flexion

Flexion is the most commonly used movement of daily living and varies according to the region of the spine. In forward bending, the movement comes from both the lumbar spine and pelvis. The pelvis tilts anteriorly and moves posteriorly to maintain the centre of gravity over the base of support. This integrated movement of the lumbar spine and pelvis is known as lumbar-pelvic rhythm, with more movement coming from the hips than the spine.

Maximum lumbar flexion is approximately 30–50°, based on the lumbar spine starting in a position of 20–30° extension. Full flexion is observed when the lumbar curve has flattened, but normally does not progress to the point where the spine curves convexly backwards. At this point, the lumbar erectors are inactive and most of the stress is on the passive support structures. Any further forward movement following full lumbar flexion is generated through hip flexion.

During the return from forward flexion, the movement should begin with hip extension, followed by a combined extension motion from both the hips and the spine. When observing flexion, it is important to understand that all spinal segments should contribute to the movement in a smooth and continuous manner.

Return from flexion should not be initiated from the lumbar region. This is often a contributing factor to back pain through increased compressive forces on the spine. Another observed deviation is forward hip-sway during return from flexion. This action reduces the load on the hip and is common in patients with weak hip extensors (sway-back posture).

A full flexion position that is greater than 50° is considered excessive. Also, if 50 per cent or more lumbar flexion occurs without hip flexion, this is considered a timing impairment of lumbar-pelvic rhythm. A similar timing problem can occur when the lumbar spine flexes more than the hips, a situation which is affected by hamstring length. Typically, females tend to flex more readily in the hips, and males in the lumbar spine.

Backward bending: Extension

Functional activities do not demand large ranges of motion in extension, and, as such, maximum lumbar extension is approximately 25°.

Many of the problems that arise in lumbar extension are due to extension stress caused by excessive tightness of the hip flexors and lumbar erectors, rather than limited range of motion. Coupled with weak, taut abdominal muscles, most of the extension movement occurs at the lower lumbar vertebrae, rather than evenly through the entire lumbar spine. During functional and sport-specific movement, the action of repeated hyperextension is a contributing factor to low back pain.

Side bending: Lateral flexion

Normal lumbar lateral flexion from a standing position will enable the fingertips to reach the level of the knee, allowing for approximately 25° of motion. Thoracic lateral flexion generally allows for up to 70° of movement due to a greater number of vertebrae. The magnitude of the lateral curve in the thoracic spine depends on the number of vertebrae involved.

As range of motion is not a reliable indicator of lateral flexion motion, it is more useful to observe the shape of the curve during side bending. During optimal lateral flexion, the lumbar vertebrae bend and form a smooth curve that is continuous with the thoracic spine.

Deviations in lateral flexion are inevitably accompanied by rotation, as one movement affects the other. Impairment of lateral flexion commonly occurs in patients who exhibit marked hypertrophy of the lumbar erector spinae. In this instance, the stiffness of the muscles limits their movement, showing up as a straighter movement of the lumbar spine, rather than a curve.

Rotation

Rotational range of motion in the lumbar spine is limited to no more than 15°, with the greatest rotational range occurring at the lumbosacral junction. The greatest amount of trunk rotation occurs in the thoracic spine (35–50°). During movement, it is important to observe which regions of the spine are involved in the motion and to what extent.

Rotational restrictions are often the result of muscle imbalances within the abdominals. Shortness of the external oblique on one side and internal oblique on the other side can limit range of motion during trunk rotation. This can easily be seen in asymmetry of the lumbar paraspinal muscles, with greater bulk on one side.

Muscle length

The spine is a multi-joint structure, and, as such, the muscles that support it must be long enough to allow normal mobility, yet short enough to contribute to optimal joint stabilisation. Although length testing alone can offer some insight into trunk flexibility,

The following tests should be performed in conjunction with movement analysis to obtain a full evaluation of trunk flexibility, both statically and dynamically.

The tests shown below focus on length of the posterior trunk muscles only, as well as the important observation of the contour and shape of the back during forward bending. The length of the anterior abdominals is not usually tested, as information regarding their shortness/weakness can be determined from comprehensive strength testing.

Muscle(s): Posterior back musculature, hamstrings.

Starting position: Client is in the long-sitting position (legs extended, feet at right angles).

Test: Instruct client to reach forwards and try to touch toes, as comfortably as possible. The therapist observes the contour of the back, in particular, the lumbar and thoracic regions.

Normal length: Normal flexion of the lumbar spine allows the spine to flatten in this region. Normal flexion of the thoracic spine allows an increase in the convexity in this region. The overall contour of the back, from lumbar through to thoracic regions, should be smooth and continuous (especially in the thoracic spine).

Normal length of the hamstrings allows adequate hip flexion so that the angle between the sacrum and couch is approximately 80°.

Shortness: Shortness in the lumbar muscles (erector spinae) normally presents as excessive thoracic flexion, as the thoracic spine compensates for lack of lumbar movement. Note that the client may still be able to touch their toes. In extreme cases, there may still be a lumbar lordosis present during forward bending.

Shortness in the hamstrings may prevent

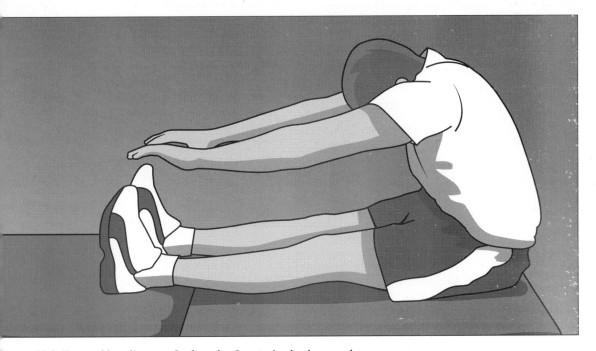

Figure 10.2. Forward-bending test for length of posterior back musculature

the client from touching their toes, and in these situations the contour of the back must be carefully observed to determine whether there is shortness in the back musculature.
Excessive length: The client is able to reach beyond the toes in forward bending. Excessive length may be present in one or all of the following muscles: hamstrings, low back and upper back.

Muscle(s): Posterior back musculature (without hip flexion).
Starting position: Client is supine, resting on forearms, with legs straight. The elbow is flexed to 90° and the arms are close to the body.
Test: The client is instructed to flex the spine, keeping the pelvis flat on the couch (no hip flexion).
Normal length: The client can flex the spine, while maintaining a flat pelvis.

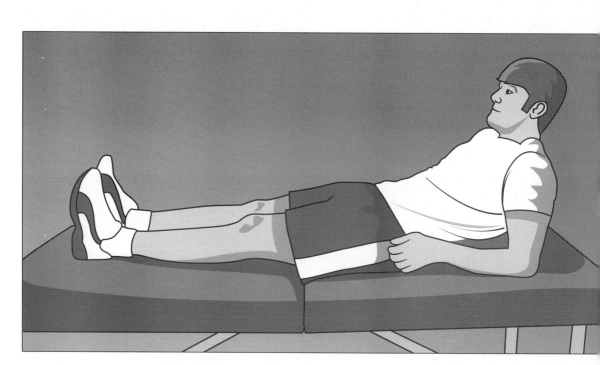

Figure 10.3. Range of motion in trunk flexion (without hip flexion)

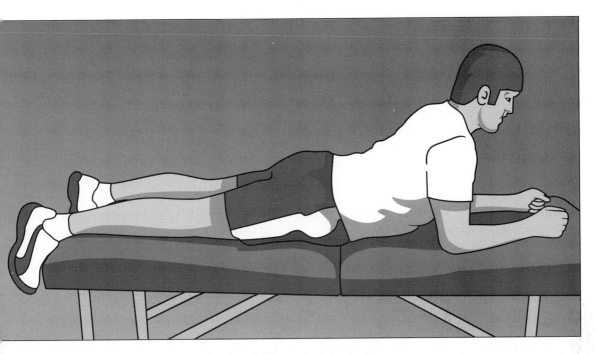

Figure 10.4. Range of motion in trunk extension (without hip extension)

Muscle(s): Posterior back musculature, anterior abdominals (without hip extension).
Starting position: Client is prone, resting on forearms. The elbows are flexed to 90°, with the arms close to the body.
Test: The client is instructed to prop themselves up on their forearms, keeping the pelvis flat on the couch (no hip extension).
Normal length: The client can extend the spine, while maintaining a flat pelvis.
Note: If the serratus anterior is weak, there may be winging of the scapula during this test, which will interfere with back extension.

Muscle strength

Strength testing for the trunk should focus on the deep and superficial abdominal muscles, and to a lesser extent on the low back muscles (extensors), as these are rarely weak. Careful assessment of these muscles will allow the therapist accurately to prescribe stretching or strengthening exercises as part of a corrective exercise programme.

The following trunk muscles should be tested:

❑ deep abdominal muscles – transversus abdominis

❑ back extensors

❑ lateral trunk flexors

❑ trunk flexors (upper and lower abdominals)

❑ trunk rotators (obliques).

The back extensors are tested in the prone position, and should be tested only if the client is able to assume this position without pain. Extension tests should not be performed routinely if the client has a history of lumbar compression.

The lateral trunk flexors are tested with

the client in a side-lying position, and the trunk flexors (anterior abdominals) are tested in the supine position.

The trunk rotators (obliques) are tested in a supine position. Care and attention must be administered when conducting trunk rotation tests, as they present more of a demand on the client.

Muscle(s): Transversus abdominis.
Pre-test: The client may need to be instructed on how to contract the transversus abdominis without moving the trunk or pelvis. This is best done in a four-point kneeling position. For further details of this manoeuvre, please refer to phase 2 of corrective exercises for the trunk in Chapter 11 (p. 136).
Starting position: The client is lying prone, with legs straight. A pressure biofeedback pad (or blood pressure cuff) is placed under the patient's belly button, inflated to

70 mmHg and allowed to stabilise. If this pressure is uncomfortable for the patient, a smaller inflation may be required. It is important for the therapist to identify an average point where the needle fluctuates due to respiration.
Test: The client is asked to breathe in and out and, while holding the breath, instructed to draw in the navel towards the spine, so that the belly button lifts off the couch. During the manoeuvre, the client should try to keep a steady spinal and pelvic position, and should not engage any other muscles, such as the glutes or the superficial abdominals.

The therapist should observe the needle movement. Once full contraction is achieved, the client can resume normal breathing. The test can be repeated if necessary to obtain a consistent result.
Normal strength: A reduction in pressure by 6–10 mmHg indicates sufficient shortness of

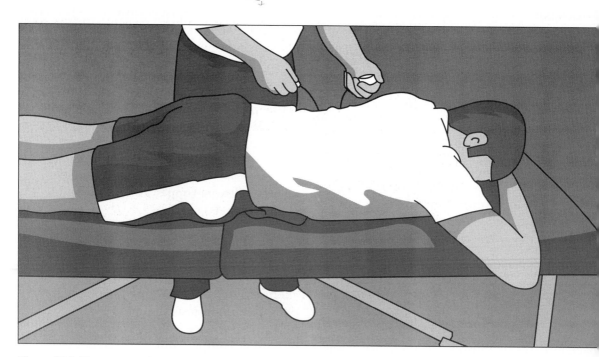

Figure 10.5. Transversus abdominis strength test

the transversus abdominis, independent of other abdominal muscles.

Weakness: Inability to reduce the pressure by more than 2 mmHg indicates that the transversus abdominis is unable to shorten independently of other abdominal muscles.

Note: Failure to drop the pressure is not always indicative of a weak transversus abdominis, but may point to excessive activation of other global muscles that serve to flatten the low back. These may include the glutes, hamstrings and lower abdominals. Special attention must be paid to observing the movements of the pelvis during the test.

A rise in pressure is normally indicative of contraction of the rectus abdominis or external obliques. As they contract, they will push on the pressure pad, causing a rise in pressure. This may not necessarily point to weakness of the transversus abdominis, but rather to overactivity of the rectus abdominis or external obliques.

Muscle(s): Back extensors.

Starting position: Client is prone, with hands clasped behind head. Therapist stabilises the legs on the couch, to avoid lifting.

Test: The client performs a trunk extension to their full range of motion, and holds.

Normal: Client can raise the trunk in extension through their range of motion, without excessive lordosis.

Weakness: Bilateral weakness of the back extensors results in a lumbar kyphosis (flattening of low back) and increased thoracic kyphosis. Unilateral weakness results in a lateral curvature of the lumbar spine, with convexity towards the weak side.

Shortness: Bilateral shortness results in an increase in lumbar lordosis. Unilateral shortness results in lateral curvature, with a concavity towards the short side. Shortness may also be caused by weak gluteus maximus (see next test).

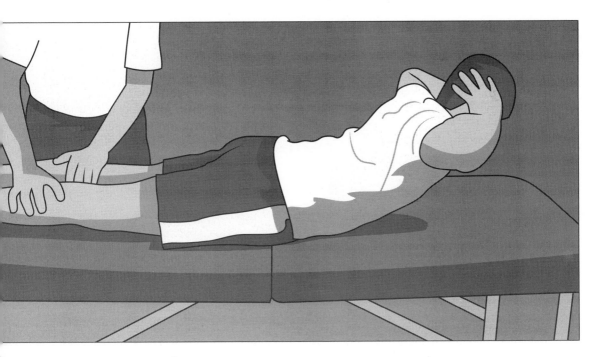

Figure 10.6. Back extensor strength test

Muscle(s): Gluteus maximus (during back extension).

Starting position: Client is prone, with hands clasped behind head.

Test: Client performs a back extension movement. Therapist observes low back posture.

Normal strength: The moment that back extension is initiated, the client exhibits a normal anterior curve in low back.

Weakness: The moment that back extension is initiated, the client exhibits an increased lordosis in low back. Full range of motion cannot be accomplished. Holding the pelvis down in the direction of posterior tilt will enable full range of motion.

Muscle(s): Lateral trunk flexors – obliques, quadratus lumborum, latissimus dorsi, rectus abdominis.

Pre-test: Test for hip abductor strength, as lateral trunk flexion in side-lying is a combination of trunk flexion and hip abduction. Adequate strength in hip abduction will stabilise the pelvis during movement.

Starting position: Client is side-lying straight, with a support between the legs. The top arm is extended down the topmost thigh, and the lower arm is across the chest, holding the opposite shoulder. The legs are held down to counterbalance the weight of the trunk.

Test: Client raises trunk directly sideways.

Normal strength: Client can raise trunk sideways to a point of maximum lateral flexion, with lowermost shoulder rising up at least 4–6 inches from the couch.

Weakness: Client cannot raise the trunk or minimally raise the lowermost shoulder off the couch.

Note: If the back hyperextends during movement, the quadratus lumborum and latissimus dorsi are short, indicating weakness of the anterior abdominals.

Figure 10.7. Lateral trunk flexor strength test

The presence of trunk rotation during lateral flexion can be indicative of an imbalance between the internal and external obliques. If the trunk rotates forwards during lateral flexion, this indicates a greater pull by the external oblique on that side. If the trunk rotates backwards, this indicates a greater pull by the internal oblique on that side. This imbalance may also be seen by performing lateral flexion over a stability ball.

Muscle(s): Lower abdominals.

Starting position: Client is lying supine, with legs straight and arms folded across chest.

Test: The therapist assists the client in raising both legs to a vertical position (legs straight – tightness of the hamstrings will affect this). Client then tilts the pelvis posteriorly to flatten the low back. This is achieved by contracting the abdominals. The client is asked to hold this tilt while slowly lowering the legs, without moving the head or shoulders. The therapist should observe the position of the low back and pelvis during lowering. The moment the pelvis starts to tilt anteriorly and the low back arches, the angle between the legs and the table is noted. This can be assisted by placing a hand under the patient's lower back.

Normal strength: If the client can lower the legs to the table (zero angle) without anterior tilt of the pelvis, then normal strength is present in the lower abdominal muscles.

If the angle between the legs and the table is 15–45°, strength is considered as being 'good' (a).

If the angle between the legs and the table is 45–75°, strength is considered as being 'fair' (b).

Weakness: If the angle between the legs and the table is 75–90°, strength is considered as being 'poor' (c) and there is marked weakness of the lower abdominal muscles.

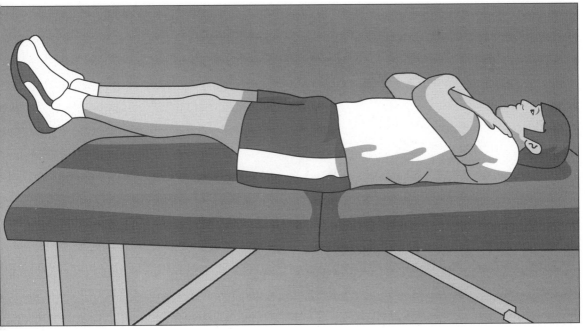

(a) good

Figure 10.8. Lower abdominal strength test

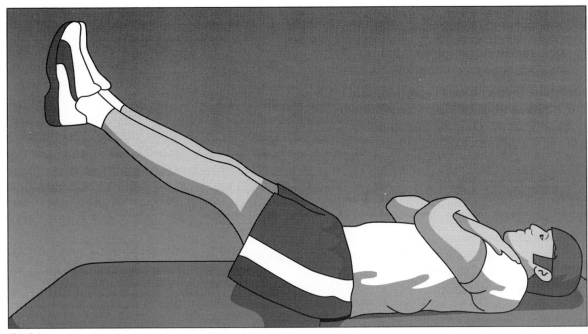

(b) fair

(c) poor

Figure 10.8. (contd) Lower abdominal strength test

Note: This test may not be suitable if the client has low back pain, or is known to have weak abdominal musculature. In this instance, the test may be modified using a single bent leg, rather than straight legs.

Muscle(s): Upper abdominals.

Pre-test: Back flexibility should be tested prior to this test, so that restricted range of motion is not misconstrued as muscle weakness.

Starting position: Client is lying supine, with legs slightly bent (knee angle of approximately 15°) and toes resting on the hands of the therapist, which are positioned about 6 inches above the level of the couch. Toes should be pointed (ankle plantar flexion). The arms are positioned alongside the body.

Test: The client performs a slow trunk curl by lifting the head and shoulders, while maintaining the same pressure on the therapist's hands with their toes. The therapist observes whether the client's toes are able to maintain constant pressure on their hands. Strength is graded according to performance of this movement with the arms in three different positions.

Normal strength: Client can perform the trunk curl with the arms by the sides of the head (fingers by ears), while maintaining the same pressure on the therapist's hands.

Strength is considered 'fair/good' if the client can perform the trunk curl with the arms across the chest, while maintaining the same pressure on the therapist's hands.

Strength is considered 'average/fair' if the client can perform the trunk curl only with the arms by the sides, while maintaining the same pressure on the therapist's hands.

Weakness: Weakness of the upper abdominal muscles is present if the client cannot

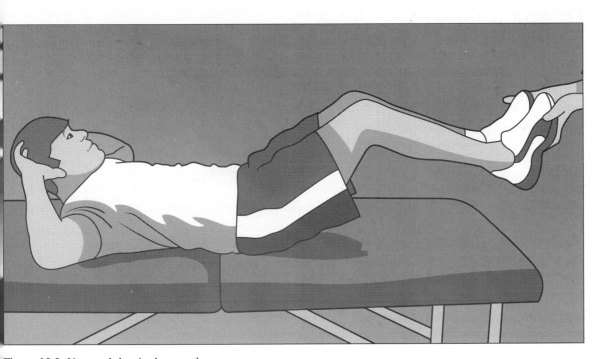

Figure 10.9. Upper abdominal strength test

perform a trunk curl with the arms by the sides, without lifting the toes. This may indicate the presence of facilitated hip flexor muscles.

Muscle(s): Trunk rotators – rectus abdominis, obliques.
Starting position: Client is supine, with legs straight, which are stabilised by the therapist.
Test: Level 1 – client holds arms by sides and flexes and rotates the trunk to the right and holds for 5 seconds. The movement is repeated to the left.

Level 2 – client extends arms forwards and flexes and rotates the trunk to the right and holds for 5 seconds. The movement is repeated to the left.

Level 3 – client holds arms across chest and flexes and rotates the trunk to the right and holds for 5 seconds. The movement is repeated to the left.

Level 4 – client holds hands by ears and flexes and rotates the trunk to the right and holds for 5 seconds. The movement is repeated to the left.
Normal strength: Client can complete testing at level 4.
Weakness: Client cannot hold flexion/rotation and the trunk begins to de-rotate and extend. Completion of levels 1–3 indicates strength grades of 'average', 'moderate' and 'good', respectively.
Note: Imbalance can exist between the internal and external obliques, and is present when there is rotation during side-lying lateral flexion (see earlier test on p. 123).

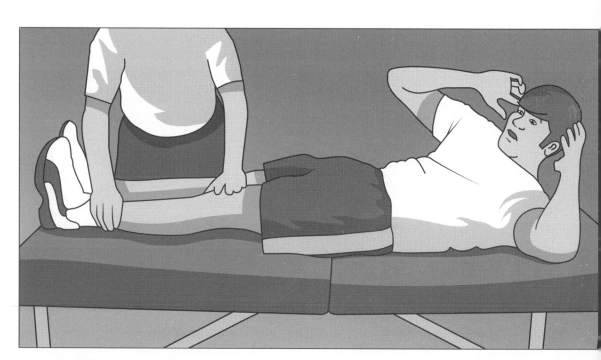

Figure 10.10. Trunk rotator strength test

Clinical perspective

Many popular training programmes for the trunk tend to emphasise abdominal and low back strength. However, one of the most important functions of the abdominal muscles is to stabilise the spine, a function often neglected, especially in sport. It is important to condition the major stabilisers of the trunk – the internal oblique and transversus abdominis – the only two muscles which pass from the anterior to the posterior parts of the trunk.

For optimal stabilisation, strength alone is insufficient: it is the speed with which the muscles contract in reaction to a force, as well as their endurance, which is important. Additionally, the ability of a client to differentiate deep abdominal function (internal oblique and transversus abdominis) from superficial abdominal function (external oblique and rectus abdominis) is also vital. In the context of corrective exercise, once the function of the deep abdominal wall has been isolated, it should then be effectively reintegrated into a number of trunk exercises and movements that are functional to the client.

11
CORRECTIVE EXERCISE FOR THE TRUNK

Corrective exercise progression

There is considerable evidence to suggest that imbalance and lack of muscle control within the trunk are important features in patients with low back pain. Therefore corrective exercise programmes must be specific to correct these deficits.

In the majority of cases of low back pain, biomechanical modification is initially required in the form of postural correction. Daily activities should be adapted to reduce position-related stresses to the lumbar spine; at the same time, it is important to address the issues of muscle weakness, tightness and control.

The long-term success of any corrective exercise programme lies in the ability to integrate strength and neuromuscular control into the functional activities of daily living and sport.

The four progressive phases of corrective exercise in relation to the trunk are described below.

Phase 1 – Muscle balance

These exercises are aimed at restoring normal length within the superficial trunk muscles, in particular the low back. This is best achieved through a combination of stretching and static postural correction. As almost all patients will be active both occupationally and recreationally, it is also important to incorporate postural correction during light functional activities, such as bending, lifting and reaching; with this in mind, emphasis should be directed towards muscle recruitment patterns, lumbar-pelvic rhythm and neutral spine alignment.

Phase 2 – Static, dynamic and reactive stabilisation

The exercises aim to improve stabilisation of the lumbar spine by restoring endurance of the deep abdominal wall and low back muscles (inner unit), as a prerequisite to conditioning the superficial layers of the abdominal wall and low back (outer unit). By re-educating all three layers of the abdominal wall, integration between the inner and outer units can take place during functional activities, enhancing spine stability. Much of this work is achieved through abdominal wall co-contraction in a variety of static and dynamic postures that challenge neutral spine alignment.

Phase 3 – Functional strength

The goal during this phase is to ensure that the stabilisation capabilities of the trunk muscles are sufficient to control the lumbar spine under increasing load. Preliminary exercises should aim to apply rotatory load to the trunk through unilateral movement of the arms or legs in a variety of positions. From here, progression can be made by using external resistance and larger extremity joint movement. The final stages should include functional exercises that are relevant to the patient's occupational and recreational environment. As all movement patterns require smooth integration of the inner and outer units, both functional strength and control of the trunk musculature in open- and closed-chain environments should be the final outcome.

Phase 4 – Functional power

This phase will further improve coordination and control of movement, to provide a high degree of functional carry-over into occupation, recreation and sport.

The preferred method of conditioning during this phase is plyometric exercise, demanding a high stabilisation requirement from the inner unit, simultaneously with quick, powerful torque production from the outer unit and extremity muscles. The result is enhanced link-sequencing and force generation from the lower extremities, through the trunk and out to the upper extremities.

For this to occur safely, muscle balance, stabilisation and functional strength must all be at optimal levels, and particular emphasis should be placed on optimal hip and trunk rotation, to ensure smooth coordination of ground reaction forces up through the body.

Corrective exercises for the trunk

Phase 1 exercises – Restoring muscle balance and flexibility

Pelvic tilts
Muscle group(s): Low back, abdominal wall
Phase/modality: Flexibility, mobility
Equipment: None

Purpose
❑ To improve mobility of the lumbar spine.
❑ To increase awareness of the lumbo-pelvic-hip complex.

Starting position
Client is lying supine, with knees bent, feet flat on floor and the spine in a natural curve (neutral alignment).

Correct performance
❑ Client gently flattens the low back and then arches, tilting the pelvis posteriorly and anteriorly. This movement is performed slowly and deliberately, and the pelvis is tilted only within a pain-free range of motion.
❑ The movement is continued for up to 2 minutes or until the movement becomes fluid and controlled.

Variations
❑ PELVIC CLOCKS – The tilting may also be performed in a circular motion. Here, begin with a posterior tilt and then slowly move the pelvis round in a clockwise direction, towards an anterior tilt. The movement is completed by continuing clockwise back to the start. The motion is

repeated in an anticlockwise direction and the exercise is repeated as above.

❑ The pelvic clocks may be performed on a stability ball to enhance proprioception. Start by sitting upright on a ball in good postural alignment. Circular pelvic tilting is performed as above, using the ball as a pivot.

Curled forward bending
Muscle group(s): Lumbar and thoracic erectors, glutes
Phase/modality: Flexibility, mobility
Equipment: None

Purpose

❑ To increase lumbar and thoracic flexibility (do not prescribe in the presence of thoracic kyphosis or osteoporosis).

Figure 11.1. Curled forward bending

❑ To increase range of motion in hip flexion.

❑ To encourage use of hip extensors, particularly in the presence of an anterior pelvic tilt.

Starting position

Client stands with feet positioned about hip-width apart.

Correct performance

❑ Client slowly reaches towards the floor, allowing the neck, trunk and hips to flex until a comfortable range of motion is reached.

❑ Client returns to an upright position by contracting the glutes and extending the hips. The movement should not be initiated by extending the spine.

Side bending
Muscle group(s): Abdominals, paraspinal muscles
Phase/modality: Flexibility, mobility
Equipment: None

Purpose

❑ To increase flexibility of the paraspinal and abdominal muscles.

❑ To encourage thoracolumbar, rather than lumbosacral, movement.

Starting position

Client is standing, with feet positioned about hip-width apart.

Correct performance

❑ Client places hands just above the iliac crests, at the lowest level of the ribs, and slowly bends to one side by tilting the shoulders rather than moving at the waist.

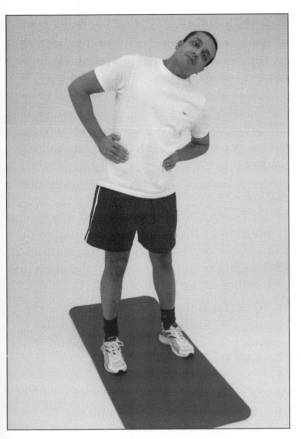

Figure 11.2. Side bending

❑ The therapist observes the movement and encourages movement of the thoracic spine, if necessary. The movement should be pain-free.

❑ Motion is repeated to the other side and continued until the movement becomes coordinated.

Spine rotation
Muscle group(s): Spinal rotators
Phase/modality: Flexibility, mobility
Equipment: None

Purpose
❑ To increase range of motion in spinal rotation.

❑ To encourage use of the thoracic spine in rotation.

Starting position
Client is lying supine, with knees bent and feet flat on floor, holding each elbow with the opposite hand ('Cossack' position). The elbows are pointing towards the ceiling.

Correct performance
❑ The client begins by slowly rotating the thoracic spine, side to side, allowing the elbows to reach towards the opposite side of the floor.

(a)

(b)

Figure 11.3. Spine rotation – (a) before, (b) after

❑ Client allows the head to turn naturally with the movement.

❑ The movement is continued until full pain-free range of motion is achieved.

❑ The legs should remain still throughout the movement, and the client is encouraged to keep the ribcage 'soft', to ensure full rotation from the thoracic spine.

Variations

This exercise may be performed in a standing or sitting position, against a wall or seated on a stability ball.

Seated low back stretch
Muscle group(s): Low back
Phase/modality: Flexibility
Equipment: Pillow

Purpose

To stretch tight low back muscles, particularly in those with excessive hamstring length.

Figure 11.4. Seated low back stretch

Starting position

Client is seated on a chair, with feet resting on the floor and a rolled-up pillow on the lap.

Correct performance

Client bends forwards over the pillow to stretch the low back, holding for up to 20 seconds.

Variations

❑ This stretch may be performed in a supine position by tilting the pelvis to flatten the low back on the floor, or by bending and bringing both knees towards the chest and holding for up to 20 seconds.

❑ To perform the stretch in a prone position, a rolled-up pillow is placed under the abdomen and a rolled-up towel under the ankles.

Nerve flossing
Muscle group(s): Paraspinal muscles, hamstrings, sciatic nerve
Phase/modality: Mobility
Equipment: None

Purpose

To increase mobility of the sciatic nerve through the intervertebral foramen.

Starting position

Client is seated upright at the end of a couch, with legs hanging freely.

Correct performance

❑ Client begins by gently flexing the cervical spine, then extends the cervical spine with simultaneous knee extension of one leg.

❑ As the knee is flexed, the cervical spine is flexed and the movement is then repeated using the other leg.

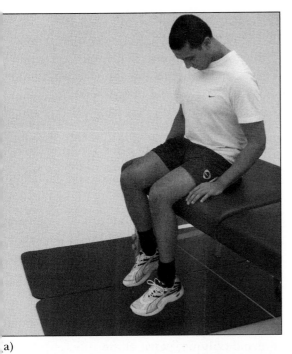

(a)

(b)

Figure 11.5. Nerve flossing – (a) before, (b) after

- The exercise is continued slowly and deliberately for up to 1 minute or until an increase in mobility is achieved.

Note: If there is excessive tension in the sciatic nerve, this exercise may exacerbate symptoms. If the client reports a reduction in symptoms the next day, then frequency of flossing can be increased.

Posterior pelvic tilt (external oblique)

Muscle group(s): External oblique, transversus abdominis
Phase/modality: Muscle balance, strength
Equipment: None

Purpose

- To strengthen the external oblique.
- To encourage use of the external oblique rather than the glutes or rectus abdominis, during posterior pelvic tilt.

Starting position

Client is lying supine, with knees bent, feet flat on floor and hands beside the head.

Correct performance

- The transversus abdominis is activated by pulling the lower abdomen up and in, and the pelvis is tilted posteriorly to flatten the low back by action of the external oblique.
- Client holds the position for up to 8 seconds, while breathing easily. The exercise is repeated 6 times.
- The therapist should observe compensatory use of the rectus abdominis or glutes to tilt the pelvis posteriorly.

Note: The client should be encouraged to carry over the awareness of holding the lower abdomen in and up, when standing. This exercise may also be performed incorporating a leg slide, using alternate legs while holding the contraction.

Cat-camel

Muscle group(s): Paraspinal muscles
Phase/modality: Mobility
Equipment: None

Purpose

To increase mobility of the spine by reducing viscous stresses.

Starting position

Client assumes a four-point kneeling position, with hands below the shoulders and knees below the hips. Spinal alignment is neutral.

(a)

(b)

Figure 11.6. Cat-camel – (a) before, (b) after

Correct performance

❑ Client flexes the spine by allowing the head and tailbone to drop downwards, and then extends the spine by lifting the head and tailbone upwards (arched back) The movement is performed slowly and deliberately.

❑ Emphasis should be placed on motion of the spine rather than end range flexibility

❑ Perform 6 cycles.

Phase 2 exercises – Restoring static, dynamic and reactive stabilisation

Abdominal hollowing

Muscle group(s): Transversus abdominis, internal oblique, pelvic floor
Phase/modality: Static stabilisation, strength, endurance
Equipment: None

Purpose

To increase awareness, strength and endurance of the deep abdominal muscles.

Starting position

Client is lying supine, in neutral spine alignment, with knees bent and feet flat on floor.

Correct performance

❑ Client draws lower abdomen upwards and inwards, to narrow the waist. This position is held for a few seconds before releasing and repeating.

❑ The therapist should observe for any compensatory movement, such as loss of neutral alignment, contraction of the rectus abdominis or glutes, or any other upper or lower extremity movement. If any of these occur, the therapist should

a)

b)

Figure 11.7. Abdominal hollowing – (a) before, (b) after

correct the faulty movement by instructing the patient.

❏ At this stage, emphasis should be placed on isolation of the deep abdominal muscles.

Progressions

Progression can occur in a number of stages:

❏ GRADING THE CONTRACTION – the client is taught to contract the deep abdominal muscles to different intensities of contraction (100 per cent, 90 per cent, down to 10 per cent). This serves to increase proprioception within the deep abdominal wall.

❏ INCREASING CONTRACTION TIME – once ability to contract is achieved, the client can then increase holding times up to 8 seconds maximum. Endurance can be further enhanced by increasing the number of repetitions. It is important that the client is instructed in the proper breathing technique while holding contractions.

❏ POSITIONAL CONTRACTIONS – the client is instructed to maintain contractions in a number of body positions, including prone lying, side-lying, four-point kneeling, two-point kneeling, sitting (stability ball) and standing.

❏ EXTREMITY MOVEMENT – the final stage of progression is to maintain the abdominal contraction while performing upper and lower extremity movement. These movements are usually performed in a number of positions (as above) and involve moving arms and legs in controlled and precise movement patterns. The aims at this stage are significantly to challenge lumbar stability and spine position using body weight. This provides a useful foundation for further functional and load-bearing movements. This approach forms the basis of a body-conditioning system known as Pilates.

Abdominal bracing

Muscle group(s): Entire abdominal wall
Phase/modality: Static stabilisation, strength, endurance
Equipment: None

Purpose

❑ To increase awareness, strength and endurance of the entire abdominal wall.

❑ To provide a primary stabilisation mechanism for the lumbar spine.

Starting position

Client is lying supine, in neutral spine alignment, with knees bent and feet flat on floor.

(a)

(b)

Figure 11.8. Abdominal bracing – (a) before, (b) after

Correct performance

❑ Client braces or 'stiffens' the muscles of the trunk and holds for a few seconds, before releasing.

❑ The therapist should be aware of the use of mental imagery to aid the patient. This may include instructions about tightening other muscles in the body and applying the same technique to the torso; asking the client to imagine they are about to be hit in the torso; asking the client to cough and notice the stiffness that it produces in the torso.

❑ Careful observation should be made to ensure the client is maintaining neutral spine alignment throughout the exercise.

Progressions

Progression can occur in a number of stages:

❑ GRADING THE CONTRACTION – the client is taught to brace the abdominal muscles to different intensities of contraction (100 per cent, 90 per cent, down to 10 per cent). This teaches the client to use the correct intensity of brace when required.

❑ INCREASING CONTRACTION TIME – once ability to contract is achieved, the client can then increase holding times up to 8 seconds maximum. Endurance can be further enhanced by increasing the number of repetitions. It is important that the client is instructed in the proper breathing technique while holding contractions.

❑ POSITIONAL CONTRACTIONS – the client is instructed to maintain contractions in a number of body positions, including prone lying, side-lying, four-point kneeling, two-point kneeling, sitting (stability ball) and standing.

Clinical perspective

There is an important difference between abdominal hollowing and abdominal bracing and their contribution to spinal stability. While abdominal hollowing is an important exercise for motor re-education in low back pain patients, the act of hollowing does not ensure optimal stability for the spine.

Abdominal bracing is more effective at enhancing spine stability as it activates all three layers of the abdominal wall. This is achieved through two mechanisms. First, during bracing, the criss-cross structure of the obliques is fully utilised to provide stiffness for the trunk; second, the abdominal muscles are more effective stabilisers of the trunk when they have a wider base, that is, when the abdomen is not hollowed. In this way, an abdominal brace provides maximal lumbar stability through co-contraction of all the abdominal muscles. This can prove to be more energy-efficient, as high levels of co-contraction in bracing are rarely required during daily functional activities.

In practice, individuals rarely have complete inactivity of the deep abdominal, except in some cases of abdominal surgery, chronic sedentary lifestyles and pathological muscle weakness/wasting. Many low back pain patients exhibit some ability to contract the deep abdominals, and, with this in mind, corrective exercise should be progressive. Once deep abdominal contraction has been restored, the bracing mechanism should be taught as the primary means of spinal stabilisation and implemented further in all functional activities.

❑ EXTREMITY MOVEMENT – the final stage of progression is to maintain the abdominal brace while performing upper and lower extremity movement. These movements are usually performed in a number of positions (as above) and involve moving arms and legs in controlled and precise movement patterns. The aims at this stage are significantly to challenge lumbar stability and spine position using body weight. This provides a useful foundation for further functional and load-bearing movements.

Oblique sling

Muscle group(s): Obliques
Phase/modality: Static stabilisation, strength
Equipment: None

Purpose

❑ To enhance awareness of the internal and external oblique force couple, as used in trunk rotation.

❑ To improve the functioning of the obliques, particularly in patients with unilateral rotational dysfunction.

❑ To increase the strength of the obliques.

Starting position

Client is lying supine, in neutral spine alignment, with knees bent and feet flat on floor. One hand should be placed over the right external oblique and the other hand over the left internal oblique.

Correct performance

❑ Client begins to draw the hands closer to one another by focusing on co-contracting the opposite internal and external oblique. To aid this process initially, a small compensatory movement of the shoulder and the opposite hip is allowed.

❏ The position is held for a few seconds before releasing. It is then repeated several times before changing sides.

Progressions

OBLIQUE CURL – Once the client has gained awareness of the obliques, they can then proceed to adding rotational spine movements. In this exercise the fingertips are placed by the sides of the head and the client curls the trunk diagonally towards the opposite hip, before returning and repeating to the other side. To facilitate integrated use of the internal and external oblique, the client should be instructed to lift the shoulder rather than the elbow, with a simultaneous lift from the opposite hip.

Note: If the client has rotational dysfunction, such as that present in scoliosis, it may be necessary to perform the oblique sling or curl unilaterally, as part of an overall corrective exercise programme. In this instance, muscle strength testing is a prerequisite.

Floor bridge

Muscle group(s): Low back, abdominals, hip extensors
Phase/modality: Dynamic stabilisation, strength
Equipment: None

Purpose

❏ To challenge and enhance lumbar stability during hip extension.

❏ To strengthen the hip extensors.

Prerequisites

❏ Pain-free range of motion in hip extension.

❏ Ability to perform an abdominal brace.

(a)

(b)

Figure 11.9. Floor bridge – (a) before, (b) after

Starting position

Client is lying supine, with knees bent and feet flat on floor. Arms are held by the sides of the body.

Correct performance

❏ Client begins by lifting the hips up towards the ceiling until there is a straight line between the knees and the shoulders. The movement should be initiated with an abdominal brace and a contraction of the glutes. Return to the start position.

❏ The movement is performed 6–10 times, before resting.

Progressions

❑ Arms across chest.

❑ Single leg.

❑ Feet on a stability ball.

Note: If the client experiences cramp in the hamstrings during the movement, the therapist should check that pelvic alignment is optimal, and correct if necessary. If the problem persists, the quadriceps should be stretched.

Four-point arm/leg reach

Muscle group(s): Low back, abdominals, hip extensors, shoulders

Phase/modality: Dynamic stabilisation, strength

Equipment: None

(a)

Purpose

❑ To challenge and enhance lumbar stability during hip extension.

❑ To strengthen the hip extensors.

❑ To condition the cross-crawl movement pattern.

Prerequisites

❑ Pain-free range of motion in hip extension.

❑ Ability to perform an abdominal brace.

❑ Adequate rotator cuff strength.

Starting position

Client assumes a four-point kneeling position, with hands below shoulders and knees below hips. Body weight should be central, midway between shoulders and hips.

Correct performance

❑ Client braces the abdominals and reaches forwards with one arm and backwards with the opposite leg. Neutral spine alignment

(b)

Figure 11.10. Four-point arm/leg reach – (a) before, (b) after

should be maintained throughout. The movement is repeated for the other side, for a total of 6 repetitions each side.

❑ The arm and leg reach should not go higher than horizontal or body level. Initially, the client may only be able to achieve a small reach, before compromising spine position and bracing ability. The reaching distance may have to be increased slowly as the client becomes stronger.

❑ The therapist should also observe any side-to-side movement of the hips and correct this by instructing the client to brace harder or decrease the distance reached. If movement still occurs, the exercise can be regressed to just moving the arms or legs alone, until adequate strength and control are achieved.

Progressions

❑ Lateral reach – the arms and legs are taken out to the sides.

❑ 'Crawling' – the client is instructed to crawl forwards and backwards while maintaining lumbar stability.

Curl-up
Muscle group(s): Abdominals (upper)
Phase/modality: Dynamic stabilisation, strength
Equipment: None

Purpose

❑ To strengthen the abdominals while minimising stresses to the lumbar spine.

❑ To challenge and enhance lumbar stability during flexion.

Prerequisites

Pain-free range of motion in flexion.

Starting position

Client is lying supine, with one leg straight and the other bent. Hands are positioned under the lumbar spine for support and feedback. It is essential that the lumbar spine is held in a neutral position throughout the movement.

(a)

(b)

Figure 11.11. Curl-up – (a) before, (b) after

Correct performance

❑ Client braces the abdominals and lifts the head and shoulders a short distance off the floor. The elbows remain on the floor. The end position is held for 1 second before returning.

❑ Particular emphasis should be placed on flexing the thoracic spine, NOT the lumbar or cervical regions. The aim is to activate the rectus abdominis and not to produce spine motion.

❑ Perform up to 10 repetitions with good technique.

Progressions

❏ The elbows can be lifted during the movement.

❏ The end position of flexion can be held for up to 8 seconds, before returning.

Note: If the client experiences neck pain, they should be instructed to place their tongue on the roof of their mouth behind the front teeth, to encourage neck stabilisation patterns. If the problem persists, isometric neck exercises may be prescribed.

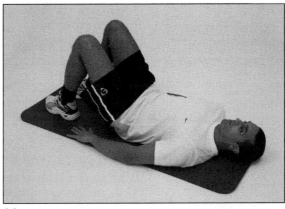

(a)

Lower abdominal curl

Muscle group(s): Abdominals (lower)
Phase/modality: Dynamic stabilisation, strength
Equipment: None

Purpose

To strengthen the lower abdominals.

Prerequisites

Pain-free range of motion in flexion.

Starting position

The client is lying supine, with knees bent and feet flat on floor. The therapist places their hand under the client's lumbar spine. The client is instructed to flatten their back into the therapist's hand, by engaging the (lower) abdominals.

Correct performance

❏ While maintaining the abdominal contraction, the client raises and lowers the flexed knee, bringing the knee above the hip and then back down. The movement is performed 8 times, before repeating with the other leg.

❏ The therapist observes whether the back is kept flat throughout the entire exercise. If the back starts to arch, the movement

(b)

Figure 11.12. Lower abdominal curl – (a) before, (b) after

must be stopped and resumed once corrected.

Progressions

❏ The first stage of progression involves gradually straightening the leg to produce a longer lever arm, until the client can perform the exercise, holding the low back flat with one leg straight.

❏ The final stage of progression involves raising and lowering both legs. In this instance, the client should begin with both legs fully bent, before progressing to straighter legs. Please note that the use of both legs is an advanced exercise.

Note: If a flat back cannot be maintained during the movement, the posterior lateral fibres of the external oblique may not be strong enough to assist the rectus abdominis in flattening the back. Muscle strength testing will be necessary to establish this.

Phase 3 exercises – Restoring functional strength

Supine hip extension: torso on ball
Muscle group(s): Hip extensors, abdominal wall
Phase/modality: Strength, stabilisation, balance
Equipment: Stability ball

Purpose
❑ To increase the strength of the hip extensors.
❑ To improve neuromuscular control of the lateral abdominal muscles, in preparation for larger kinetic chain movements.
❑ To improve whole body balance.

Prerequisites
❑ Good level of core strength.
❑ Optimal scapula control to ensure retraction and depression.

Starting position
❑ Client sits on the stability ball and rolls down, while comfortably placing the head, neck and shoulder blades on the ball, with both feet positioned straight ahead.
❑ The hips are lifted until they are in line with knees; hands are placed across the chest. The hips should remain level throughout the exercise. The scapulae are slightly retracted and depressed and the abdominals are braced.

(a)

(b)

Figure 11.13. Supine hip extension: torso on ball – (a) before, (b) after

Correct performance
❑ Client begins to perform hip flexion by lowering the hips towards the ball, followed with extension, by pushing through the heel of the planted foot. The movement should be done slowly and extension must be initiated through abdominal bracing and glute contraction.
❑ The therapist should observe the hips and shoulders to ensure they are level throughout the entire movement and that proper spinal position is maintained throughout.

Progressions

❏ Eyes closed.

❏ Holding a weight on the legs.

Supine hip extension: feet on ball

Muscle group(s): Hip extensors, abdominal wall

Phase/modality: Strength, stabilisation, balance

Equipment: Stability ball

Purpose

❏ To increase the strength of the hip extensors.

❏ To improve neuromuscular control of the lateral abdominal muscles, in preparation for larger kinetic chain movements.

❏ To improve whole body balance.

Prerequisites

❏ Good level of core strength.

❏ Optimal scapula control to ensure retraction and depression.

❏ Normal hamstring length.

Starting position

Client is lying supine, with legs straight and heels resting on a stability ball, hip-width apart. Part of the ball should be resting against the calf muscles. Arms are resting on the floor beside the body.

Correct performance

❏ Client braces the abdominals and performs hip extension by lifting the hips up, until a straight line is formed from the knees to the shoulders. The movement

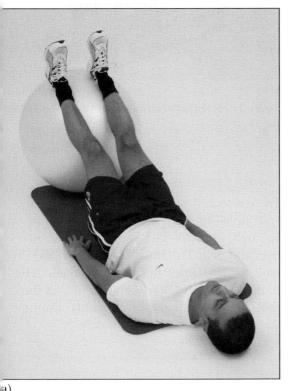
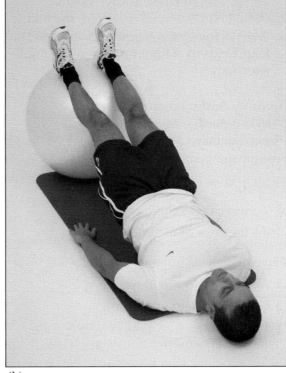

(a)   (b)

Figure 11.14. Supine hip extension: feet on ball – (a) before, (b) after

should be initiated by contracting the glutes.

❑ Return to the start position and perform a total of 8–10 repetitions.

❑ The therapist should observe the hips and spine for any faulty movements and correct if necessary. Excessive wobbling should be controlled through appropriate levels of abdominal bracing and may indicate weakness in the lateral abdominals.

Progressions

❑ Eyes closed.

❑ Feet closer together on ball.

❑ Hands across chest.

❑ Adding knee flexion – as hip extension is performed, there is simultaneous knee flexion, by 'pulling' the ball in towards the glutes using the heels. Knee flexion should end in a position where the ball is close to the glutes (approximately 100° knee flexion). This is an advanced exercise.

Stability ball abdominal curl
Muscle group(s): Abdominals
Phase/modality: Strength, balance
Equipment: Stability ball

Purpose

❑ To increase strength of abdominals.

❑ To improve whole body balance.

Prerequisites

❑ Adequate thoracic flexion.

❑ Good level of core strength.

❑ Pain-free range of motion in extension.

(a)

(b)

Figure 11.15. Stability ball abdominal curl – (a) before, (b) after

Starting position

From a seated position on the ball, client rolls down to allow the whole spine to rest on the ball, with the back comfortably arched over the ball. The head should be tilted backwards slightly, but not excessively. The hands are placed across the chest and the feet are positioned approximately shoulder-width apart. The abdominals are appropriately braced.

Correct performance

❑ Client begins curling the trunk by lifting the head and shoulders off the ball and bringing the lower ribs towards the iliac crest. This position is held for 1 second before returning to the start. The movement is repeated 8–10 times.

❑ The movement should be initiated by curling the head first (chin to chest), followed by flexing the thoracic spine to lift the shoulders. The end position is achieved when the client can no longer curl the trunk and full abdominal contraction is felt.

Clinical perspective

The abdominal curl over a stability ball has a different and distinct place in corrective exercise compared to the traditional floor curl-up, for three reasons:

❑ Being positioned over a stability ball allows the trunk to be curled through a much larger range of flexion and is therefore functional to daily activities.

❑ Performing exercise on a stability ball will challenge the neuromuscular system to a greater degree, conditioning important righting and tilting reflex pathways.

❑ A curl-up on the stability ball causes almost double the amount of co-contraction of the abdominal musculature. Correspondingly, the spine load also increases.

Use of the stability ball for the curl-up exercise can be an effective way to challenge and enhance lumbar stability. In practice, it is essential that the client establishes adequate spine stability and load-bearing capacity on a stable surface, before attempting to tolerate additional spinal compression.

Progressions

❑ The fingertips may be placed on the sides of the forehead.

❑ Brace the abdominals to a greater intensity during the movement.

Stability ball back extension
Muscle group(s): Back extensors, abdominals
Phase/modality: Strength, endurance
Equipment: Stability ball

(a)

(b)

Figure 11.16. Stability ball back extension – (a) before, (b) after

Purpose

❏ To increase the strength and endurance of the back extensors.

❏ To enhance lumbar stability in extension movements.

Prerequisites

❏ Good level of core strength.

❏ Pain-free range of motion in extension. Although the exercise does not require an end range extension position, it does produce significantly higher extensor forces, which may be contraindicated in some patients.

Starting position

Client is lying prone over a stability ball, with knees slightly bent to provide balance and stability. The hands are placed by the sides of the head (not touching) and the abdominals are braced to an appropriate level.

Correct performance

❏ Client begins by slightly flexing and then extending the spine, continuing for up to 15 repetitions.

❏ The movement should be performed slowly and deliberately, ensuring that the spine does not extend past neutral alignment.

❏ The aim of this exercise is to focus on maximum recruitment of the back extensor muscles, rather than full range of motion. The use of mental imagery may assist the client in this task.

Progressions

❏ Moving the ball further towards the pelvis.

❏ Holding a small weight in one hand will significantly increase the challenge of stabilisation, consequently recruiting more motor units.

Russian twist: feet on stability ball

Muscle group(s): Obliques
Phase/modality: Strength, stabilisation, balance, coordination
Equipment: Stability ball

Purpose

❏ To strengthen the obliques.

❏ To integrate the abdominal wall into rotational actions.

Prerequisites

❏ Good awareness of the oblique sling.

❏ Adequate hip flexor flexibility.

Starting position

Client is lying supine, with knees flexed to 90° and heels resting on the ball, approximately hip-width apart. Hands are by the sides of the body and the abdominals are lightly braced.

Correct performance

❏ Client slowly allows the ball to rotate to the left, just a few inches. From here, client activates the right external oblique and left internal oblique to draw the ball back to the centre (oblique sling) and repeats on the other side, using the opposite obliques, performing 6–8 repetitions each side.

❏ The shoulders should remain on the floor throughout the movement.

❏ If the therapist observes unstable movement, the distance rotated should be decreased to improve control. If the problem persists, the client should be instructed to practise the 'oblique sling' exercise, until good coordination and strength of the obliques is achieved.

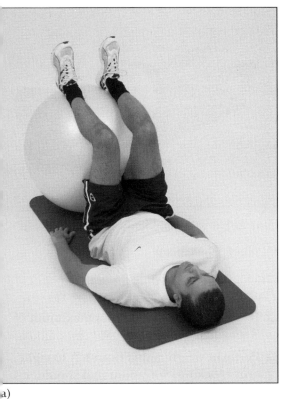 

(a)   (b)

Figure 11.17. Russian twist: feet on stability ball – (a) before, (b) after

Progressions

❑ Increase distance rotated.

❑ Faster activation of the oblique sling.

❑ Hands across chest (advanced).

Variations

Russian twist: body on ball. If the client can hold a bridge position on the stability ball for 1 minute and exhibit good technique with the basic Russian twist exercise, they can try this variation.

❑ The client assumes a bridge position, with hands clasped together, pointing towards the ceiling. The arms remain perpendicular to the trunk throughout the movement. The abdominals are braced.

❑ Maintaining a stable pelvis, the trunk is slowly rotated to each side. As strength develops, range of motion and speed can be increased.

❑ It is important to maintain proper spinal alignment. Hips should not drop while rotating.

Iso-abdominals: prone

Muscle group(s): Abdominals, glutes, shoulders

Phase/modality: Strength, static stabilisation

Equipment: None

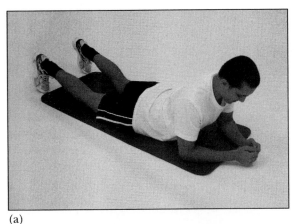

(a)   (b)

Figure 11.18. Iso-abdominals: prone – (a) before, (b) after

Purpose

❏ To increase isometric strength of the abdominals.

❏ To enhance integration of the entire abdominal wall.

Prerequisites

❏ Adequate core and glute activation.

❏ Diaphragmatic breathing while bracing.

Starting position

Client assumes a prone position, with elbows and shoulders flexed to 90°. The elbows should be positioned under the shoulders.

Correct performance

❏ Client begins by bracing the abdominals, tightening the glutes and lifting the body up onto the forearms.

❏ Client holds body position and optimal spinal alignment for 3 seconds, before returning and resting.

❏ Repeat up to 10 times, keeping neutral spine alignment from cervical through to lumbar spine.

❏ Focus on quality, NOT duration.

Progressions

❏ Increase holding time to a maximum of 8 seconds.

❏ Perform weight shifts from left to right arm (rocking) for additional shoulder stability.

❏ Raise alternate legs for additional core stabilisation.

Iso-abdominals: side-lying

Muscle group(s): Abdominals, shoulders
Phase/modality: Strength, static stabilisation
Equipment: None

Purpose

To increase the isometric strength of the obliques.

Prerequisites

❏ Client must be instructed in diaphragmatic breathing.

❏ Adequate abdominal bracing.

Starting position

Client is lying on the right side, with knees bent. Optimal postural alignment must be

a)

b)

Figure 11.19. Iso-abdominals: side-lying – (a) before, (b) after

maintained throughout movement. Client places right elbow directly under right shoulder.

Correct performance

❑ Client begins by bracing the abdominals and lifting body up onto right forearm.
❑ Client holds body position and optimal spinal alignment for 3 seconds, before returning and resting.
❑ Repeat up to 10 times, keeping neutral spine alignment from cervical through to lumbar spine. Repeat on the left side.
❑ Focus on quality, NOT duration.

Progressions

Increase holding time to a maximum of 8 seconds.

Forward ball roll

Muscle group(s): Abdominals, shoulders, arms
Phase/modality: Strength, stabilisation
Equipment: Stability ball

Purpose

❑ To integrate isometric abdominal strength into upper and lower extremity movements.
❑ To improve multi-planar lumbar stability.

Prerequisites

❑ Adequate rotator cuff strength.
❑ Instruction in diaphragmatic breathing.
❑ Good level of core strength.

Starting position

Client assumes a kneeling position in front of the ball and places clasped hands at the centre of the ball, ensuring neutral spine alignment and bracing abdominals.

Correct performance

❑ Client begins to roll forwards slowly, keeping the spine in good alignment. The forward movement comes from the simultaneous action of knee extension and shoulder flexion. The hips should remain the same distance away from the ball at all times.
❑ The therapist should observe for arching in the low back, which may indicate a lack of stability. In this instance, a tighter brace may be the solution. If the problem persists, instruct the client to perform a shorter movement.

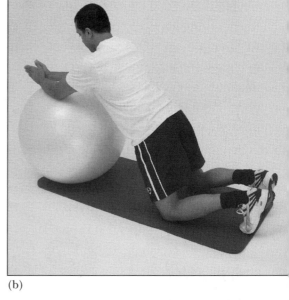

(a)   (b)

Figure 11.20. Forward ball roll – (a) before, (b) after

Progressions

Increase the distance moved.

Supine lateral ball roll

Muscle group(s): Abdominals, total body
Phase/modality: Strength, stabilisation, balance, coordination
Equipment: Stability ball

Purpose

❑ To strengthen the abdominals and low back in all three planes of motion.

❑ To improve static stabilisation of the muscles of the trunk.

Prerequisites

This is an advanced exercise and the client must possess good flexibility and strength in the lumbo-pelvic-hip complex.

Starting position

From a seated position on the ball, client rolls down into a bridge position, allowing the head and shoulders to rest on the ball. Arms are straight and out to the sides and a wooden dowel is held across the chest. The abdominals are braced.

Correct performance

❑ Client slowly rolls the whole body along the ball to the right, until the right shoulder begins to come off the ball, ensuring that the hips and shoulders are level throughout the movement. This position is held for 2–3 seconds, before rolling over to the other side and repeating. Perform 3–4 repetitions each side, before resting.

(a)   (b)

Figure 11.21. Supine lateral ball roll – (a) before, (b) after

❏ It is important that the abdominals are braced throughout the movement and that the whole body rolls as one unit.

❏ The therapist can observe the wooden dowel to ensure it remains horizontal throughout and that the spine is not twisting in any way.

Progressions

❏ Increase the holding time to up to 8 seconds.

❏ Increase the distance moved. This will place increasing stresses on the trunk musculature to stabilise the entire body.

Note: This is an advanced exercise that should be placed towards the end of the functional phase. It is designed to train a number of skills, including strength, endurance, agility, balance, coordination and flexibility – with this in mind, careful attention should be paid to technique and execution.

Squat

Muscle group(s): Abdominals, low back, legs
Phase/modality: Strength, stabilisation
Equipment: None

Purpose

❏ To improve lumbar stabilisation during functional movements.

❏ To enhance the body's ability to transfer force along the kinetic chain, during extension and flexion. Particularly useful for activities and sports where force is generated from the ground up.

Prerequisites

❏ Pain-free range of motion in shoulder flexion.

(a)   (b)

Figure 11.22. Squat – (a) before, (b) after

❑ If a lower- or upper-crossed posture is noted, a proper stretching programme must be completed before attempting this exercise, to ensure ideal lumbar alignment and stability.

❑ Good flexibility in the calf muscles.

❑ The client must exhibit good core strength and stabilisation.

Starting position

In a standing position, client places the feet shoulder-width apart, places arms across chest and assumes good postural alignment. The spine should remain in neutral alignment throughout the movement. The abdominals should be lightly braced.

Correct performance

❑ Client performs triple flexion of the hip, knee and ankle, and squats down to a position where the thighs are parallel with the floor. In this position, the knees should not overshoot the toes and should be tracking over the second toe of each foot (not bowing inwards or outwards). The spine is still in neutral alignment and the hips are pushed backwards to maintain balance over the feet.

❏ From this position, client braces the abdominals further and contracts the glutes, while performing triple extension of the ankle, knee and hip, to return to the start position. Perform 10–12 repetitions.

❏ It is important to contract the glutes at the beginning of the upward push, as this will allow the pelvis to initiate the movement, prior to the spine.

❏ The therapist should observe spinal alignment, knee position and the coordination of triple extension/flexion. There should be particular emphasis on the sequencing of abdominal and glute contraction at the start of the upward phase.

❏ If there is muscle weakness in the legs, the squat can be modified into a half- or quarter-squat, where the client only completes the range of motion available to them. Tightness in the calves may prevent full range of motion and these muscles should be stretched prior to attempting this exercise.

Progressions
❏ Slower tempo.
❏ Use of a weighted barbell. This progression involves holding a barbell across the upper back and requires adequate strength in shoulder abduction, along with good scapula control.

Dead lift
Muscle group(s): Abdominals, low back, legs
Phase/modality: Strength, stabilisation
Equipment: Dumb-bells

Purpose
❏ To improve lumbar stabilisation during functional movements.

❏ To enhance the body's ability to transfer force along the kinetic chain, during extension and flexion. Particularly useful for activities and sports where force is generated from the ground up.

Prerequisites
❏ If a lower- or upper-crossed posture is noted, a proper stretching programme must be completed before attempting this exercise, to ensure ideal lumbar alignment and stability.

❏ Good flexibility in the calf muscles.

❏ The client must exhibit good core strength and stabilisation.

Starting position
In a standing position, client places the feet shoulder-width apart, holding a pair of light dumb-bells. The spine should remain in neutral throughout the movement. Client lightly braces the abdominals.

Correct performance
❏ Client performs triple flexion of the hip, knee and ankle, and bends down to a position where the thighs are almost parallel with the floor, as if to place the dumb-bells beside the body. In this position, the knees should not overshoot the toes and should be tracking over the second toe of each foot (not bowing inwards or outwards). The spine is still in neutral alignment and the hips are pushed backwards to maintain balance over the feet.

❏ From this position, client braces the abdominals further and contracts the glutes, while performing triple extension of the ankle, knee and hip, to return to the start position. Perform 10–12 repetitions.

(a)

(b)

Figure 11.23. Dead lift – (a) before, (b) after

❑ It is important to contract the glutes at the beginning of the upward push, as this will allow the pelvis to initiate the movement, prior to the spine.

❑ The therapist should observe spinal alignment, knee position and the coordination of triple extension/flexion. There should be particular emphasis on the sequencing of abdominal and glute contraction at the start of the upward phase.

❑ If there is muscle weakness in the legs, the dead lift can be modified into a half- or

quarter-lift, where the client only completes the range of motion available to them. Tightness in the calves may prevent full range of motion and these muscles should be stretched prior to attempting this exercise.

Progressions

❑ Use of heavier dumb-bells.

❑ Use of a barbell.

Note: The dead-lift pattern is almost identical to the squat, except that the weight is lowered to the floor. This exercise (and the

Clinical perspective

The squat and dead lift are functional movement patterns and are performed by almost everyone on a daily basis. They are used in activities such as rising up from a chair and lifting heavy bags off the floor, as well as a large number of sport-specific movements. As many of these activities are repeated many times throughout the day, rehabilitation and conditioning programmes should be tailored to the individual's demands.

By focusing on strength-endurance the squat/dead-lift pattern can be used as an effective corrective exercise tool. For example, a mother who has a two-year-old child may bend down to lift her child approximately 30 times a day. Along with a number of other bending/lifting activities, this may amount to a total of about 50 movements. To increase her functional capacity to squat/dead-lift safely, with good lumbar stabilisation, a corrective exercise programme can be prescribed that includes squatting or lifting, progressively, up to 50 repetitions daily. The use of an appropriately weighted medicine ball (estimated weight of the child) may be used to improve functional strength.

For patients who regularly lift uneven loads with both hands, for example, shopping bags, the dead-lift pattern can be suitably modified using medicine balls of different weights, or an unevenly weighted barbell.

squat) is extremely functional for patients who exhibit faulty lifting and bending movement patterns and can be adapted to incorporate load bearing where necessary.

High-low wood-chop

Muscle group(s): Abdominals, total body
Phase/modality: Strength, stabilisation, balance
Equipment: Cable, exercise band

Purpose

❑ To enhance lumbar stabilisation through functional whole body movement.

❑ To re-educate the torso rotation mechanism and strengthen the oblique musculature.

Prerequisites

❑ Functional flexibility of the shoulder/arm, without compensation in the spine.

❑ Adequate strength and flexibility in the anterior and lateral abdominals and in the lumbar spine.

❑ Adequate leg strength.

Starting position

❑ Client starts in a standing position, with a shoulder-width stance, facing away from the cable machine and holding the handle with both hands above the right shoulder. In this position, the left hand should grip the handle first, with the right hand over the top of the left hand.

❑ Good spinal alignment should be maintained, with a strong abdominal brace, prior to the movement.

Correct performance

❑ Starting from optimal posture, client initiates a rotational movement from the trunk outwards, towards the left. Client should not pull with the shoulders or arms. The cable handle is pulled downwards and across the body.

❑ Use a slow tempo to start with. Avoid beginning the movement from a forward flexed position.

 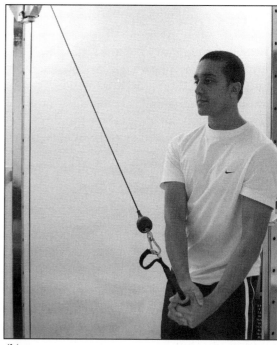

(a)   (b)

Figure 11.24. High-low wood-chop – (a) before, (b) after

❑ Do not push so quickly that the shoulders round forwards; movement should be generated from the core instead of the arms.

❑ Allow the torso and arms to move back to the start position and repeat up to 10 times.

Progressions

❑ As stability is developed, progress to lateral weight shifting (moving weight from right to left leg and vice versa), so that the movement resembles a 'wood-chopping' motion.

❑ The wood-chop may also be progressed by performing the exercise seated on a stability ball. This will increase awareness of the obliques, providing the ball is kept still throughout the movement.

❑ LOW-HIGH WOOD-CHOP – cable is adjusted so that the line of resistance starts low and moves high.

❑ LATERAL WOOD-CHOP – cable is adjusted so that the line of resistance is horizontal.

❑ This exercise can also be progressed to a functional power movement, by accelerating through the chop downwards and slowly returning to the start. Adding speed in this way requires a high level of core strength and stabilisation, combined with perfect movement technique, and is only suitable for high-performance conditioning programmes (sport-specific).

Phase 4 exercises – Restoring functional power

(all power movements require a thorough cardiovascular and neuromuscular warm-up prior to performance)

Power crunch

Muscle group(s): Abdominals
Phase/modality: Power, strength, stabilisation
Equipment: Stability ball, dumb-bell, medicine ball

Purpose

To increase strength and power of the trunk flexors.

Prerequisites

❑ Ability to perform a stability ball crunch with good form.

❑ Good abdominal strength.

Starting position

❑ As with the basic stability ball crunch, except that a medicine ball or dumb-bell is held firmly on the chest.

❑ The therapist should kneel behind the ball to stabilise, if necessary.

Correct performance

❑ The crunch is performed as normal, except that the concentric movement should be more explosive, building up the speed over 10–12 repetitions. The exercise should stop when there is a noticeable loss

(a)

(b)

Figure 11.25. Power crunch – (a) before, (b) after

of speed or when 12 repetitions have been achieved.

❏ It is essential that momentum is not used to perform this movement (that is, no bouncing on the stability ball).

❏ Focus on perfect technique rather than the number of repetitions.

Note: This is a very advanced exercise and should only be performed if deemed necessary, both from a functional and muscle balance perspective.

Russian power twist: body on ball
Muscle group(s): Obliques
Phase/modality: Power, strength, stabilisation, balance
Equipment: Stability ball, medicine ball

Purpose
To develop power in rotational movement.

Prerequisites
❏ Good level of strength in the lateral abdominal musculature.

❏ Ability to perform the Russian twist using own body weight.

Starting position
Client begins in a bridge position on the ball, holding a small medicine ball in both hands vertically above chest. Client braces abdominals and should aim to keep the spine in good alignment throughout the exercise.

(a)   (b)

Figure 11.26. Russian power twist: body on ball – (a) before, (b) after

Correct performance

The performance is the same as the body weight Russian twist, except rotation speed is increased as the repetitions increase. Perform 10–12 repetitions, or as many as possible before the speed begins to decrease.

Progressions

Increase weight.

Note: This is an advanced exercise and the therapist should watch carefully for good technique and alignment throughout the movement.

Oblique medicine ball toss

Muscle group(s): Obliques, total body
Phase/modality: Power, strength, coordination
Equipment: Medicine ball

Purpose

❑ To increase functional power and strength in the obliques.

❑ To condition task-specific acceleration and deceleration in rotational movements.

Prerequisites

❑ Good level of strength in the lateral and anterior abdominal musculature.

❑ Ability to perform the wood-chop and/or Russian twist.

Starting position

Standing upright, with knees slightly bent, in good postural alignment, client holds the medicine ball with both hands and braces the abdominals.

Correct performance

❑ With a partner standing about 6–8 feet away, to one side, client passes the ball just in front of partner. When throwing the

(a)

Figure 11.27. Oblique medicine ball toss – (a) before

ball, aim to rotate the body using a smooth integrated movement from the legs, hips, torso and shoulders/arms. When catching the ball, allow the body to decelerate by absorbing the weight through the shoulders/arms, torso, hips and legs, before accelerating again and throwing it back.

❑ Perform 10 passes before repeating on the other side.

Progressions

❑ Increase the weight of the medicine ball.

❑ Increase the throwing distance.

(b)   (c)

Figure 11.27. (contd) Oblique medicine ball toss – (b) during, (c) after

Vertical/horizontal oscillations with a Bodyblade®

Muscle group(s): Abdominals, total body
Phase/modality: Power, strength, stabilisation, balance
Equipment: Bodyblade®

Purpose

To condition the entire kinetic chain in power, strength and reactive stabilisation.

Prerequisites

❑ Good core strength and frontal plane stability.

❑ Adequate flexibility in the shoulder complex.

Starting position

In a standing position, feet shoulder-width apart, client assumes good postural alignment, with scapulae slightly adducted

(a)   (b)

Figure 11.28. (a) Vertical oscillations with a Bodyblade®; (b) Horizontal oscillations with a Bodyblade®

and depressed. Client holds the Bodyblade® with arms straight and both hands in the centre, using an interlocking grip. The flat surface of the Bodyblade® should be facing laterally. The abdominals are braced.

Correct performance

Client begins to oscillate the Bodyblade® side to side at a steady rate, using quick hand action. As a steady oscillation is achieved, the hand movement is increased to increase the amount of flexing in the blade. Increase to a maximum speed and hold this oscillation for as long the body can be stabilised.

Note: The therapist should observe the client for any position changes of the blade which may result in a redirection of forces to the body.

Variations

The Bodyblade® may be held horizontally, as shown (see Figure 11.31b). A number of other body and limb positions can be used to condition a number of upper body muscles. All variations will require significant stabilisation from the superficial and deep abdominal muscles.

Barbell clean and press
Muscle group(s): Abdominals, shoulders, total body
Phase/modality: Power, strength, stabilisation, balance
Equipment: Barbell

Purpose
- Enhances lumbar stability during power movements.
- Increases total body strength and power. It is important to remember that the strength and power developed here are completely relative to the posture of the client during the exercise, and the range of motion that the client moves through.
- Enhances the body's ability to transfer force along the kinetic chain.

Prerequisites
- The client must exhibit good lifting/squatting technique and be able to perform the upright row and shoulder press exercises.
- If a lower- or upper-crossed posture is noted, a proper stretching programme must be completed before attempting this exercise, to ensure ideal lumbar alignment and stability.
- The client must exhibit good core strength and stabilisation.
- The client must be properly progressed through stability and strength phases, in order to ensure that there is adequate flexibility, core strength and time for

adaptation, thereby reducing chance of injury.
- The therapist must have a justifiable reason and system of programme progression to implement this advanced exercise. This exercise is useful in activities where there are distinct stages of link sequencing/power transfer – for example, lifting up a child and placing them into a high chair, or during a tennis serve.

Starting position
- Client begins with feet shoulder-width apart and toes pointing forwards.
- Client bends the knees slightly and bends at the waist, grasping the barbell with both hands slightly wider than shoulder-width apart (palms facing body).
- Abdominals are braced.

Correct performance
- Client performs an explosive triple extension movement in the lower extremities – ankle, knee and hip extension – and drives the elbows high. The barbell must travel in a vertical, linear fashion (close to body).
- As bar reaches shoulder height, client externally rotates the arms and 'catches' the weight in front of the shoulders, simultaneously dropping into a half-squat position, to get under the weight. From here, the glutes are contracted to stand into a full upright position, with bar resting on the chest.
- Bracing the abdominals, client sinks into a half-squat position to pre-stretch the glutes and quickly follows this with another explosive movement, pushing the barbell up into a shoulder press. This movement

(a)

(b)

(c)

Figure 11.29. Barbell clean and press – (a) before, (b) during, (c) after

should start from a glute contraction, as if pushing the floor away, and at the same time pushing the bar upwards. Stand tall at the top with good posture and a strong abdominal brace.

❑ The barbell is carefully lowered to the ground. Reset posture and perform 6–8 repetitions.

Progressions

❑ Increase the weight gradually, while maintaining good technique.

❑ This advanced exercise should be performed in 'chunks' before attempting the whole sequence. The client should be competent in performing a dead lift, upright row and shoulder press; these movements can then be combined successively. For example, once the dead lift can be performed, the client can attempt a dead lift with the upright row (also known as the 'clean'); once this double sequence is perfected, the final pressing movement can be added, to complete the entire motion.

4 The Pelvis, Hip and Knee

The pelvis or the 'pelvic girdle' is made up of the two hip bones, the sacrum and the coccyx, and forms the essential functional link between the trunk and the lower extremity. Movement of the pelvic girdle is largely dependent on movement of the spine. In contrast to the shoulder girdle, the pelvic girdle offers more strength than movement and is assisted by some of the most powerful muscles of the body.

The sockets of the pelvic girdle (acetabula) articulate with the femur to form the hip joint, producing movement of the lower extremity. The larger depth of the hip joint socket limits large ranges of movement, allowing for weight bearing instead: therefore, flexibility in the hip joint is sacrificed for stability.

The distal end of the femur articulates with the tibia at the knee joint, the largest joint in the human body. The knee joint functions in both weight bearing and locomotion and is subject to enormous stresses in all planes of motion; to meet these demands it has a complex yet strong ligamentous system, combined with a functional muscular system.

Understanding the mechanics of the pelvis, hip and knee is of particular importance in corrective exercise, as almost all movements involving the lower extremity involve the integrated action of the pelvis, hip joints and knee joints. While these joints work together to produce movement, they must also contribute to stability of the entire kinetic chain. With this in mind, corrective exercise should be tailored towards function, rather than isolation of individual muscles.

Mechanical dysfunction of the pelvis, hip and knee commonly presents as combinations of muscle imbalance and movement impairment, all of which can develop into chronic degenerative conditions and predictable pain patterns. These can be helped with corrective exercise.

This section aims to review the functional anatomy of the pelvic girdle and knee joint and discusses a number of evaluation strategies. The final chapter outlines corrective exercise to facilitate and enhance muscular control of hip and thigh movement.

12
FUNCTIONAL PELVIS, HIP AND KNEE ANATOMY

Overview of pelvis, hip and knee anatomy

The pelvis, hip and knee (and ankle) form the basic structures involved in lower extremity mobility and stability. The considerable range of motion of the thigh and leg is achieved through the dynamic relationship between the pelvic girdle and

hip joint and the knee joint. Structurally, movement is brought about by articulation of the pelvis and femur at the hip joint, and articulation of the femur and tibia at the knee joint. Functionally, movement is achieved via a multitude of one- and two-joint muscles that mobilise and stabilise these joints. The skeletal anatomy of the pelvis, hip and knee is shown in figure 12.1.

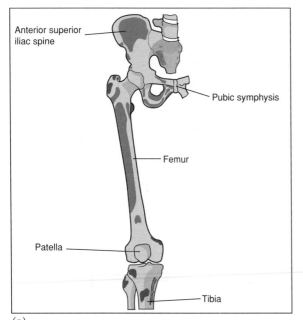

Anterior superior iliac spine

Pubic symphysis

Femur

Patella

Tibia

(a)

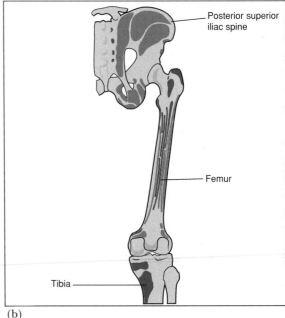

Posterior superior iliac spine

Femur

Tibia

(b)

Figure 12.1. Skeletal anatomy of the pelvis, hip and knee – (a) anterior, (b) posterior views

Structure and function of the pelvis, hip and knee

The pelvic girdle consists of two hip bones (innominate bones) and provides a strong and stable support for the lower extremities. Each hip bone is composed of three separate bones at birth: the ilium, pubis and ischium. These bones eventually fuse at a depression called the acetabulum, which forms the socket for the hip joint.

The hip joint is formed by the articulation of the head of the femur with the acetabulum. The deep, cup-shaped acetabulum is reinforced with strong ligamentous and cartilaginous support, designed to protect it against the impact of the femoral head during forceful movement, as well as preventing excessive hip joint movement.

The femur, or thigh bone, is the largest, heaviest and strongest bone of the body. It articulates proximally with the hip and distally with the tibia, forming the knee joint. The patella, or kneecap, is located anterior to the knee joint. It is held in place by the quadriceps tendon above and the patellar ligament below. It functions to increase the leverage of the quadriceps tendon, to maintain the position of the tendon when

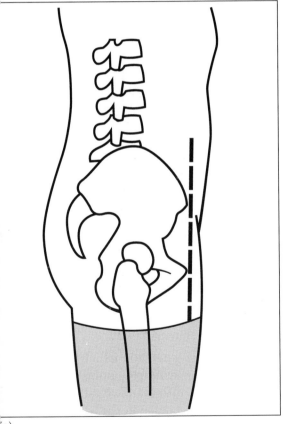

(a)

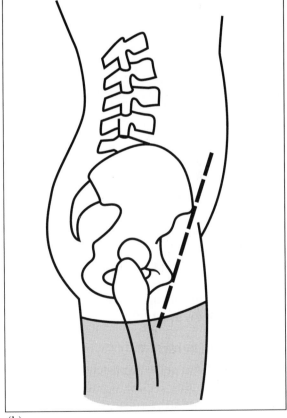

(b)

Figure 12.2. Movements of the pelvis – (a) neutral, (b) anterior tilt, (c) posterior tilt, (d) lateral tilt

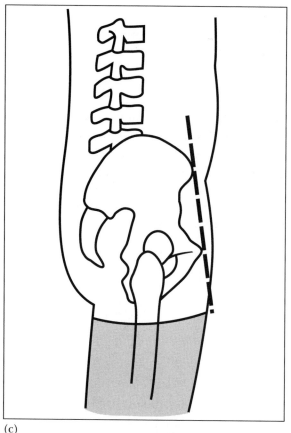

(c)

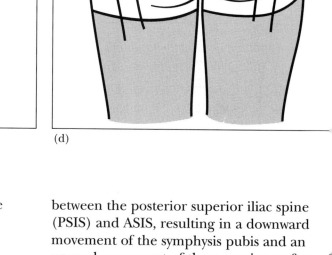

(d)

Figure 12.2. (contd) Movements of the pelvis

the knee is bent and to protect the knee joint.

Movements of the pelvis

Movement of the pelvis is a product of lumbar spine and hip joint motion, allowing the pelvis to tilt forwards, backwards and sideways (see Figure 12.2).

Anterior tilt (forward tilt)

A position of the pelvis in which the anterior superior iliac spine (ASIS) is anterior to the symphysis pubis in the vertical plane. Anterior tilt may also be observed as an increase in the angle from the horizontal

between the posterior superior iliac spine (PSIS) and ASIS, resulting in a downward movement of the symphysis pubis and an upward movement of the posterior surface of the sacrum.

In standing posture, anterior tilting is associated with increased lumbar lordosis and hip flexion.

Posterior tilt (backward tilt)

A position of the pelvis in which the ASIS is posterior to the symphysis pubis in the vertical plane. Anterior tilt may also be observed as a decrease in the angle from the horizontal between the PSIS and ASIS, resulting in an upward movement of the

ymphysis pubis and a downward movement
of the posterior surface of the sacrum.

   In standing posture, posterior tilting is
associated with a flattening of the lumbar
curve and hip extension.

Lateral tilt

A position of the pelvis where one ASIS is
higher than the other. In standing posture, a
lateral tilt is associated with lumbar lateral
flexion and adduction of the hip joint on the
side of the high ASIS; the opposite hip joint
will be in abduction.

Rotation

A rotation of the pelvis in the horizontal
plane around a longitudinal axis.

Movements of the hip joint

Movements at the hip joint are generally
described as movements of the femur (when
the pelvis is fixed) or movements of the
pelvis (when the femur is fixed). This
includes flexion and extension; abduction
and adduction; lateral and medial rotation;
and circumduction (see Figure 12.3).

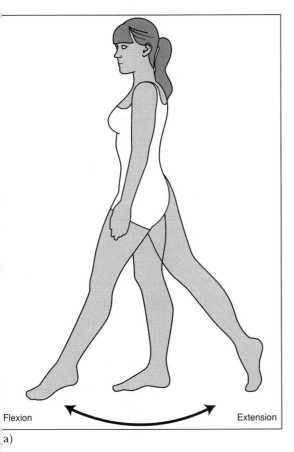

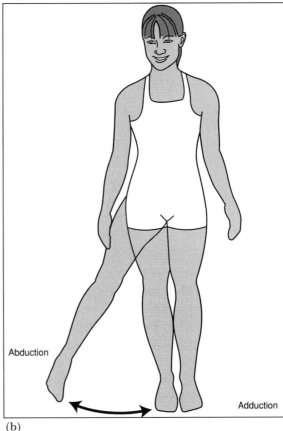

Flexion   Extension

(a)

Abduction

Adduction

(b)

Figure 12.3. Movements of the hip joint – (a) flexion and extension, (b) adduction and abduction, (c) medial and
lateral rotation

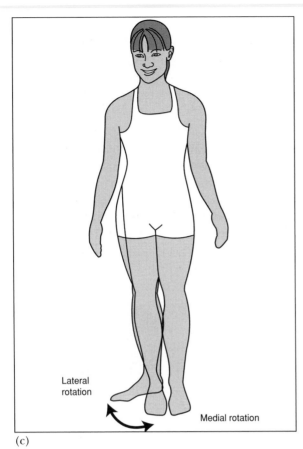

Lateral rotation

Medial rotation

(c)

Figure 12.3. (contd) Movements of the hip joint

movement of the pelvis and trunk in a posterior direction when the legs are fixed.

The range of hip joint extension is 0–10° and may be restricted by the rectus femoris. The rectus femoris is therefore placed in a shortened position when testing range of motion in extension.

Hyperextension involving excessive posterior movement of the femur is only possible when the femur is laterally rotated. This movement may be restricted in some people.

Abduction

A lateral movement of the femur away from the mid-sagittal plane when the pelvis and trunk are fixed; or movement of the trunk so that the pelvis moves laterally downwards towards a fixed thigh.

The range of motion in abduction is approximately 45°, with greater range of motion being possible when coupled with lateral rotation of the femur. Abduction is limited by the adductor muscles.

Adduction

A medial movement of the femur towards the mid-sagittal plane when the pelvis and trunk are fixed; or movement of the trunk so that the pelvis moves laterally upwards, away from the fixed thigh.

The range of motion in adduction is approximately 10° and can be limited by the abductor muscles.

Lateral rotation

A movement in which the anterior surface of the thigh moves away from the mid-sagittal plane, resulting in an outwardly turned knee. Rotation may also occur from counter-rotation of the pelvis on the femur. Lateral rotation is usually restricted to approximately 45°.

Flexion

A movement of the femur in an anterior direction when the pelvis is fixed; or bringing the pelvis towards the fixed thighs, such as bending from a standing position.

The range of hip joint flexion is 0–125° and may be restricted by the tension of the hamstring muscles. The hamstrings are therefore placed in a shortened position when testing range of motion in flexion.

Extension

A movement of the femur in a posterior direction when the pelvis is fixed; or

Medial rotation

A movement in which the anterior surface of the thigh moves towards the mid-sagittal plane, resulting in an inwardly turned knee. Rotation may also occur from counter-rotation of the pelvis on the femur. Medial rotation is usually restricted to approximately 45°.

Circumduction

A combination of flexion, abduction, extension and adduction, performed in sequence.

Movements of the knee joint

The primary movements that occur at the knee joint are flexion and extension, with a limited degree of rotation (see Figure 12.4).

Flexion

A movement of the tibia in a posterior direction in the sagittal plane, resulting in approximation of the posterior surfaces of the calf and thigh. The range of flexion is approximately 0–140°. During early flexion, the tibia also rotates medially on the femur (non-weight bearing). Stability of the knee joint in flexion is provided by the anterior cruciate ligament, as well as femoral anterior glide.

Extension

A movement of the tibia in an anterior direction in the sagittal plane, to a position of straight alignment (0°). The final phase of extension is accompanied by a slight outward rotation of the tibia (non-weight bearing). Stability of the knee joint in extension is provided by the posterior cruciate ligament, as well as femoral posterior glide.

Hyperextension is an abnormal movement beyond the zero position of extension; however, in many occupational and recreational postures, there may be a few degrees of 'normal' extension beyond zero.

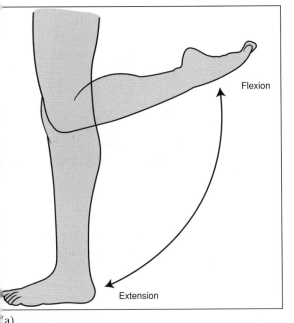

(a)

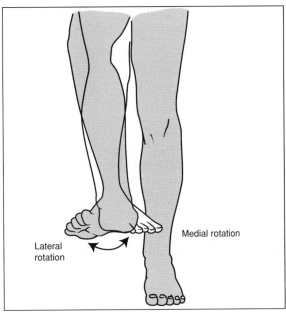

(b)

Figure 12.4. Movements of the knee joint – (a) flexion and extension, (b) medial and lateral rotation

Rotation

Medial rotation is rotation of the anterior surface of the tibia towards the mid-sagittal plane. Movement away from the mid-sagittal plane is lateral rotation.

This slight amount of rotation can only take place when the knee is flexed in non-weight bearing. In this position, the ligamentous support becomes slack. When the knee is extended (zero position), for example, in weight bearing, the joint becomes 'locked', preventing rotation.

Muscles of the pelvis

Muscles involved in movement of the pelvis are shown in Figure 12.5. As pelvic movement is dependent on lumbar spine movement (as well as hip joint movement), a number of important trunk muscles have a significant action on the pelvis, particularly when the lower extremity is fixed. Their role in pelvic movement is described below.

External oblique

A large, flat muscle, with obliquely oriented fibres, that tilts the pelvis posteriorly when acting bilaterally. Unilaterally, the lateral fibres act to move the iliac crest in a superior direction (upwards). The external oblique also combines with the contralateral internal oblique to form a force couple for rotation of the trunk or pelvis.

Adequate performance of this important postural muscle is significant in controlling rotation and for lumbar support, and specific training is often necessary. Weakness of the external oblique is more common in females and can be associated with an increase in the infrasternal angle, causing the ribs to flare outwards.

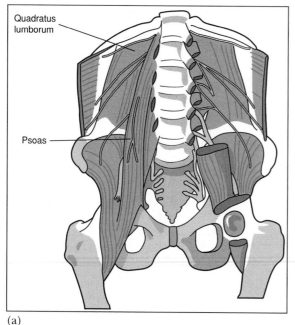

(a)

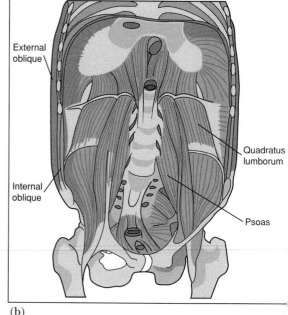

(b)

Figure 12.5. Muscles of the pelvis – (a) anterior, (b) posterior

Internal oblique

A fan-shaped muscle with obliquely oriented fibres that tilts the pelvis posteriorly and flexes the thorax, when acting bilaterally. Unilaterally, the internal oblique tilts the same side of the pelvis, moving it in a superior direction (upwards).

Rectus abdominis

A large, beaded muscle that flexes the thorax and tilts the pelvis posteriorly. This muscle is often more dominant than the internal and external oblique, affecting the control of pelvic and trunk rotation.

Iliopsoas

A long muscle that flexes the hip or tilts the pelvis anteriorly when the legs are fixed.

Erector spinae (lumbar)

A long muscle that is divided into three groups, which, when acting bilaterally, cause anterior pelvic tilt. Unilateral action causes lateral pelvic tilt.

Quadratus lumborum

A muscle with obliquely oriented fibres, which laterally tilts the pelvis when acting unilaterally, with the trunk fixed. If the pelvis is fixed, it acts to flex the trunk laterally.

Muscles of the hip joint

The following muscles (see Figure 12.6) all have an action at the hip joint, contributing to movement or stabilisation of the thigh. Although these muscles have attachments on the pelvis, their main action on the pelvis is regarded as one of stability, rather than mobility.

Iliopsoas

As a muscle affecting the hip joint as well as the pelvis, the iliopsoas flexes the hip and weakly rotates it laterally. It may also serve as a stabiliser for the hip joint in a standing position.

Tensor fasciae latae (TFL) and iliotibial band (ITB)

The TFL flexes, medially rotates and abducts the hip, as well as tensing the ITB. Acting together as a unit, the TFL-ITB and gluteus maximus act to stabilise the pelvis and knee in weight bearing.

TFL shortness is commonly mistaken for iliopsoas shortness, and in the non-weight-bearing leg can contribute to lateral tibial torsion. When the TFL is short, the iliopsoas and posterior gluteus medius are often weak. In this instance, if the lower extremity is fixed, TFL shortness can result in rotation of the pelvis and lumbar spine.

Gluteus maximus

The largest and most superficial of the three buttock muscles, the gluteus maximus extends and laterally rotates the hip. The upper fibres contribute to hip abduction and the lower fibres contribute to hip adduction. Over 75 per cent of the fibres insert into the ITB. Shortness of the muscle may contribute to lumbar flexion during sitting postures.

Weakness of the gluteus maximus (along with the other posterior hip muscles) may compromise control of the femur at the hip joint, particularly during the stance phase of walking, and is a common observation in sway-back postures.

As well as extending the hip when the trunk is fixed, the gluteus maximus is also very active during triple extension of the ankle, knee and hip, such as during heavy lifting. In this instance, the gluteus maximus is most active during the mid to end range of the movement.

Gluteus medius

The second largest of the three buttock muscles, the gluteus medius is divided into anterior and posterior portions, according to function. The posterior gluteus medius (PGM) acts to extend, abduct and laterally rotate the hip, and is prone to weakness and lengthening. The weakened muscle is usually associated with pain in the muscle belly, with the source of pain being faulty alignment of the femoral head in the acetabulum. The pain can occur during contraction or palpation and with hip joint movement.

The anterior fibres of the gluteus medius abduct, medially rotate and weakly flex the hip, and this portion of the muscle is usually strong.

The gluteus medius is an important stabiliser of the hip in standing posture and gait. When weight is shifted to one leg, the gluteus medius (and other abductors) contracts to stabilise the hip and prevent a drop of the pelvis on the other side (Trendelenburg's sign).

Gluteus minimus

The smallest of the three buttock muscles, the gluteus minimus abducts, medially rotates and weakly flexes the hip. This muscle works in conjunction with the gluteus medius: whereas the medius is primarily an abductor, then a medial rotator, the minimus is primarily a medial rotator, then an abductor.

Piriformis

A small muscle that is one of a group of six deep lateral rotators of the hip. The piriformis laterally rotates, extends and abducts the hip when the hip is flexed. Shortness of this muscle can contribute to sciatic pain. The piriformis and other lateral rotators are secondary to the gluteus maximus in their mechanical advantage in lateral rotation; therefore, in the presence of a weak gluteus maximus, the piriformis may become short and facilitated, thereby contributing to piriformis syndrome.

Pectineus

A short, thick muscle that adducts, medially rotates and weakly flexes the hip.

Adductors (brevis, longus and magnus)

The adductor brevis and longus both adduct and flex the hip and are also active during medial rotation. The adductor magnus also adducts the hip, with the anterior fibres flexing the hip and the posterior fibres extending the hip. This muscle is also active during medial and lateral rotation.

Muscles of the hip and knee joint

The muscles of the hip joint include several muscles that act equally or more effectively a the knee joint (see Figure 12.6). These are known as two-joint muscles.

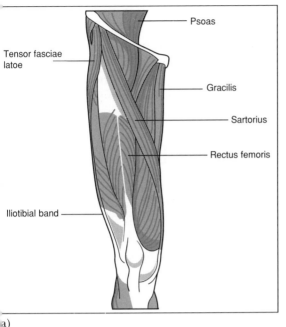

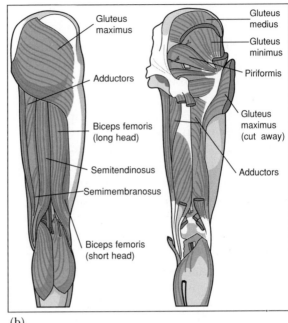

(a)   (b)

Figure 12.6. Muscles of the hip and knee joint – (a) anterior, (b) posterior

Rectus femoris

As part of the quadriceps femoris group, the rectus femoris is a two-joint muscle that flexes the hip and extends the knee. This muscle is also active during abduction and lateral rotation.

Sartorius

A long, slim, two-joint muscle that crosses the thigh obliquely in a lateral to medial direction. It flexes, laterally rotates and abducts the hip; and in a non-weight-bearing position, it acts to flex and rotate the knee medially.

Gracilis

A long, thin muscle that adducts the hip and flexes the knee. When the knee is flexed in non-weight bearing, this muscle also assists in medial rotation of the tibia.

Hamstrings

The hamstring group consists of three muscles: biceps femoris, semimembranosus and semitendinosus.

The biceps femoris (also known as the lateral hamstrings) extends and laterally rotates the hip, and also flexes and laterally rotates the knee in non-weight bearing. The semimembranosus and semitendinosus muscles (also known as the medial hamstrings) extend and medially rotate the hip, as well as flexing and rotating the knee medially.

Imbalances between the medial versus the lateral hamstrings may result in faulty recruitment patterns of the lower extremity.

Clinical perspective

The multiple functions of the hamstrings at the hip and lower extremity often predispose these muscles to strain, which may be due to overuse when synergistic muscles are underused. For example, hamstring strain is often seen in runners who exhibit sway-back posture. The posterior pelvic tilt and associated hip extension seen in this posture, alongside atrophy and weakness of the gluteus maximus, may result in strain.

Dominant hamstring muscles may also substitute for quadriceps function, by producing knee extension (as a result of hip extension) when the foot is fixed on the floor.

This is commonly seen in cyclists, who have medially rotated hips as the medial hamstrings are used more than the lateral hamstrings when cycling.

If the lateral hamstrings become dominant, they may reduce the activity of the deep hip lateral rotators.

Muscles of the knee

The true knee joint muscles are the vastus intermedius, vastus lateralis, vastus medialis and popliteus (see Figure 12.7). Although the tibialis anterior, peroneus longus and soleus do not contribute to knee joint action, they are listed here for their contribution to lower extremity movement patterns.

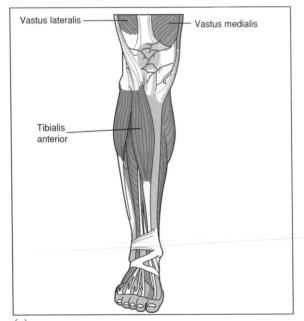

(a)

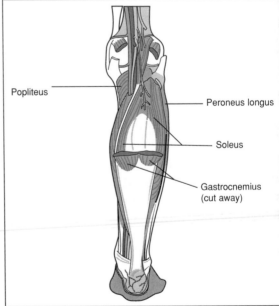

(b)

Figure 12.7. Muscles of the knee joint – (a) anterior, (b) posterior

Vastus intermedius, lateralis and medialis

As part of the quadriceps femoris group, the vasti muscles arise from a common origin on the greater trochanter and attach to the tibia. Because they are one-joint muscles, they are powerful extensors of the knee, regardless of hip joint position. Their greatest activity is during the last phase of knee extension. The vastus medialis is an important stabiliser of the knee in weight bearing through its role in medial glide of the patella, thus preventing lateral dislocation.

Popliteus

A small muscle, located behind the knee joint, which flexes the knee and medially rotates the tibia. Its primary function is to stabilise and protect the knee joint from anterior dislocation of the femur.

Gastrocnemius and soleus

The gastrocnemius muscle is a two-joint muscle that flexes the knee and plantar-flexes the ankle. The soleus is a one-joint muscle that plantar-flexes the foot at the ankle joint.

Tibialis anterior

A long muscle than runs the entire length of the tibia and dorsiflexes the ankle and inverts the foot. This muscle is antagonistic to the peroneus longus.

Clinical perspective

When the gastrocnemius-soleus complex is weak, the client is unable to plantar-flex the ankle fully against resistance. In order to complete plantar flexion, the client may substitute by using the other plantar flexors, such as the peroneus longus or tibialis posterior. In turn, these may become short. Correction of this compensation can be made by encouraging the client to 'lift the heels' when plantar-flexing, rather than 'going up onto the toes'.

Clinical perspective

The tibialis anterior may be particularly prone to overuse in running patterns where the individual has a posterior-displaced centre of gravity. In this instance, there is prolonged dorsiflexion, with minimal plantar flexion, resulting in overuse of the tibialis and potential anterior shin splints.

Peroneus longus

A long muscle that is situated on the lateral aspect of the leg, which plantar-flexes the ankle and everts the foot. Shortness of the muscle is present in clients with pronated feet.

Table 12.1.   Summary of muscles involved in pelvis, hip and knee movements

Movement	Prime mover	Synergist
	Pelvis	
Anterior tilt	Iliopsoas	Tensor fasciae latae
	Erector spinae	Sartorius
	Rectus femoris	Pectineus
Posterior tilt	Rectus abdominis	External oblique
	Internal oblique	Hamstrings
Lateral tilt	Erector spinae	Iliopsoas
	Quadratus lumborum	Gracilis
	adductors	Pectineus
Rotation	External oblique	Erector spinae
	Internal oblique	Rectus abdominis
	Gluteals	
	Lateral rotators	
	Hip	
Flexion	Iliopsoas	Sartorius
	Rectus femoris	Adductors (longus, brevis)
	Tensor fasciae latae	Pectineus
		Anterior gluteus medius
		Gluteus minimus
Extension	Gluteus maximus	Adductor magnus (superior fibres)
	Posterior gluteus medius	Piriformis
	Semimembranosus	
	Semitendinosus	
	Biceps femoris (long head)	
Abduction	Gluteus medius	Tensor fasciae latae
	Gluteus minimus	Sartorius
		Piriformis
Adduction	Adductors	Pectineus
		Gracilis
		Gluteus maximus (lower fibres)
Medial rotation	Anterior gluteus medius	Pectineus
	Gluteus minimus	Adductors (brevis, longus)
	Tensor fasciae latae	
	Semimembranosus	
	Semitendinosus	

Table 12.1.   Summary of muscles involved in pelvis, hip and knee movements (continued)

Movement	Prime mover	Synergist
	Hip	
Lateral rotation	Gluteus maximus Lateral rotators Biceps femoris	Iliopsoas Piriformis Sartorius Posterior gluteus medius
	Knee	
Flexion	Hamstrings	Gracilis Sartorius Popliteus Gastrocnemius
Extension	Quadriceps femoris	Tensor fasciae latae
Medial rotation	Popliteus Semimembranosus Semitendinosus	Sartorius Gracilis
Lateral rotation	Biceps femoris	Tensor fasciae latae

13
EVALUATION OF THE PELVIS, HIP AND KNEE

Evaluation of the pelvis, hip and knee will enable the therapist to identify movement impairment and muscle dysfunction, and put together a systematic approach to corrective exercise. Knowledge of the biomechanics of the lower extremity will allow the therapist to individualise the client's rehabilitation and help to prevent injury or impairment.

This chapter outlines assessment of the lower extremity in relation to alignment of the pelvis, hip and knee, as well as muscle length and strength. Combining the results of these assessments will help to build a progressive corrective exercise programme.

Alignment analysis

Evaluation of static alignment of the pelvis, hip joint and knee as part of lower extremity postural assessment should examine the client anteriorly, posteriorly and laterally (plumb line). The plumb line can offer an accurate visual line of reference to assess deviations from the ideal alignment in the sagittal plane (see Figure 13.1), and anterior or posterior horizontal lines of reference can provide insight into pelvic asymmetry in the frontal plane.

Basic alignment of the pelvis, hip joint and knee joint is outlined below.

Normal alignment of the pelvis

Ideal, or 'neutral', alignment of the pelvis is present when the anterior superior iliac spine (ASIS) is in the same vertical plane as the symphysis pubis, producing a pelvic tilt of up to 10° between the ASIS and posterior superior iliac spine (PSIS).

In practice, structural variations in pelvic

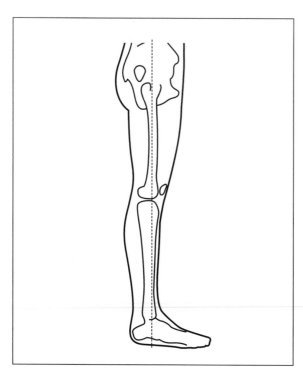

Figure 13.1. Ideal plumb alignment of the pelvis, hip and knee

ilt exist, especially between males and females, and the therapist should not expect any one angle to be an indication of normal alignment.

When a pelvic tilt is present, there may also be changes in the alignment of the spine, hip joint and knee. If correction of a tilt causes unwanted changes in alignment of the spine, hip joint and knee, the impairment is probably structural.

Misalignment may also occur around the vertical axis, resulting in pelvic rotation or torsion, and may be determined by observing deviations from the frontal plane between the left and right ASIS.

Normal alignment of the hip joint

Ideal alignment of the hip joint is present when the side-view line of reference passes slightly posterior to the centre of the hip joint (see Figure 13.2). Deviations either side

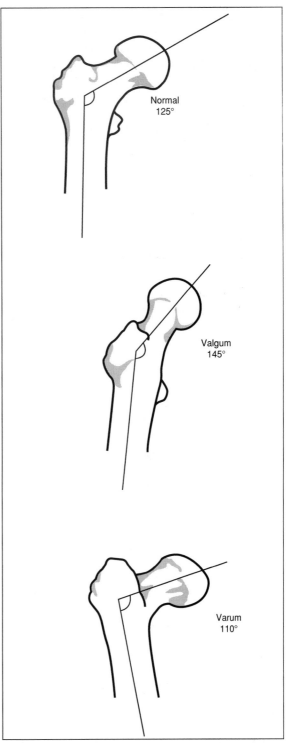

Figure 13.3. Angle of inclination of the femoral neck

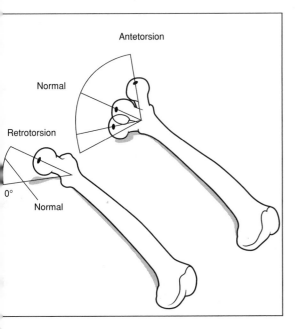

Figure 13.2. Angle of declination of the femoral neck

of this reference may indicate hip flexion or extension, both of which may have implications on the pelvis and knee joint.

Structural variations of the hip joint should be assessed carefully to ensure that corrective exercise prescription is applicable to the client's available range of motion. The two main structural variations that are commonly seen are deviations from the normal angle of declination and inclination.

The angle of declination, also known as the angle of torsion, is the angle between the neck of the femur and the transverse axis of the femoral condyle. The normal angle is approximately 15° anterior.

The angle of inclination is the angle formed between the neck of the femur and the longitudinal axis of the femoral shaft. The normal angle is approximately 125°.

Normal alignment of the knee joint

In the sagittal plane, ideal alignment of the knee joint is present when the side-view line of reference passes slightly anterior to the axis of the knee joint (see Figure 13.1). In this position, the femur lies in the same plane as the tibia. Structural variations of knee flexion and hyperextension can occur, with the latter being more common.

In the frontal plane, ideal alignment of the knee joint is present when the knee is located vertically over the second toe. Structural and acquired variations from the ideal alignment can result in knock knees (genu valgum) or bow legs (genu varum).

Common alignment problems

Many muscles of the pelvis and hip joint are also common to the knee joint; therefore

postural alignment problems frequently involve all three structures. Common problems to look for when assessing static alignment of the pelvis, hip and knee include the following.

Hip extension

Hip joint extension is an alignment fault in clients with posterior pelvic tilt and hyperextended knees. It is common in sway-back postures and particularly in activities such as distance running and contemporary dance. The result of prolonged hip hyperextension (greater than 10°) is weakening of the anterior joint capsule and

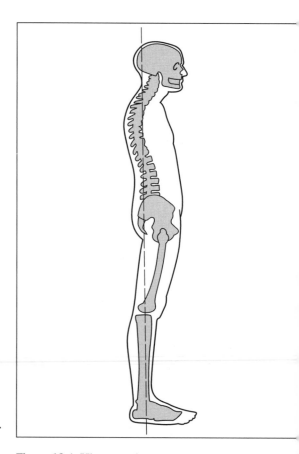

Figure 13.4. Hip extension

iliopsoas, as well as the development of femoral anterior glide syndrome.

Hip flexion

Hip flexion is a common postural fault in clients with increased lumbar lordosis and excessive anterior pelvic tilt. The presence of hip flexion in standing can be the result of weakness in the rectus abdominis or external oblique and glutes, as well as shortness in the hip flexors.

Hip joint lateral asymmetry (apparent leg length discrepancy)

In this common postural fault, one iliac crest is higher than the other (more than half an inch), resulting in a lateral pelvic tilt and lateral lumbar flexion (and rotation). The hip on the side of the high iliac crest is in adduction and the other hip is in abduction. This alignment is often associated with low back, hip and, sometimes, ankle pain.

Weak muscles include the hip abductors, and when the adducted hip is placed into slight abduction, the iliac crests often become level.

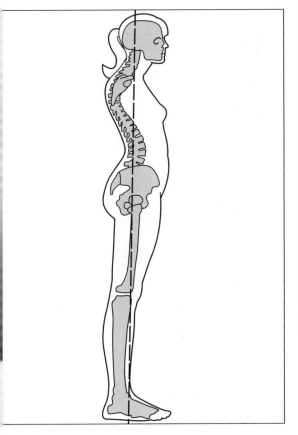

Figure 13.5. Hip flexion

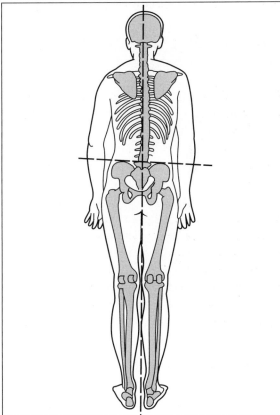

Figure 13.6. Hip joint lateral asymmetry

Hip antetorsion

In this structural misalignment, the angle of the head and neck of the femur is rotated anteriorly beyond the normal alignment of 15°. Excessive hip medial rotation and genu valgum (knock knees) may also appear to be present in the client with antetorsion. If the client sits with the hip in maximum medial or lateral rotation, hip pain can develop. With correct alignment of the femurs in the hip joints, the feet appear pigeon-toed. However, many clients will habitually position the feet forwards in standing and walking, thus rotating the hip laterally and causing the head of the femur to point anteriorly. This may result in pain.

Hip retrotorsion

In this structural condition the angle of the head and neck of the femur is rotated posteriorly with respect to the femoral shaft. The range of medial rotation is limited and lateral rotation is excessive. If a client with retrotorsion crosses their legs in prolonged sitting, the excessive medial rotation can result in hip pain, due to irritation of the anterior capsule. There will also be an accompanied stretch-weakening of the hip abductors and lateral rotators. With correct alignment of the femurs in the hip joints, the feet appear turned out.

Figure 13.7. Hip antetorsion

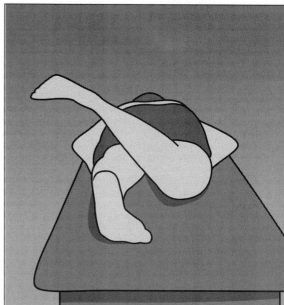

Figure 13.8. Hip retrotorsion

Clinical perspective

Structural variations of the femur resulting in hip torsion are common. Knowledge of these variations is necessary for accurate prescription of corrective exercise as variation can contribute to back, hip and knee pain.

In exercise and sport, the presence of hip antetorsion and retrotorsion can cause a number of compensatory movement patterns. In activities where hip lateral rotation is required, such as ballet, the presence of antetorsion can often result in compensatory lateral tibial rotation, which may cause knee pain.

In activities and sports that require rotation while the feet are fixed, such as tennis and golf, the presence of retrotorsion may cause compensatory lumbar rotation and facet joint compression, as the hip reaches the limit of medial rotation. In this instance, the individual should be instructed to place the feet in an appropriate lateral position to allow for optimal hip medial range of motion.

Knee hyperextension

Knee hyperextension is a common structural or acquired fault and is present when the femur is positioned anterior to the tibia. In this position, the posterior joint capsule is stretched with slackness in the anterior cruciate ligament. Knee hyperextension may also be associated with bowing of the tibia in the sagittal plane, although bowing can often occur independently. The condition is normally accompanied by hip extension and a sway-back posture.

Genu valgum (knock knees) and genu varum (bow legs)

Genu valgum is an acquired or structural variation in the angle of the femur, resulting in knock knees (see Figure 13.9). In the structural condition, the feet are likely to be neutral or supinated, indicating the presence of antetorsion. Acquired misalignment is usually caused by hip medial rotation, with the feet pronated. In this instance, the hip lateral rotators may be weak.

Genu varum is an acquired or structural variation in the angle of the tibia or femur, resulting in bow legs (see Figure 13.9). The client with genu varum will often walk with an abnormal gait. Excessive genu varum can be an indicator of degenerative knee joint disease. Hip medial rotation with knee hyperextension can give rise to acquired genu varum. In this instance, the feet are often laterally rotated and pronated. Correction of the hip rotation often eliminates genu varum and foot pronation.

Tibial torsion

Tibial torsion is a rotation of the shaft of the tibia, often in a lateral direction, and is almost always associated with shortness of the iliotibial band.

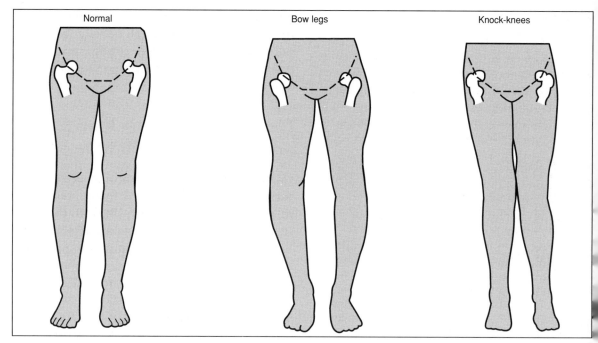

| Normal | Bow legs | Knock-knees |

Figure 13.9. Bow legs and knock knees

Movement analysis

There are a number of tests that are useful when evaluating movement of the pelvis, hip and knee. The results of these tests are not necessarily intended for end range of motion assessment, but rather to observe important functional movements that highlight muscle recruitment patterns and imbalance. Using movement for diagnosis of muscle dysfunction places emphasis on correcting the pattern of muscular recruitment and not only on palliative treatment of the painful muscle. As structural variations are common within the hip and knee, these should be taken into account when interpreting movement capability and prescribing exercise.

Active range of motion tests

The following tests outline some of the important movements that can be used to gain a basic understanding of the client's range of motion.

Hip abduction

From a standing position, ask the client to spread legs as wide as possible. Good range of motion is indicated by an ability to abduct each leg to at least 45° from the midline.

Hip adduction

From a standing position, ask the client to bring their legs together and alternately cross one in the front of the other. Good range of motion is indicated by an ability to achieve at least 10° of adduction.

Hip flexion

From a standing or supine position, ask the client to bring each knee towards the chest, without flattening the low back or using assistance. Good range of motion in flexion is indicated by an ability to flex the hip to approximately 120°.

Hip extension

From a seated position on a chair, ask the client to fold their arms across their chest and stand up. Good functional extensor strength and ability to return from flexion is indicated by an ability to stand up while keeping the back straight, without the need for assistance from the arms.

Hip flexion and adduction

From a seated position on a chair, ask the client to cross one thigh over the other. Good functional range of motion in hip flexion and adduction is indicated by an ability to cross thighs comfortably.

Hip flexion, abduction and external rotation

From a seated position on a chair, ask the client to place the outside of one foot on the opposite knee. Good functional range of motion in the combined movement of flexion, abduction and external rotation is indicated by an ability to perform the movement comfortably.

Hip medial/lateral rotation

From a prone lying position, with one knee in 90° flexion, ask the client to drop the knee outwards. Good range of motion in medial rotation is indicated by an ability to rotate the hip to approximately 30° from the vertical. If the knee is dropped inwards, good range of motion in lateral rotation is indicated by an ability to rotate the hip to at least 40° from the vertical.

The results of the active range of motion for medial and lateral rotation can be used as preliminary measurements for the presence of hip antetorsion: if medial rotation seems excessive (greater than 50°) and lateral rotation is limited (less than 15° from vertical), antetorsion is suggested. The Craig test can be used to gain further information regarding the degree of antetorsion. Assessment of the angle of torsion at the hip joint is important in prescribing hip abduction exercises to ensure that the range of motion is appropriate for the client's femoral alignment.

Test: Craig test.

Starting position: The client is lying prone, with one knee flexed to 90°. The therapist moves the hip through the full ranges of medial and lateral rotation, while palpating the greater trochanter.

Outcome: The position in the range of rotation at which the trochanter is most prominent is the position in which the femoral head is optimally situated in the acetabulum. If this angle is greater than 15° from the vertical in the direction of hip medial rotation, the femur is considered to be in antetorsion.

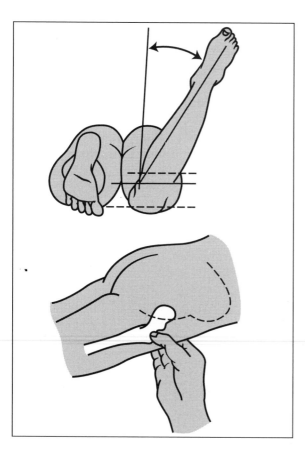

Figure 13.10. The Craig test

Functional movement tests

Squat and gait analysis are two important functional movements that can be used to gain an understanding of lower extremity muscle balance. The following tests outline the basic procedures for evaluating the squat pattern and walking gait. Deviations commonly seen during squatting and walking, and the subsequent muscle imbalances, are summarised in Table 13.1. The results of these tests should be correlated with those of muscle testing before prescribing corrective exercise.

Test: Squat.

Starting position: Client is standing, with feet placed shoulder-width apart and arms across chest.

Movement: Instruct the client to squat down, under control, to a position that is comfortable. If they are unsure of how to squat, an analogy of sitting on a chair may be useful. The client should perform as many repetitions as are necessary to observe the movement from all angles (anterior, posterior and lateral views). If the client is weak, ensure adequate rest is taken between repetitions. Specific observations are made of the pelvis, hips, knees and feet.

Test: Walking gait.

Starting position: Client is standing.

Movement: Instruct the client to walk up and down the room at a moderate pace (or on a treadmill, if available). They should be instructed to walk without trying to correct themselves in any way. Specific observations are made of the pelvis, hips, knees and feet.

Muscle length

Adequate length of the hip flexors and hip extensors is required for optimal function of the hip and knee, as well as the management and prevention of some cases of low back

Table 13.1.   Common deviations observed during squatting and walking

Observation	Weak muscles	Short muscles
Feet flatten	Gluteus medius, anterior tibialis, posterior tibialis	Gastrocnemius, peroneals
Feet externally rotate	Gluteus medius	Soleus, biceps femoris, piriformis
Knees turn inwards	Gluteus medius, gluteus maximus	Adductors, iliotibial band
Knees turn outwards	Adductors	Biceps femoris, iliopsoas, piriformis
Low back arches	Gluteus maximus, gluteus medius, core musculature	Iliopsoas, rectus femoris, erector spinae, latissimus dorsi
Low back rounds	Core musculature, gluteus maximus	External oblique, rectus abdominis, hamstrings
Asymmetrical weight shift	Gluteus medius, gluteus maximus, transversus abdominis, multifidi	Gastrocnemius-soleus, biceps femoris, iliotibial band, iliopsoas, piriformis

pain. Changes in the length of these muscles may produce compensatory changes in stability and movement at the knee, as well as in the thoracic and lumbar spine. The following muscle tests will determine whether the range of motion at the hip and knee joint is normal, limited or excessive. These results can then be used to determine the degree of muscle imbalance.

Muscle(s): Hip flexors – iliopsoas, rectus femoris, tensor fasciae latae, sartorius.
Starting position: Client begins by sitting at the end of a couch, with thighs half off the edge. The therapist places one hand behind the subject's back and another behind one knee, as the client rolls back into a supine position. The client holds the knee close to the chest, just enough to allow the lumbar curve to flatten, without excessive posterior pelvic tilting.
Notes: If testing for excessive length of the hip flexors, the hip joint should be at the edge of the couch, with the thigh completely off the end.
Test: The other thigh is allowed to drop down towards the couch, with the knee naturally flexing over the edge.
Normal length: All four hip flexor muscles are normal length if the posterior thigh touches the couch and the knee flexes to approximately 80° (while the low back and sacrum are flat on the couch). The knee flexion indicates that the rectus femoris and sartorius are normal in length.
Note: As there are four muscles involved in this length test, the variations observed are discussed individually below.

Iliopsoas (one-joint hip flexor)

Normal length: The posterior thigh touches the couch, with the low back and sacrum flat.
Shortness: The posterior thigh does not touch the couch (see Figure 13.11 (b)), with the low back and sacrum flat.
Excessive length: When the hip joint is positioned at the end of the couch, the thigh drops below couch level.

Rectus femoris (two-joint hip flexor)

Normal length: The knee flexes to 80° in the test position.
Shortness: Knee flexion is less than 80° in the test position. If the client is placed in a kneeling position, shortness of the rectus femoris will pull the pelvis into an anterior tilt, resulting in an increase in lumbar lordosis (compared to standing) (see Figure 13.11 (c)).

Tensor fasciae latae

Shortness: Abduction of the hip as it extends; lateral deviation of the patella, in the presence or absence of hip abduction; compensatory extension of the knee, if the hip is not allowed to abduct; medial rotation of the hip; lateral rotation of the tibia. Although this indicates shortness of the tensor fasciae latae, the modified Ober test should be used specifically to test the length of this muscle (see p. 195).

Sartorius

Shortness: A combination of at least three of the following indicates shortness: hip abduction, flexion and external rotation; knee flexion (see Figure 13.11 (d)).

Muscle(s): Hamstrings – biceps femoris (short head), semimembranosus, semitendinosus, biceps femoris (long head).
Starting position: Client is supine, with knees extended and low back and sacrum flat on couch. If low back does not flatten due to hip flexor shortness, a small pillow may be placed under the knees to flex the hips just enough to allow the back to flatten.
Test: The therapist stabilises one leg and raises the other, with knee extended and foot relaxed. The client may assist in raising the leg.
Normal length: With the low back and sacrum flat, an angle of 80° is achieved between the couch and the leg.
Shortness: The angle between the couch and the leg is less than 80°. (If the client performs a seated forward bend, the angle between the sacrum and the table is less than 80°, indicating limited flexion of the pelvis towards the thigh; in this instance, there may be compensatory movement of the thoracic spine to achieve forward bending.)
Excessive length: An angle greater than 90° is achieved.
Note: Excessive posterior tilting of the pelvis during the test will give a false indication of the length of the hamstrings, with the apparent length being greater than actual length. Anterior tilt of the pelvis during

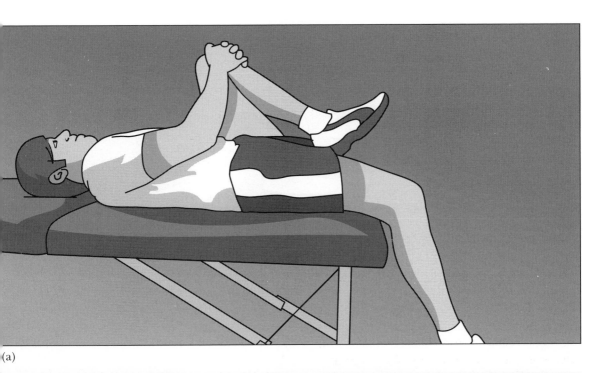

(a)

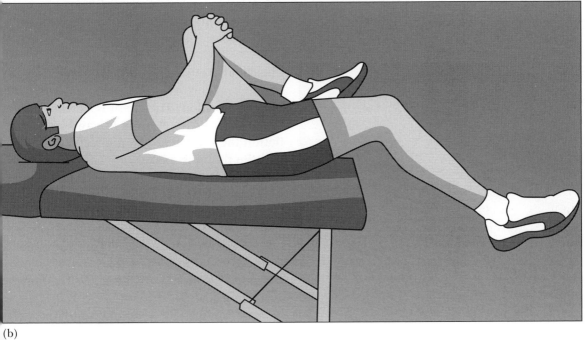

(b)

Figure 13.11. Test for length of hip flexor muscles – (a) normal length, (b) shortness in the iliopsoas

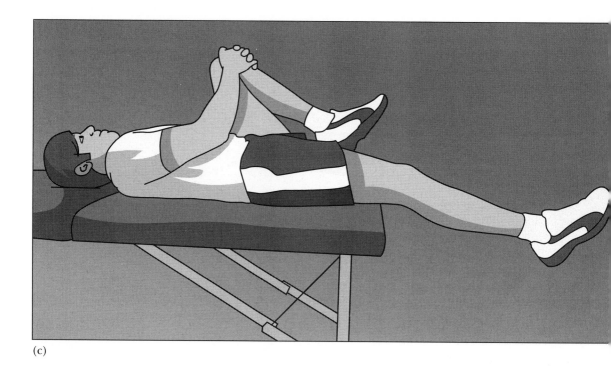

(c)

(d)

Figure 13.11. (contd) Test for length of hip flexor muscles – (c) shortness in the rectus femoris, (d) shortness in the sartorius

testing will make the hamstrings appear shorter than the actual length.

Muscle(s): Tensor fasciae latae and iliotibial band.

Starting position: The client is side-lying, with the lower leg flexed at the hip and knee to flatten the low back. The top leg is straight, and the therapist places one hand just below the topmost iliac crest, applying slight pressure upwards to stabilise the pelvis and keep the trunk in contact with the table.

Test: The therapist raises the top leg into a position of abduction and slight extension (without rotation). The leg is held in an extended position and allowed to drop into adduction towards the couch.

Normal length: The leg drops approximately 10° below horizontal, with the knee extended and the pelvis in neutral.

Shortness: The extended leg remains above horizontal, indicating shortness of the tensor fasciae latae and iliotibial band.

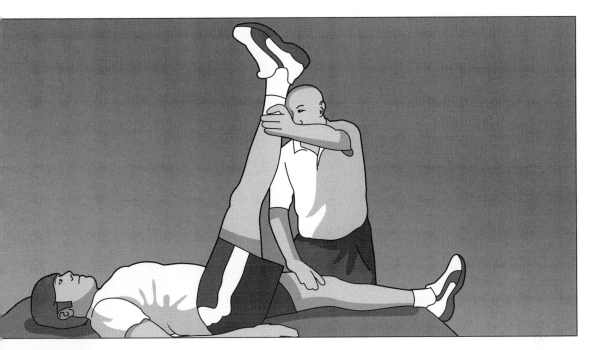

Figure 13.12. Test for length of hamstring muscles

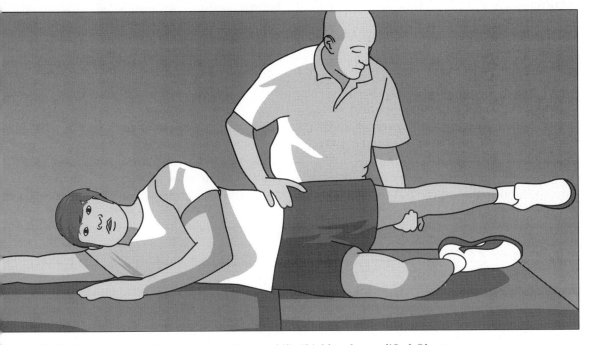

Figure 13.13. Test for length of tensor fasciae latae and iliotibial band – modified Ober test

Muscle strength

Muscle strength testing of the lower extremity will determine the ability of the pelvic, hip and knee muscles to provide stability and movement. Weakness or shortness of these muscles can contribute to a number of common postural faults and/or low back pain.

Muscle(s): Hip flexors.
Starting position: Client is sitting, with knees bent over the side of the couch.
Test: Client flexes hip (with a flexed knee) a few inches off the couch, against resistance on the anterior thigh. To test the iliopsoas, full hip flexion should be performed and held.
Weakness: A decreased ability to flex the hip against resistance, resulting in lumbar kyphosis or sway-back posture in standing. Unilateral weakness may result in lumbar scoliosis.
Shortness: Increased lumbar lordosis with anterior pelvic tilt during tests. This will also be seen in upright posture.
Note: When resisted hip flexion is accompanied by lateral rotation and abduction, the sartorius may be short or the tensor fasciae latae weak. Medial rotation may be evidence of a stronger tensor fascia lata over the sartorius.

If the client has weak trunk muscles and cannot stabilise the pelvis, the test may be

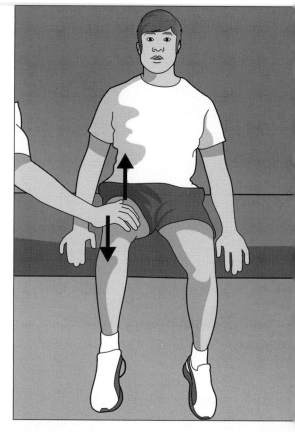

Figure 13.14. Test for strength of hip flexors

performed in the supine position, with legs straight. In this case, pressure is applied (in the direction of extension) to a slightly abducted and laterally rotated hip.

Muscle(s): Medial rotators.

Starting position: Client is sitting on a couch, with knees bent over the side, holding on to the edge.

Test: The thigh is medially rotated. Counter-pressure is applied to the medial side of the lower thigh, as well as to the lateral aspect of the lower leg.

Weakness: Inability to maintain medial rotation against resistance, resulting in a dominance of lateral rotation of the lower extremity in standing and walking.

Shortness: Inability to rotate the hip laterally in the test position. This can also be observed in weight bearing, with a subsequent tendency towards knock knees. There will also be an inability to sit cross-legged.

Muscle(s): Lateral rotators.

Starting position: Client is sitting on a couch, with knees bent over the side, holding on to the edge.

Test: The thigh is laterally rotated. Counter-pressure is applied to the lateral side of the lower thigh, as well as to the medial aspect of the lower leg.

Shortness: Excessive range of lateral rotation, with limited medial rotation. In standing there may be an outward turning of the feet.

Weakness: Inability to hold the test position, with a tendency towards knock knees in standing posture.

Figure 13.15. Test for strength of medial rotators

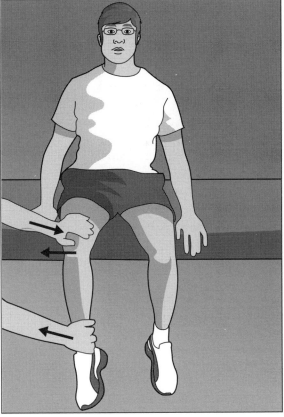

Figure 13.16. Test for strength of lateral rotators

Muscle(s): Tensor fasciae latae.
Starting position: Client is supine, with legs straight.
Test: The hip is abducted, flexed and medially rotated, while keeping the knee extended. Pressure is applied against the lower leg in the direction of extension and adduction.
Weakness: Inability to maintain the medial rotation against pressure. In the standing position, this may cause a tendency towards a bow-leg position and lateral rotation of the hip.
Shortness: In standing, shortness of this muscle can be observed as anterior pelvic tilt, hip flexion and a tendency towards knock knees.

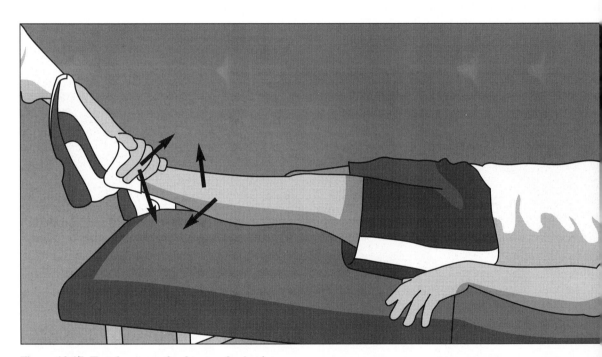

Figure 13.17. Test for strength of tensor fasciae latae

Muscle(s): Posterior gluteus medius.

Starting position: Client is side-lying, with lower leg flexed and pelvis slightly rotated forwards. The uppermost iliac crest is stabilised by the therapist.

Test: The hip is abducted, with slight extension and lateral rotation, with the knee in extension. Pressure is applied to the lateral aspect of the lower leg in the direction of adduction and flexion.

Weakness: An inability to hold the test position, with a tendency for the gluteus medius to cramp. During walking, weak abductors in the stance leg will cause the hip joint to adduct, rather than abduct. Consequently, the opposite side of the pelvis drops downwards. This is known as the Trendelenburg sign.

Shortness: In standing, there may be a lateral pelvic tilt, low on the side of tightness.

Note: The hip abductors may test normal as a group, whereas a test of the gluteus medius may uncover weakness.

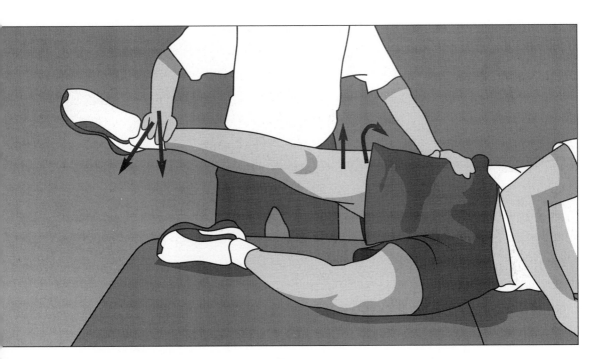

Figure 13.18. Test for strength of posterior gluteus medius

Muscle(s): Hip adductors.

Starting position: Client is side-lying, with legs straight. The therapist is standing behind, holding the upper leg in 15–20° abduction. The client may hold on to the side of the couch.

Test: The lower leg is adducted away from the table (no hip rotation, flexion or extension), against pressure applied on the medial aspect of the thigh.

Weakness: Marked weakness occurs when the client is unable to maintain the pressure and the thigh drops down.

Shortness: In standing, the pelvis will be high on the side of tightness, so much so that plantar flexion may be required to maintain balance.

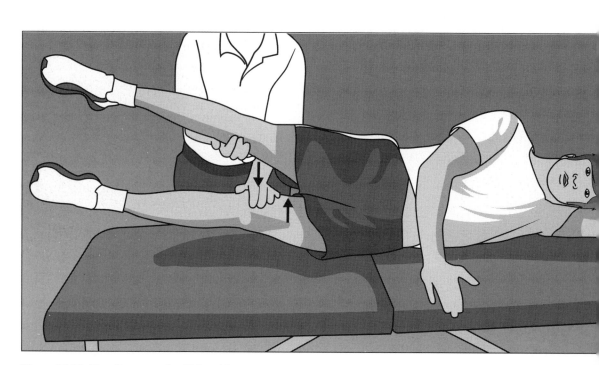

Figure 13.19. Test for strength of hip adductors

Muscle(s): Gluteus maximus.

Starting position: Client is prone, with the knee flexed to 90°. The therapist stabilises the sacrum.

Test: The hip is extended, maintaining knee flexion, while pressure is applied against the posterior thigh in the direction of hip flexion.

Weakness: Inability to hold the test position against pressure. In standing, the client may find walking difficult, with weight being displaced more posteriorly. In the forward-bend position, there may be difficulty in raising the trunk back to an upright position, without the use of the arms.

Note: It is important to test the gluteus maximus for strength as a prerequisite for back extensor testing.

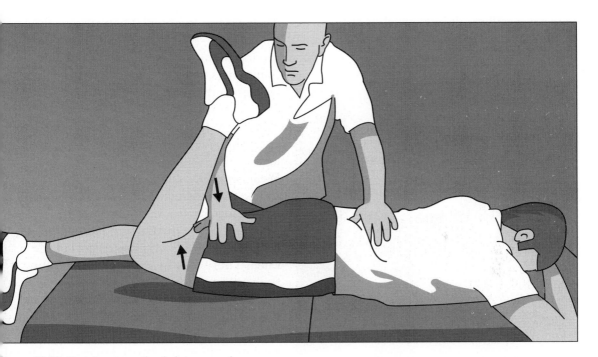

Figure 13.20. Test for strength of gluteus maximus

Muscle(s): Quadriceps femoris.
Starting position: Client is sitting, with knees over the side of the couch.
Test: The knee is extended against pressure applied on the anterior leg, just above the ankle.
Weakness: An inability to extend the knee fully shows marked weakness and may interfere with squatting and stair climbing. In the standing position, the weakness results in hyperextension of the knee, which may require the client to 'snap' or 'lock' the knee back during walking.
Shortness: Shortness of the rectus femoris, in particular, will result in restriction of knee flexion during hip extension movements, or restriction of hip extension when the knee is flexed. This may impact activities such as running or sprinting.
Note: Dominance of the rectus femoris will result in the client leaning backwards during the test, in order to obtain the greatest mechanical advantage. Dominance of the tensor fasciae latae will cause medial rotation of the hip during testing.

Muscle(s): Hamstrings (medial and lateral).
Starting position: Client is prone, with the knee flexed to 50°. The therapist stabilises the posterior thigh.
Test: To test the medial hamstrings, the knee is flexed 50–70°, with the hip and knee in medial rotation. To test the lateral hamstrings, the knee is flexed 50–70°, with the hip and knee in lateral rotation. In both cases, pressure is applied to the posterior leg just above the ankle, in the direction of knee extension. No pressure should be exerted against the rotation.
Weakness: Inability to maintain rotation indicates weakness of medial or lateral hamstrings. In the standing position, weakness of the medial and lateral hamstrings allows hyperextension of the knee. There may be anterior pelvic tilting if the weakness is bilateral, and pelvic rotation if unilateral weakness exists. Lateral hamstring weakness can result in a tendency towards bow legs, and medial hamstring weakness allows for knock knees, with lateral tibial rotation.
Shortness: Shortness may result in a knee-flexion posture in standing that is accompanied by posterior pelvic tilting and flattening of the lumbar curve.
Note: If the rectus femoris is very short, there will be limited knee flexion during testing. In this instance, there may be compensatory hip flexion, as observed by anterior pelvic tilting and excessive lumbar lordosis.

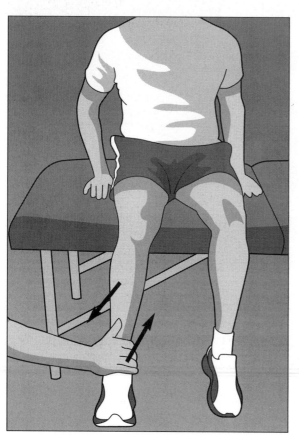

Figure 13.21. Test for strength of quadriceps femoris

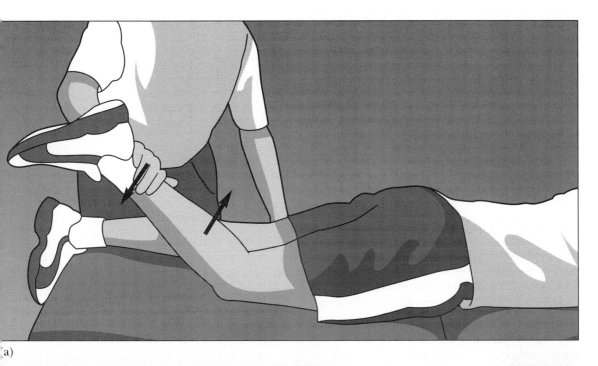

(a)

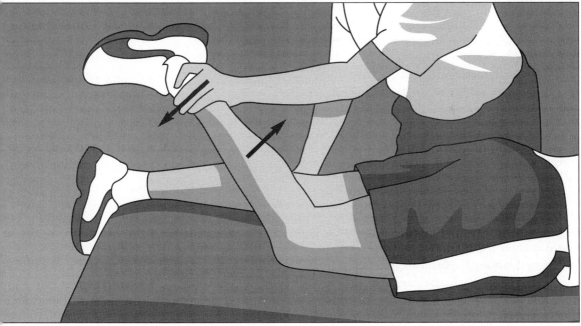

(b)

Figure 13.22. Test for strength of hamstrings – (a) medial hamstrings, (b) lateral hamstrings

14
CORRECTIVE EXERCISE FOR THE PELVIS, HIP AND KNEE

Corrective exercise progression

The objectives of corrective exercise prescription for the pelvis, hip and knee are multifaceted. Because the hip region and lower extremity provide the first step in the transference of ground reaction forces through the kinetic chain, it becomes important to condition these structures in an integrated way, once balance and alignment have been restored.

The vast majority of daily activities utilise the pelvis, hip and knee, including sitting, standing, bending and walking. Therefore any impairment of these basic movement patterns must be identified and corrected, using optimal exercises that provide adequate functional progression.

Muscle balance and stability should be restored to the pelvis, hip and knee as a first step in corrective exercise. Following this, the client is then ready to progress onto functional strength exercises that condition these structures for load-bearing and load-transferring activities. Many of these movement patterns fall into the two main categories of squatting and lifting. It is important to note that during these activities movement of the pelvis, hip and knee is integrated with the trunk and shoulder. With this in mind, continual attention to alignment and body mechanics is required by therapist and client.

The final stages of corrective exercise focus on whole body movements that enable the pelvis, hip and knee to coordinate and transfer ground reaction forces through the torso and up to the shoulder, in a controlled manner.

The following exercises are divided into four progressive phases.

Phase 1 – Muscle balance

These exercises are aimed at restoring normal length of the pelvic, hip and thigh muscles, through a combination of passive and active stretching techniques, with the intention of re-establishing optimal range of motion. When joint mobility is within normal limits, subsequent movement can continue to be normal and pain patterns will be alleviated.

Phase 2 – Static, dynamic and reactive stabilisation

The aim of these exercises is to improve stabilisation of the hip and knee joint, by improving the neuromuscular control of specific movement patterns. Many of these exercises involve minimal joint movements in a multi-planar environment, allowing the lient to build control and confidence of movement. The use of stability balls and rocker-boards is strongly encouraged during this phase.

Phase 3 – Functional strength

The goal during this phase is to ensure that the stabilisation capabilities of the hip and knee muscles are sufficient to control the leg under increasing load. These exercises generally involve simple movement patterns, but with a larger range of motion that fully utilises the client's own body weight, or added resistance, in both open- and closed-chain situations. From here, a number of important functional variations can be performed that may be specific to the client's occupational and recreational environment.

Phase 4 – Functional power

The aim of this phase is further to improve coordination and control of movement, to provide a high degree of functional carry-over into occupation, recreation and sport. These exercises involve the addition of speed to the movement, often using plyometric exercise. The result is enhanced link-sequencing and force generation from the lower extremities, through the trunk and out to the shoulders and arms.

For this to occur safely, muscle balance, stabilisation and functional strength must all be at optimal levels and particular emphasis should be placed on optimal hip and trunk rotation, to ensure smooth coordination of ground reaction forces up through the body.

Corrective exercises for the hip

Phase 1 exercises – Restoring muscle balance and flexibility

Hip flexor stretch
Muscle group(s): Hip flexors – iliopsoas, tensor fasciae latae, rectus femoris, sartorius
Phase/modality: Flexibility
Equipment: None

Purpose

To stretch the hip flexors (one-joint and two-joint).

Starting position

❑ FLOOR STRETCH (one-joint) – Client is lying supine, with knees bent, both feet flat on the floor. The low back is flat.

❑ COUCH STRETCH (two-joint) – Client is lying supine on the couch, holding both knees towards the chest, and far enough up the couch to allow the thigh to drop down and the lower leg to hang off the edge. The low back is flat.

Correct performance

❑ FLOOR STRETCH – the client brings one leg up towards the chest and holds it, while keeping the low back flat to the floor. The other leg is extended straight out, and the gluteals on that side are contracted, while the back of the leg is pushed into the floor. This position is held for 8–10 seconds and repeated 6 times, before swapping legs.

❑ COUCH STRETCH – from the start position, the client allows one leg to lower towards the couch and holds for 20–30 seconds, while keeping the low back flat.

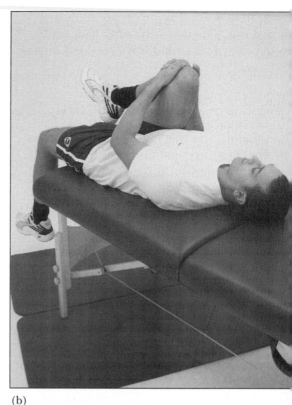

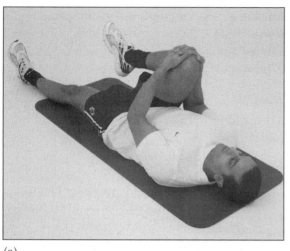

(a)   (b)

Figure 14.1. Hip flexor stretch – (a) floor, (b) couch

Variations

❏ During the couch stretch, if lowered thigh begins to abduct, it should be pulled in towards the midline. The abduction may represent shortness of the tensor fascia lata. This action may also be performed by a therapist.

❏ If the knee extends, this indicates shortness of the rectus femoris. In this instance, the lower leg may be actively pulled inwards to a point where the ankle is positioned under the knee to provide an appropriate stretch. This action may also be performed by a therapist.

Standing abductor stretch
Muscle group(s): Abductors
Phase/modality: Flexibility
Equipment: None

Purpose
To increase range of motion of the lateral hip muscles.

Starting position
Client is standing, with the leg to be stretched crossed in behind.

Correct performance
❏ The client laterally flexes away from the stretching leg until a stretch is felt.
❏ This position is held for 20–30 seconds, repeating 2–3 times and swapping legs if necessary.

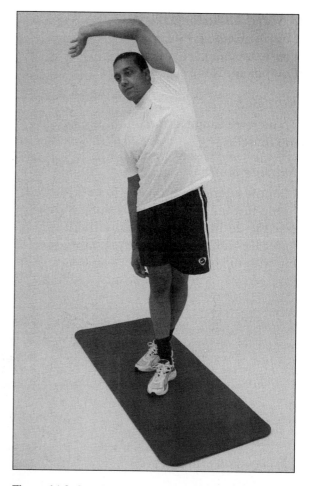

Figure 14.2. Standing abductor stretch

Assisted abductor stretch

Muscle group(s): Abductors
Phase/modality: Flexibility
Equipment: None

Purpose

To increase range of motion of the lateral hip muscles.

Starting position

Client is supine, with the leg to be stretched in hip flexion and knee extension, as shown (see Figure 14.3). The therapist holds the lower leg with one hand and stabilises the hip with the other.

Correct performance

❑ The therapist gently adducts the leg and stops when a resistance barrier is felt. This position is held for 20–30 seconds, before relaxing and repeating 2–3 times.

❑ The stretch is repeated on the other leg.

Variations

This stretch may also be performed using PNF.

Figure 14.3. Assisted abductor stretch

Standing adductor stretch

Muscle group(s): Adductors
Phase/modality: Flexibility
Equipment: None

Purpose

To increase range of motion of the hip adductors.

Starting position

The client is standing, with one leg straight and the opposite leg bent, with both feet facing forwards, as shown (see Figure 14.4).

Correct performance

❑ The client moves sideways towards the bent leg until a stretch is felt in the inner thigh of the straight leg.

❑ The stretch is held for 20–30 seconds and repeated 2–3 times before swapping legs.

Figure 14.4. Standing adductor stretch

Assisted adductor stretch
Muscle group(s): Adductors
Phase/modality: Flexibility
Equipment: None

Purpose
To increase range of motion of the hip adductors.

Starting position
Client is lying supine, with both legs straight.

Correct performance
❑ The therapist stabilises the contralateral hip with one hand and gently abducts the leg to be stretched by pulling, just below the knee, until a stretch is felt.

❑ The position is held for 20–30 seconds and repeated 2–3 times before swapping sides.

Variations
This stretch may also be performed using PNF.

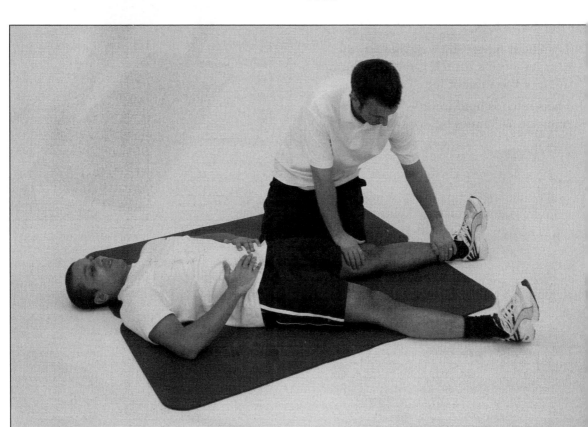

Figure 14.5. Assisted adductor stretch

Piriformis stretch

Muscle group(s): Piriformis, hip lateral rotators
Phase/modality: Flexibility
Equipment: None

Purpose

❑ To stretch the piriformis.

❑ To increase range of motion and function of the hip joint.

Starting position

Client is lying supine, with the left leg straight and the right knee flexed. The right foot is positioned on the lateral aspect of the left thigh, just above the knee, as shown (see Figure 14.6).

Correct performance

❑ The client gently pulls the right knee towards the left hip until a stretch is felt deep in the right gluteals.

❑ This position is held for 20–30 seconds before repeating 2–3 times on each side.

ITB stretch

Muscle group(s): Tensor fasciae latae-iliotibial band
Phase/modality: Flexibility
Equipment: None

Purpose

❑ To improve the performance of the hip abductor muscles.

❑ To stretch the tensor fasciae latae-iliotibial band.

❑ To improve isometric strength of the lateral abdominal musculature.

Starting position

Client is side-lying, with lower hip and knee bent, and the pelvis slightly rotated forwards. The top leg is straight and positioned forwards, with the knee turned up slightly.

Figure 14.7. Iliotibial band stretch

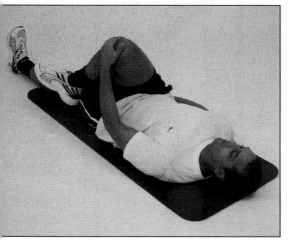

Figure 14.6. Piriformis stretch

Correct performance

❑ The top leg is abducted and then extended, so it is positioned slightly behind the body. The leg is then dropped towards the floor and allowed to hang for 15–20 seconds.

❑ The pelvis should not move and the low back should not be allowed to arch during the movement.

Prone hip rotation
Muscle group(s): Hip rotators
Phase/modality: Flexibility
Equipment: None

Purpose

❑ To stretch the hip rotators.

❑ To decrease compensatory motion of the pelvis during hip movement.

Starting position

The client is lying prone, with forehead resting on hands, as shown (see Figure 14.8). The lower abdominals are upwards and inwards to stabilise the spine and pelvis. One knee is flexed to 90°.

Correct performance

❑ The client rotates the hip by allowing the foot to move in towards the opposite leg and then away.

❑ The movement is repeated 10 times in each direction, before swapping legs.

(a)

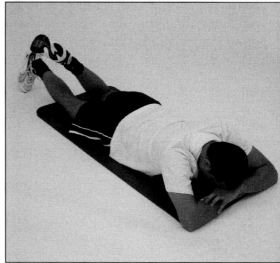
(b)

Figure 14.8. Prone hip rotation – (a) before, (b) after

Side-lying adductor roll-up

Muscle group(s): Adductors, medial rotators
Phase/modality: Flexibility
Equipment: None

Purpose

To increase range of motion in adduction and medial rotation.

Starting position

The client is side-lying, with top leg bent at the hip and knee and positioned over the lower leg, as shown (see Figure 14.9). The lower leg is straight and neutral spine alignment is maintained throughout the movement.

Correct performance

❑ The client internally rotates the lower leg, allowing the toes to point upwards. All the motion should be generated from the hip, while keeping the leg completely straight.

❑ The movement is repeated 8–10 times before swapping legs.

Figure 14.9. Side-lying adductor roll-up

Four-point rocking

Muscle group(s): Low back, gluteals
Phase/modality: Flexibility
Equipment: None

Purpose

❑ To stretch the gluteals and low back muscles.

❑ To decrease compressive forces acting on the spine.

❑ To improve hip-bending motion.

Starting position

The client is in a four-point kneeling stance, as shown (see Figure 14.10), with the spine in neutral alignment. The hips are centred over the knees, and the shoulders over the wrists.

Correct performance

❑ Client rocks gently backwards, aiming the buttocks towards the ceiling, allowing the low back to remain in neutral. Do not let the low back arch upwards. The movement should be aided by pushing back with the hands.

❑ Return to the start position by initiating the movement back, using the gluteals and bracing the abdominals.

❑ Repeat slowly 8 times.

(a)

(b)

Figure 14.10. Four-point rocking – (a) before, (b) after

Standing quadriceps stretch
Muscle group(s): Quadriceps femoris
Phase/modality: Flexibility
Equipment: None

Purpose
To stretch the quadriceps and hip flexors.

Starting position
The client is standing in optimal alignment, holding one ankle. A wall may be used to lean against for balance.

Correct performance
❏ The client is instructed to perform a posterior pelvic tilt, while squeezing the gluteals of the stretching leg.
❏ This position is held for 20–30 seconds and repeated 2–3 times before swapping legs.

Prone quadriceps stretch
Muscle group(s): Quadriceps femoris
Phase/modality: Flexibility
Equipment: None

Purpose
To stretch the quadriceps and hip flexors.

Starting position
Client is lying prone, with forehead resting on one hand and the other hand holding the ankle of the stretching leg.

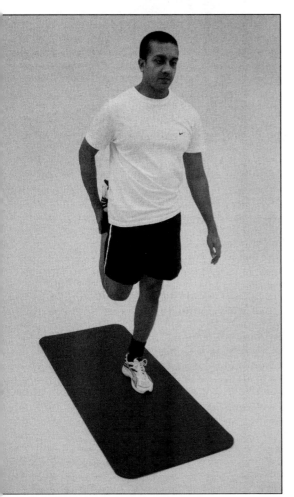

Figure 14.11. Standing quadriceps stretch

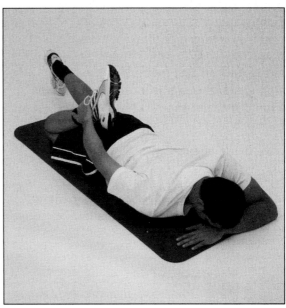

Figure 14.12. Prone quadriceps stretch

Correct performance

❑ The client is instructed to perform a posterior pelvic tilt, while squeezing the gluteals of the stretching leg.

❑ This position is held for 20–30 seconds and repeated 2–3 times before swapping legs.

Variations

This stretch can be performed using PNF. **Note:** This stretch may be contraindicated in those with existing low back pain.

Standing hamstring stretch (spiral)
Muscle group(s): Hamstrings (medial and lateral)
Phase/modality: Flexibility
Equipment: Couch

Purpose

To increase functional flexibility of the hamstrings.

Starting position

Client is standing in optimal alignment, with one leg resting straight on couch. The therapist should ensure that the couch is set at the appropriate height for the client to be able to stand in neutral spinal alignment. The foot of the support leg should be facing forwards and the hips should be square to the stretching leg.

Correct performance

❑ The client performs an anterior tilt of the pelvis to stretch the hamstrings. If this is

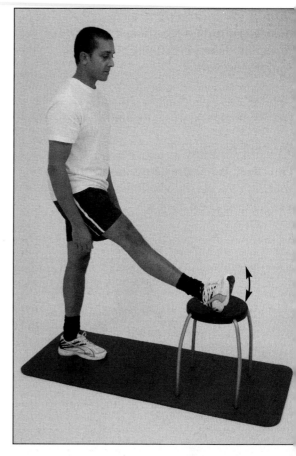

Figure 14.13. Standing hamstring stretch (spiral)

insufficient to induce a stretch, the level of the couch should be set higher.

❑ The stretching leg is then slowly rotated from the hip, alternating left to right, while maintaining good spine alignment.

❑ The movement is repeated 8 times in each direction, before swapping legs.

Supine hamstring stretch

Muscle group(s): Hamstrings
Phase/modality: Flexibility
Equipment: None

Purpose

To increase flexibility of the hamstrings.

Starting position

The client is lying supine, in neutral alignment, with one leg straight. The other leg is slightly bent at the knee, held by one hand below the back of the knee and one hand above the knee, on the posterior thigh.

Correct performance

❑ The leg to be stretched is gently pulled towards the chest, until a stretch is felt in the hamstrings. It is important that the lumbar spine remains in neutral alignment and the knee remains slightly flexed – do not allow the knee to bend further.

❑ This position is held for 20–30 seconds, before repeating 2–3 times and swapping legs.

Seated hamstring stretch

Muscle group(s): Hamstrings
Phase/modality: Flexibility
Equipment: Stability ball

Purpose

To stretch the hamstrings.

Figure 14.15. Seated hamstring stretch with stability ball

Figure 14.14. Supine hamstring stretch

Starting position

Client is seated on a stability ball, in optimal spinal alignment, with both legs straight out in front. The lower abdominals are drawn upwards and inwards to stabilise the spine, and the ankles are dorsiflexed.

Correct performance

❑ An anterior pelvic tilt is performed while maintaining a straight-leg position, and the client then slowly leans forwards from the hips until a stretch is felt in the hamstrings.

❑ This position is held for 20–30 seconds and repeated 2–3 times.

Variations

This stretch may be performed using one leg at a time.
Note: Some individuals will not need to lean forwards. The anterior pelvic tilt alone will create a hamstring stretch. Maintenance of the anterior pelvic tilt is an important part of this stretch – leaning too far forwards should not be encouraged, as compensatory stretching may occur at the lumbar or thoracic spine.

Standing calf stretch

Muscle group(s): Gastrocnemius, soleus
Phase/modality: Flexibility
Equipment: None

Purpose

To stretch the gastrocnemius and soleus muscles.

Starting position

The client is facing a wall, with arms stretched out for support. One leg is brought forwards, and the leg to be stretched is placed further back. The toes of the rear leg should be facing forwards, with the foot flat on the floor.

Correct performance

Gently shift weight forwards onto front leg, while maintaining a straight back leg, until a stretch is felt in the calf. This position is held for 20–30 seconds and repeated 2–3 times before changing legs.

Variations

The rear leg may be slightly bent to stretch the soleus muscle.

Supine calf stretch

Muscle group(s): Gastrocnemius
Phase/modality: Flexibility
Equipment: None

Purpose

To stretch the gastrocnemius.

Starting position

The client is lying supine, with a straight leg over the therapist's knee. The therapist places one hand on the anterior thigh, just above the knee, and the other hand on the sole of the foot.

Correct performance

❑ The therapist applies resistance in the direction of dorsiflexion, until a comfortable stretch is felt. The knee should be kept straight throughout. This position is held for 20–30 seconds and repeated 2–3 times before changing legs.

❑ The client may assist the stretch by actively dorsiflexing the ankle.

Variations

This stretch may also be performed using PNF.

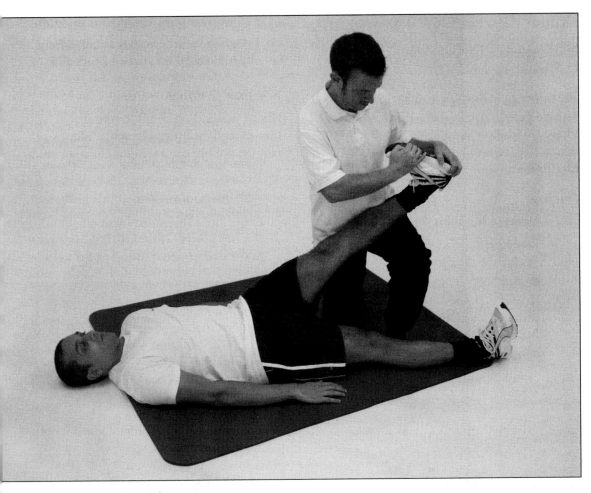

Figure 14.16. Supine calf stretch

Phase 2 exercises – Restoring static, dynamic and reactive stabilisation

Forward bending from standing

Muscle group(s): Gluteals, low back
Phase/modality: Stabilisation – static, dynamic; strength
Equipment: None

Purpose

❑ To increase hip joint flexibility.

❑ To improve performance of the gluteals.
❑ To improve the lumbar stabilisation mechanism.

Starting position

Client is standing in good alignment, with feet placed comfortably apart. Hands may rest on a table or on thighs if the client is weak.

Correct performance

❑ Begin the movement by slowly bending at the hip joints, while keeping the spine in neutral alignment. Bend as far as possible.

(a)

(b)

Figure 14.17. Forward bending – (a) before, (b) after

Return to standing by tightening the gluteals and abdominals, while moving the hips back inwards.

❑ If short hamstrings limit the movement, allow the knees to bend slightly.

Supine leg raise
Muscle group(s): Hip flexors, abdominals
Phase/modality: Stabilisation – static, dynamic
Equipment: None

Purpose
To improve the performance of the abdominals in controlling pelvic motion.

Starting position
Client is lying supine, with knees and hips flexed, feet flat on floor.

Correct performance
❑ The client contracts the deep abdominal muscles by pulling the navel upwards and inwards, and lifts one foot off the floor until the knee and hip are flexed to 90° (tabletop position).

❑ Maintaining the abdominal contraction, the leg is returned to the floor and the movement performed for a total of 10 repetitions, before changing legs.

Variations
The hands may be lifted a few inches above the floor to increase the performance of the abdominal muscles.

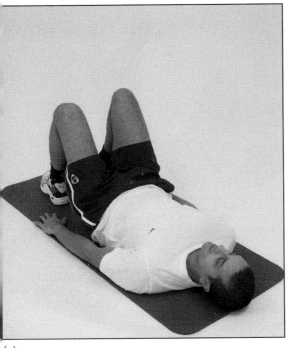

(a)

(b)

Figure 14.18. Supine leg raise – (a) before, (b) after

Supine leg drop

Muscle group(s): Hip flexors, abdominals, hip adductors
Phase/modality: Stabilisation – static, dynamic
Equipment: None

Purpose

❏ To improve the performance of the abdominals in controlling pelvic motion.
❏ To strengthen the hip adductors.

Starting position

Client is lying supine, with both knees and hips flexed. One leg is raised off the floor, with the knee positioned above the hip and flexed to 90° (tabletop position).

Correct performance

❏ The client contracts the deep abdominal muscles by pulling the navel upwards and inwards. Maintaining the leg in the tabletop position, the hip is horizontally abducted, allowing the leg to drop towards the floor. The pelvis and lumbar spine must remain in neutral throughout the movement.

❏ The abdominal contraction is maintained as the leg is returned to the start position. The movement is performed for a total of 10 repetitions, before changing legs.

Variations

The hands may be lifted a few inches above the floor to increase the performance of the abdominal muscles.

(a)

(b)

Figure 14.19. Supine leg drop – (a) before, (b) after

Supine leg slide
Muscle group(s): Hip flexors, abdominals
Phase/modality: Stabilisation – static, dynamic
Equipment: None

Purpose
To improve the performance of the abdominals in controlling pelvic motion.

Starting position
Client is lying supine, with legs straight.

Correct performance
❑ The client contracts the deep abdominal muscles by pulling the navel upwards and inwards, and slides one foot along the floor until the hip and knee are flexed and the foot is resting flat on the floor.

❑ Maintaining the abdominal contraction, slide the foot down and return to the start position.

❑ The movement is alternated from side to side, for a total of 20 repetitions each side.

Variations
The hands may be lifted a few inches above the floor to increase the performance of the abdominal muscles.

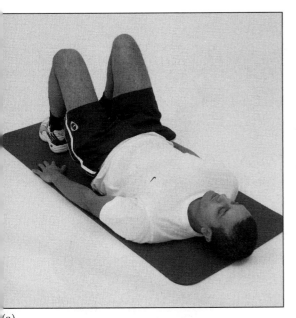 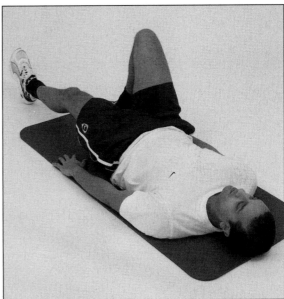

(a)   (b)

Figure 14.20. Supine leg slide – (a) before, (b) after

Side-lying hip abduction
Muscle group(s): Hip abductors, abdominals
Phase/modality: Stabilisation – static, dynamic
Equipment: None

Purpose
❑ To improve performance of hip abductors.
❑ To improve performance of the lateral abdominal musculature.

Starting position
Client is side-lying, with lower leg bent and top leg straight.

Correct performance
❑ The top leg is lifted upwards, towards the ceiling. The pelvis remains in neutral and the low back does not arch or flatten during the movement.
❑ The leg is lowered and the movement repeated for a total of 10 repetitions, before changing legs.

Variations
This exercise may be regressed by allowing the top leg to bend slightly before starting the movement.

(a)   (b)

Figure 14.21. Side-lying hip abduction – (a) before, (b) after

Side-lying hip adduction

Muscle group(s): Hip adductors, abdominals
Phase/modality: Stabilisation – static, dynamic
Equipment: None

Purpose

❏ To improve performance of hip adductor muscles.

❏ To stretch hip abductors.

Starting position

The client is side-lying, with the leg to be exercised lowermost. The hip and knee are straightened and the pelvis is held in neutral alignment. The top leg is rotated at the hip and the knee is bent, with the foot flat on the floor in front of the lower leg. The top hand can be placed on the floor to stabilise the trunk.

Correct performance

❏ The client contracts the abdominals by pulling the navel upwards and inwards, and lifts the lower leg up towards the top leg.

❏ The leg is returned and the movement repeated for a total of 10 repetitions, before changing legs.

(a)

(b)

Figure 14.22. Side-lying hip adduction – (a) before, (b) after

Isometric glutes
Muscle group(s): Gluteus maximus
Phase/modality: Static stabilisation
Equipment: None

Purpose
To improve performance of the gluteus maximus.

Starting position
The client is lying prone, with legs straight.

Correct performance
The client tightens the buttock muscles while thinking about 'turning the legs outwards'. This position is held for up to 8 seconds, before relaxing and repeating 10 times.

Prone hip extension
Muscle group(s): Gluteus maximus, hamstrings, abs
Phase/modality: Stabilisation – static, dynamic
Equipment: None

Purpose
- ❏ To improve performance of the gluteus maximus and hamstrings.
- ❏ To stretch the hip flexor muscles.
- ❏ To improve performance of the back extensor and abdominal muscles.

Starting position
The client is lying prone, with legs straight.

Correct performance
- ❏ The client contracts the abdominals by pulling the navel upwards and inwards. One leg is lifted off the floor by tightening the gluteus maximus. The leg is lifted only high enough to maintain a stable pelvis – do not allow the pelvis to rock.
- ❏ This position is held for up to 8 seconds before relaxing, and the movement is performed for 10 repetitions on each leg.

Variations
This exercise can be performed by first flexing the knee to 90°. This position shortens the hamstrings and allows for

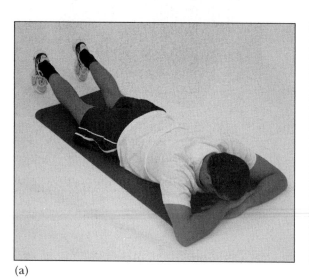

(a)

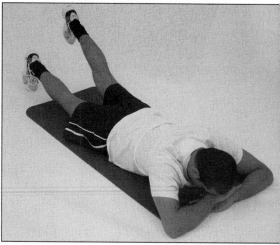

(b)

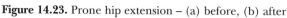

Figure 14.23. Prone hip extension – (a) before, (b) after

increased performance by the gluteus maximus and back extensors.

Seated knee extension

Muscle group(s): Quadriceps femoris, hip flexors

Phase/modality: Stabilisation – static, dynamic

Equipment: None

Purpose

- To improve control of the anterior thigh and back extensor muscles.

- To control hip rotation during knee movement.

- To stretch the hamstring and calf muscles.

Starting position

Client is seated, with neutral spine alignment. Hips and knees should be flexed to approximately 90°. The hands can be placed on the low back to monitor neutral alignment during the movement.

Correct performance

- Client slowly extends one knee as far as possible, while maintaining a neutral spine, keeping the abdominals contracted throughout.

- This position is held for up to 8 seconds before returning. Perform the movement 10 times on each leg.

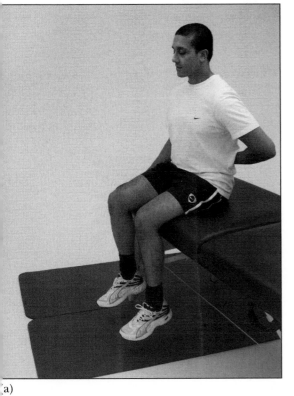 

(a)   (b)

Figure 14.24. Seated knee extension – (a) before, (b) after

Band shuffle

Muscle group(s): Hip abductors, hip flexors, abdominals

Phase/modality: Stabilisation – static, dynamic; balance

Equipment: Exercise band

Purpose

❑ To improve functional performance of the hip abductors.

❑ To improve performance of the abdominals during hip abduction.

Prerequisites

Good postural and abdominal control.

Starting position

Client is standing, with an exercise band placed around the mid-lower leg. Feet are positioned shoulder-width apart, toes pointing forwards and knees slightly bent.

Correct performance

❑ The client contracts the abdominals by pulling the navel upwards and inwards, and performs a slow, controlled lateral movement, side to side and forwards.

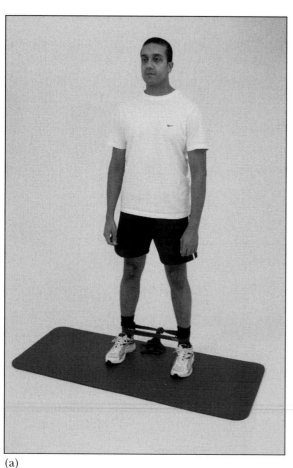

(a)

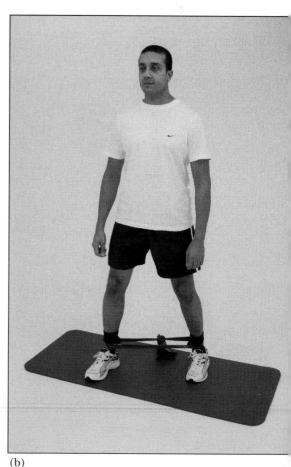

(b)

Figure 14.25. Band shuffle – (a) before, (b) after

- ❏ The client should be encouraged to generate strength from the trunk musculature. The knees should always remain over the second toes and not be allowed to fall inwards or outwards.
- ❏ The movement should be performed for 2–3 minutes.

Standing balance

Muscle group(s): Trunk, hip and legs
Phase/modality: Stabilisation, balance, strength
Equipment: Rocker-board, Vew-Do™ board

Purpose

- ❏ To improve performance of total body stabilisation and strength.
- ❏ To improve the functional strength of the lower extremity.
- ❏ To improve postural control during balance (sport-specific).

Prerequisites

- ❏ Good postural and abdominal control.
- ❏ Good ability to stabilise statically in an upright position.

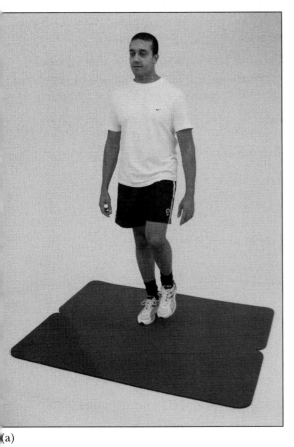

(a)

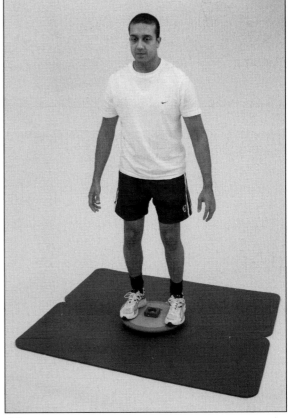

(b)

Figure 14.26. Standing balance – (a) single leg, (b) rocker-board (intermediate)

(c)

Figure 14.26. (contd) Standing balance – (c) Vew-Do™ board (advanced)

Starting position

Client is standing, with good spinal alignment and abdominals contracted.

Correct performance

❑ SINGLE-LEG BALANCE – while maintaining good posture, the client lifts one leg off the floor and holds this position for up to 8 seconds, before swapping legs. The movement is alternated between legs for a total of 8 repetitions each side. The knee should be positioned over the second toe throughout the movement.

❑ ROCKER-BOARD – the client is instructed to maintain balance on the rocker-board, without the edges touching the floor. Good postural alignment should be kept throughout the movement.

❑ VEW-DO™ BOARD – in this advanced exercise, the client maintains balance while standing on a Vew-Do™ board.

Variations

Increase the balance time.

Wall slide

Muscle group(s): Anterior/posterior thigh, abdominals

Phase/modality: Stabilisation, strength, balance

Equipment: Stability ball

Purpose

To improve performance, strength and coordination of the trunk and lower extremity.

Starting position

Client is standing, with the stability ball placed in the low back against a wall. Feet are positioned shoulder-width apart, with knees over the second toes.

Correct performance

❏ The client contracts the abdominals by pulling the navel upwards and inwards, and slowly lowers the hips by approximately 6 inches. Neutral spine alignment is maintained throughout the movement. The return is initiated by contracting the buttocks and tightening the abdominals further.

❏ The knees are positioned over the toes throughout the movement.

❏ The movement is repeated 10 times, before resting, and the exercise may be repeated 2–3 times in total.

Variations

As the client gets stronger, the hips may be lowered further, until maximum range of motion is achieved (hips reach knee height).

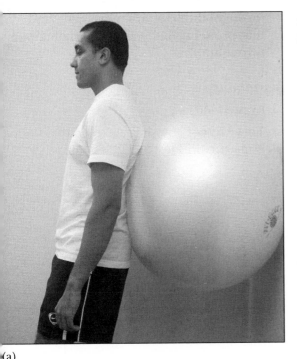

(a)   (b)

Figure 14.27. Wall slide – (a) before, (b) after

Supine isometric bridge

Muscle group(s): Hip extensors, abdominal wall
Phase/modality: Stabilisation, strength, balance
Equipment: Stability ball

Purpose

❏ To increase the strength of the hip extensors.

❏ To improve neuromuscular control of the lateral abdominal muscles, in preparation for larger kinetic chain movements.

❏ To improve whole body balance.

Figure 14.28. Supine isometric bridge

Prerequisites

❏ Good level of core strength.

❏ Optimal scapula control.

Starting position

Sit on the stability ball and roll down, while comfortably placing the head, neck and shoulder blades on the ball, with both feet positioned straight ahead.

Correct performance

❏ The hips are lifted until they are in line with knees, and hands are placed across the chest. The scapulae are slightly retracted and depressed and the abdominals are braced.

❏ This position is held for up to 8 seconds, before resting momentarily. Up to 10 repetitions are performed in total.

❏ The therapist should observe the hips and shoulders to ensure they are level throughout the entire movement, and that proper spinal position is maintained throughout.

Variations

❏ Eyes closed.

❏ This exercise may be regressed to a floor isometric bridge.

Supine bridge lateral roll

Muscle group(s): Legs, total body
Phase/modality: Stabilisation, strength, balance
Equipment: Stability ball

Purpose

☐ To strengthen the entire kinetic chain in all three planes of motion.

☐ To improve static stabilisation of the muscles of the pelvis, hip and knee.

Prerequisites

This is an advanced exercise and the client must possess good flexibility and strength in the lumbo-pelvic-hip complex.

Starting position

From a seated position on the ball, the client rolls down into a bridge position, allowing the head and shoulders to rest on the ball. Arms are straight and out to the sides, and a wooden dowel can be held across the chest to maintain alignment. The abdominals are braced.

Correct performance

☐ The client slowly rolls the whole body along the ball to the right, until the right shoulder begins to come off the ball, ensuring that hips and shoulders are level throughout the movement. This position is held for 2–3 seconds, before rolling over to the other side and repeating. Perform 3–4 repetitions each side, before resting.

☐ It is important that the abdominals are braced throughout the movement and that the whole body rolls as one unit.

☐ The therapist can observe the wooden dowel to ensure it remains horizontal throughout and that the spine is not twisting in any way.

(a)   (b)

Figure 14.29. Supine bridge lateral roll – (a) before, (b) after

Variations

❑ Increase the holding time to up to 8 seconds.

❑ Increase the distance moved. This will place increasing stresses on the trunk musculature to stabilise the entire body.

Note: This is an advanced exercise that is designed to train a number of skills, including strength, endurance, agility, balance, coordination and flexibility – with this in mind, careful attention should be paid to technique and execution.

Walking re-education

Muscle group(s): Legs, abdominals
Phase/modality: Stabilisation, balance, coordination
Equipment: None

Purpose

❑ To prevent excessive rotation of pelvis and lumbar spine during walking gait.

❑ To improve control of the pelvis and spine via the abdominal muscles.

❑ To improve awareness of knee position during walking gait.

❑ To improve performance of the plantar flexors and gluteals during walking gait.

Starting position

Client is standing and contracts the abdominals by pulling the navel upwards and inwards.

Correct performance

❑ LIMITING PELVIC ROTATION – client places hands on pelvis and practises walking while trying to prevent pelvic rotation. It may be necessary to take smaller steps initially, particularly if the abdominals are weak or if the hip flexors are tight.

❑ LIMITING HIP MEDIAL ROTATION/HIP ADDUCTION – at heel strike, the client is instructed to contract the gluteals to prevent excessive hip medial rotation.

❑ LIMITING KNEE HYPEREXTENSION – at heel strike, the client is instructed not to allow the knee to hyperextend. There should be good use of the plantar flexors during this movement (see below, FACILITATING ANKLE PLANTAR FLEXION).

❑ LIMITING KNEE ROTATION – the client steps forwards with the foot turned slightly outwards. On heel strike, the gluteals are contracted to maintain this medial rotation at the knee, and the knee should be in slight flexion, ready for the weight shift. There should be good use of the plantar flexors during this movement (see below, FACILITATING ANKLE PLANTAR FLEXION). Hip antetorsion may contribute to excessive medial rotation and should not be considered a dysfunction.

❑ FACILITATING ANKLE PLANTAR FLEXION – on heel strike, the client should think about pushing back on the floor to control the forward movement of the knee. As the foot approaches toe-off, the client pushes the ball of the foot into the floor and lifts the heel.

Phase 3 exercises – Restoring functional strength

Standing hip flexion/glute contraction

Muscle group(s): Hip flexors, gluteals, abdominals

Phase/modality: Strength

Equipment: None

Purpose

❑ To improve performance of gluteal muscles.

❑ To improve isometric control by the abdominal muscles.

Prerequisites

Pain-free range of motion in standing hip flexion.

Starting position

Client is standing, with feet close together.

Correct performance

❑ Client begins by shifting weight to the stance leg and tightening the buttock muscles on this side. Client contracts the abdominals, by pulling the navel upwards and inwards, and flexes the opposite hip and knee, lifting the leg off the floor. This position is held for up to 8 seconds, maintaining full contraction of the gluteals and abdominals.

Figure 14.30. Standing hip flexion/glute contraction

❑ Keep the pelvis and shoulders level and do not allow the knee to rotate medially or the ankle to pronate.

❑ Perform 8–10 repetitions before changing legs.

Four-point reach

Muscle group(s): Hip and knee extensors, back extensors, abdominals, shoulders
Phase/modality: Strength, balance, endurance, coordination
Equipment: None

Purpose

❑ To improve performance of the lumbo-pelvic-hip complex.

❑ To improve balance control.

❑ To improve performance of the abdominal muscles.

❑ To enhance the cross-crawl movement pattern.

Starting position

Client is in a four-point kneeling stance, with hands positioned below the shoulders, and knees below the hips. The spine is in neutral alignment, with the head in line with the body. The client contracts the abdominals by pulling the navel upwards and inwards.

Prerequisites

❑ Pain-free range of motion in hip extension.

❑ Ability to perform an abdominal hollow and brace.

❑ Adequate rotator cuff strength.

Correct performance

❑ Client braces the abdominals and reaches forwards with one arm and backwards with the opposite leg. Neutral spine alignment should be maintained throughout. The movement is repeated for the other side, for a total of 6–8 repetitions each side.

❑ The arm and leg reach should not go higher than horizontal, or body level. Initially, the client may only be able to achieve a small reach, before compromising spine position and bracing ability. The reaching distance may have to be increased slowly as the client becomes stronger.

(a)

(b)

Figure 14.31. Four-point reach – (a) before, (b) after

❑ The therapist should also observe any side-to-side movement of the hips and correct this by instructing the client either to brace harder or to decrease the distance reached. If movement still occurs, the exercise can be regressed to moving the arms or legs alone, until adequate strength and control is achieved.

Variations

❑ Lateral reach – the arms and legs are taken out to the sides.

❑ 'Crawling' – the client is instructed to crawl forwards and backwards, while maintaining lumbar stability.

❑ Hold the end position for longer (maximum of 8 seconds).

Supine floor bridge

Muscle group(s): Hip extensors, back extensors, abdominals
Phase/modality: Strength, balance, endurance
Equipment: None

Purpose

❑ To improve performance of gluteals and low back.

❑ To improve control of abdominal muscles.

❑ To challenge and enhance lumbar stability during hip extension.

Prerequisites

❑ Pain-free range of motion in hip extension.

❑ Ability to perform an abdominal hollow and brace.

Starting position

The client lies supine, with knees bent and feet flat on floor. Arms are held by the sides of the body. The client contracts the abdominals by pulling the navel upwards and inwards.

Correct performance

❑ Begin by lifting the hips up towards the ceiling until there is a straight line through the knees, hips and shoulders. The movement should be initiated with an abdominal brace and a contraction of the gluteals. Return to the start position.

❑ The movement is performed 6–10 times, before resting.

(a)   (b)

Figure 14.32. Supine floor bridge – (a) before, (b) after

Variations

❏ Arms across chest.

❏ Single leg.

❏ Feet on a stability ball.

❏ The end position may be held for up to 8 seconds.

Note: If the client experiences cramp in the hamstrings during the movement, the therapist should check that pelvic alignment is optimal, and correct if necessary. If the problem persists, the quadriceps should be stretched and more emphasis should be placed on initiating the movement with the gluteals and abdominals.

Supine hip extension: feet on ball

Muscle group(s): Hip extensors, abdominals

Phase/modality: Strength, balance, endurance

Equipment: Stability ball

Purpose

❏ To increase the strength of the hip extensors.

❏ To improve neuromuscular control of the lateral abdominal muscles, in preparation for larger kinetic chain movements.

❏ To improve whole body balance.

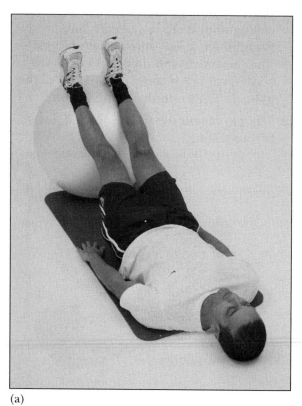

(a)

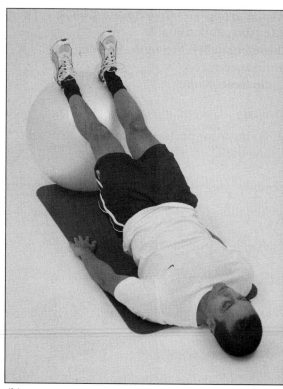

(b)

Figure 14.33. Supine hip extension: feet on ball – (a) before, (b) after

Prerequisites

❏ Good level of core strength.

❏ Optimal scapula control, to ensure retraction and depression.

❏ Normal hamstring length.

Starting position

The client lies supine, with legs straight and heels resting on a stability ball, hip-width apart. Part of the ball should be resting against the calf muscles. Arms are resting on the floor, beside the body. The client contracts the abdominals by pulling the navel upwards and inwards in preparation for the movement.

Correct performance

❏ Client braces the abdominals and performs hip extension by lifting the hips up, until a straight line is formed from the knees to the shoulders. The movement should be initiated by contracting the glutes.

❏ Return to the start position and perform a total of 8–10 repetitions.

❏ The therapist should observe the hips and spine for any faulty movements and correct if necessary. Excessive wobbling should be controlled through appropriate levels of abdominal bracing, and may indicate weakness in the lateral abdominals.

Variations

❏ The end position may be held for up to 8 seconds, to improve muscular endurance of the hip and back extensors.

❏ Eyes closed.

❏ Feet closer together on ball.

❏ Hands across chest.

❏ Adding knee flexion – as hip extension is performed, there is simultaneous knee flexion, by 'pulling' the ball in towards the glutes using the heels. Knee flexion should end in a position where the ball is close to the glutes (approximately 100° knee flexion). This is an advanced exercise.

Supine hip extension: torso on ball

Muscle group(s): Hip and back extensors, abdominals

Phase/modality: Strength, balance, endurance

Equipment: Stability ball

Purpose

❑ To increase the strength of the hip extensors.

❑ To improve neuromuscular control of the lateral abdominal muscles, in preparation for larger kinetic chain movements.

❑ To improve whole body balance.

Prerequisites

❑ Good level of core strength.

❑ Optimal scapula control, to ensure retraction and depression.

Starting position

❑ The client sits on the stability ball and rolls down, while comfortably placing the head, neck and shoulder blades on the ball, with both feet positioned straight ahead.

❑ The hips are lifted until they are in line with knees, and hands are placed across the chest. The hips should remain level (horizontally) throughout the exercise. The scapulae are slightly retracted and depressed and the abdominals are braced. The client contracts the abdominals by pulling the navel upwards and inwards in preparation for movement.

Correct performance

❑ Client begins to perform hip flexion by lowering the hips towards the ball, moving only as far as is comfortable. This movement is followed with hip extension, by pushing through the heels of the feet, to return to the start position. The movement should be done slowly and extension must be initiated through abdominal bracing and glute contraction.

❑ The therapist should observe the hips and shoulders to ensure they are level throughout the entire movement, and that proper spinal position is maintained throughout.

Variations

❑ Holding the end position, following extension, for up to 8 seconds, to improve muscular endurance.

(a)   (b)

Figure 14.34. Supine hip extension: torso on ball – (a) before, (b) after

❑ Eyes closed.

❑ Holding a weight on the legs.

Squat

Muscle group(s): Legs, abdominals, low back, shoulders

Phase/modality: Strength, balance, coordination

Equipment: None

Purpose

❑ To strengthen the legs and lumbo-pelvic-hip musculature.

❑ To improve lumbar stabilisation during functional movements.

❑ To enhance the body's ability to transfer force along the kinetic chain, during extension and flexion. Particularly useful for activities and sports where force is generated from the ground up.

Prerequisites

❑ If a lower- or upper-crossed posture is noted, a proper stretching programme must be completed before attempting this exercise, to ensure ideal lumbar alignment and stability.

(a)

(b)

Figure 14.35. Squat – (a) before, (b) after

❑ Good flexibility in the posterior thigh and leg muscles.

❑ Good core strength and stabilisation.

Starting position

In a standing position, client places the feet shoulder-width apart, with arms across chest and good postural alignment. The spine should remain in neutral alignment throughout the movement. The abdominals should be contracted by pulling the navel upwards and inwards, or by performing an abdominal brace.

Correct performance

❑ Client performs triple flexion of the hip, knee and ankle, and squats down to a position where the thighs are parallel with the floor. In this position, the knees should not overshoot the toes and should be tracking over the second toe of each foot (not bowing inwards or outwards). The spine is still in neutral alignment and the hips are pushed backwards to maintain balance over the feet.

❑ From this position, brace the abdominals further and contract the glutes, while performing triple extension of the ankle, knee and hip, to return to the start position. Perform 10–12 repetitions.

❑ It is important to contract the glutes at the beginning of the upward push, as this will allow the pelvis to initiate the movement, prior to the spine.

❑ The therapist should observe spinal alignment, knee position and the coordination of triple extension/flexion. There should be particular emphasis on the sequencing of abdominal and glute contraction at the start of the upward phase.

❑ If there is muscle weakness in the legs, the squat can be modified into a half- or quarter-squat, where the client completes only the range of motion available to them. Tightness in the calves may prevent full range of motion and these muscles should be stretched prior to attempting this exercise.

Variations

❑ If the client does not possess the coordination, balance or strength to perform the squat, this exercise may be regressed to the wall slide (see Phase 2, above, p. 231).

❑ Slower tempo.

❑ Use of a weighted barbell. This progression involves holding a barbell across the upper back, and requires adequate strength in shoulder abduction, along with good scapula control.

❑ Single-leg squat.

❑ Standing on a rocker-board/balance-board.

Lunge

Muscle group(s): Legs, abdominals, low back
Phase/modality: Strength, balance, coordination
Equipment: None

Purpose

❑ To strengthen the legs and lumbo-pelvic-hip musculature.

❑ To improve lumbar stabilisation during functional movements.

❑ To enhance the body's ability to transfer force along the kinetic chain, during extension and flexion. Particularly useful for activities and sports where force is generated from the ground up.

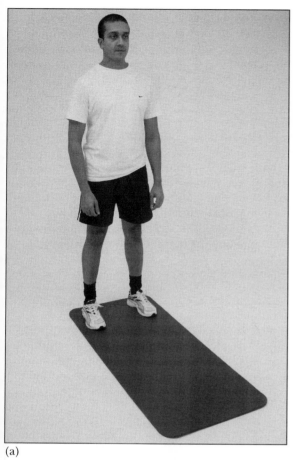

(a)

(b)

Figure 14.36. Lunge – (a) before, (b) after

❑ To improve overall balance and coordination.

Prerequisites

❑ If a lower- or upper-crossed posture is noted, a proper stretching programme must be completed before attempting this exercise, to ensure ideal lumbar alignment and stability.

❑ Good flexibility in the posterior thigh and leg muscles.

❑ The client must exhibit good core strength and stabilisation.

Starting position

In a standing position, client places the feet shoulder-width apart, allowing the arms to hang by the sides of the body and assuming good postural alignment. The spine should remain in neutral alignment throughout the movement. The abdominals should be contracted by pulling the navel upwards and inwards, or by performing an abdominal brace.

Correct performance

❑ Maintaining good spinal alignment, the client begins by stepping forwards and slightly laterally, allowing the hip to drop downwards and slightly forwards, until the thigh is almost parallel to the floor.

❏ From this position, the client contracts the abdominals and glutes and performs triple extension of the ankle, knee and hip, to return to an upright stance. Neutral spine alignment must be maintained throughout the movement.

❏ The movement is repeated on alternate legs, for a total of 8 repetitions each side.

Variations

❏ If the client does not possess the balance or coordination to perform this exercise, it can be regressed to a static lunge. In this exercise, the client maintains the forward position and lunges on the spot. Hands may be placed on a wall for extra support.

❏ Use of dumbbells.

❏ Walking lunge – the client lunges forwards, followed by a stepping through to the upright stance, followed by another lunge with the opposite leg. The movement is continued as a series of walking lunges.

❏ Balance-board lunge (advanced) – one foot may be placed on a balance-board, to perform static lunges.

❏ Backward lunge (advanced) – from an upright position, the client steps backwards, followed by a lunge back to the start position. The movement is alternated between legs.

Dead lift
Muscle group(s): Legs, abdominals, low back, shoulders
Phase/modality: Strength, balance, coordination
Equipment: Barbell

(a)

(b)

Figure 14.37. Dead lift – (a) before, (b) after

Purpose

❏ To strengthen the legs and lumbo-pelvic-hip musculature.

❏ To improve lumbar stabilisation during functional movements.

❏ To enhance the body's ability to transfer force along the kinetic chain, during extension and flexion. Particularly useful for activities and sports where force is generated from the ground up.

❏ To improve overall balance and coordination.

Prerequisites

❏ If a lower- or upper-crossed posture is noted, a proper stretching programme must be completed before attempting this exercise, to ensure ideal lumbar alignment and stability.

❏ Good flexibility in the posterior thigh and leg muscles.

❏ The client must exhibit good core strength and stabilisation.

Starting position

In a standing position, client places the feet shoulder-width apart, holding a barbell. The spine should remain in neutral throughout the movement. The client contracts the abdominals by pulling the navel upwards and inwards.

Correct performance

❏ Client performs triple flexion of the hip, knee and ankle, and bends down to a position where the thighs are almost parallel with the floor, as if to place the barbell on the floor. In this position, the knees should not overshoot the toes and should be tracking over the second toe of each foot (not bowing inwards or outwards). The spine is still in neutral alignment and the hips are pushed backwards to maintain balance over the feet.

❏ From this position, client braces the abdominals further and contracts the glutes while performing triple extension of the ankle, knee and hip, to return to the start position. Perform 10–12 repetitions.

❏ It is important to contract the glutes at the beginning of the upward push, as this will allow the pelvis to initiate the movement prior to the spine.

❏ The therapist should observe spinal alignment, knee position and the coordination of triple extension/flexion. There should be particular emphasis on the sequencing of abdominal and glute contraction at the start of the upward phase.

❏ If there is muscle weakness in the legs, the dead lift can be modified into a half- or quarter-lift, where the client completes only the range of motion available to them. Tightness in the calves may prevent full range of motion and these muscles should be stretched prior to attempting this exercise.

Variations

❏ Use of heavier weight.

❏ Use of unevenly weighted barbell.

Note: The dead-lift pattern is almost identical to the squat, except that the weight is lowered to the floor. This exercise (and the squat) is extremely functional for patients who exhibit faulty lifting and bending movement patterns, and can be adapted to incorporate load bearing where necessary.

Phase 4 exercises – Restoring functional power

Squat push
Muscle group(s): Total body
Phase/modality: Power, stabilisation, balance, coordination
Equipment: Medicine ball, dumb-bell

Purpose

❏ Improves concentric acceleration, dynamic stabilisation and eccentric deceleration of the entire kinetic chain.

❏ Enhances the body's ability to transfer force along the kinetic chain, during extension and flexion.

❏ Particularly useful for activities and sports where force is generated from the ground up, towards the upper extremities (for example, tennis, basketball, golf, boxing).

Prerequisites

❏ Client must demonstrate a good squat, dead-lift and shoulder-press pattern.

❏ Pain-free range of motion in shoulder flexion.

❏ If a lower- or upper-crossed posture is noted, a proper stretching programme must be completed before attempting this exercise, to ensure ideal lumbar alignment and stability.

❏ The client must exhibit good core strength and stabilisation.

(a)

(b)

Figure 14.38. Squat push – (a) before, (b) after

Starting position

Client is standing, with feet positioned about shoulder-width apart, holding the weight with both hands on the chest. The client contracts the abdominals by pulling the navel upwards and inwards, in preparation for the movement.

Correct performance

❑ Client begins the movement by squatting down to a point where the thighs are parallel to the floor. The abdominals are braced, ready for acceleration.

❑ Client accelerates the weight upwards, by focusing on the smooth integration of ankle dorsiflexion, knee and hip extension and shoulder flexion. The end position is where the arms are extended overhead and the body is in optimal postural alignment.

❑ Slowly return to the bottom position and repeat until the speed cannot be maintained, or when 12 repetitions have been completed.

❑ It is important to brace the abdominals just before the point of acceleration, to protect the spine from overextension at the top of the movement.

Variations

❑ Increase the weight.

❑ Perform a squat raise (see Chapter 8, Phase 4, p. 101).

Clean and press

Muscle group(s): Total body
Phase/modality: Power, strength, stabilisation, balance, coordination
Equipment: Barbell

Purpose

❑ Increases total body strength and power. It is important to remember that the strength and power developed here are completely relative to the posture of the client during the exercise and the range of motion that the client moves through.

❑ Enhances the body's ability to transfer force along the kinetic chain.

Prerequisites

❑ The client must exhibit good lifting/squatting technique and be able to perform the upright row and shoulder press exercises.

❑ If a lower- or upper-crossed posture is noted, a proper stretching programme must be completed before attempting this exercise, to ensure ideal lumbar alignment and stability.

❑ The client must exhibit good core strength and stabilisation.

❑ The client must be properly progressed through stability and strength phases, in order to ensure that there is adequate flexibility, core strength and time for adaptation, thereby reducing chance of injury.

❏ The therapist must have a justifiable reason and system of programme progression to implement this advanced

(a)

exercise. This exercise is useful in activities where there are distinct stages of link sequencing/power transfer – for example, lifting up a child and placing them into a high chair or during a tennis serve.

Starting position

❏ Client begins with feet shoulder-width apart and toes pointing forwards.

❏ Client flexes the knees and hips and bends down, grasping the barbell with both hands slightly wider than shoulder-width apart (palms facing body).

❏ The abdominals are braced in preparation for the movement.

(b)

(c)

Figure 14.39. Clean and press – (a) before, (b) during, (c) after

Correct performance

❑ Client performs an explosive triple extension movement in the lower extremities – ankle, knee and hip extension – and drives the elbows high, making sure the barbell travels in a vertical, linear fashion (close to body).

❑ As bar reaches shoulder height, client should externally rotate the arms and 'catch' the weight in front of the shoulders, simultaneously dropping into a half-squat position, to get under the weight. From here, the glutes are contracted to stand into a full upright position, with bar resting on the chest.

❑ The abdominals are braced again, sinking into a half-squat position to pre-stretch the glutes, and quickly following with another explosive movement, pushing the barbell up into a shoulder press. This movement should start from a glute contraction, as if pushing the floor away, and at the same time pushing the bar upwards. Stand tall at the top, with good posture and a strong abdominal brace.

❑ Carefully lower the barbell back to the ground. Reset posture and perform 6–8 repetitions.

Variations

❑ Increase the weight gradually, while maintaining good technique.

❑ This advanced exercise should be performed in 'chunks' before attempting the whole sequence. The client should be competent in performing a dead lift, upright row and shoulder press; these movements can then be combined successively. For example, once the dead lift can be performed, the client can attempt a dead lift with the upright row (also known as the 'clean'); once this double sequence is perfected, the final pressing movement can be added, to complete the entire motion.

Box jumps
Muscle group(s): Total body
Phase/modality: Power, strength, balance, coordination
Equipment: Box

Purpose

❑ To increase total body strength and power, and to enhance the body's ability to transfer force along the kinetic chain.

❑ To improve acceleration and deceleration mechanics.

❑ To enhance static, dynamic and reactive stabilisation.

Prerequisites

❑ The client should exhibit good squatting/lifting technique.

❑ A proper stretching programme must be completed before attempting this exercise, to ensure ideal lumbar alignment and stability.

❑ The client must exhibit good core strength and stabilisation.

❑ The client must be properly progressed through stability and strength phases, in order to ensure that there is adequate flexibility, core strength and time for adaptation, thereby reducing chance of injury.

Starting position

Following a thorough dynamic warm-up, the client stands in front of the box, with feet placed shoulder-width apart. The abdominals are contracted by pulling the navel upwards and inwards.

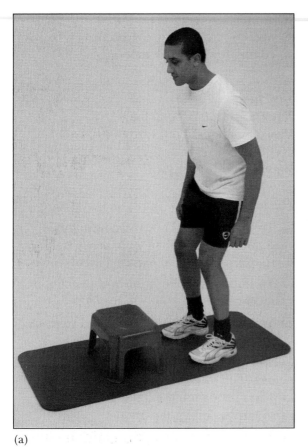 

(a)   (b)

Figure 14.40. Box jumps – (a) before, (b) after

Correct performance

❑ Client braces the abdominals, flexes the hips and knees slightly and, with both feet, jumps upwards and forwards onto the box, landing with feet parallel and shoulder-width apart. The landing should be flat-footed, with the force absorbed through the knee and hip. Once the force has been absorbed, the client should stand upright, in good postural alignment, looking straight ahead.

❑ The movement is repeated 8–10 times before resting.

Variations

❑ A jump-down can be performed, forwards or backwards. Jumps may also be performed sideways, to improve frontal plane power and stabilisation.

❑ Two-legged jump to one-legged landing; one-legged jump to two-legged landing; or one-legged jump to one-legged landing.

Multi-planar hops
Muscle group(s): Total body
Phase/modality: Power, strength, stabilisation, balance
Equipment: None

(a)

(b)

(c)

(d)

Figure 14.41. Multi-planar hops – (a) start, (b) sagittal plane hop, (c) frontal plane hop, (d) transverse plane hop

Purpose

- To increase multi-planar neuromuscular stability.
- To increase total body strength and power, and to enhance the body's ability to transfer force along the kinetic chain.
- To improve acceleration and deceleration mechanics.

Prerequisites

- The client must be able to perform a two-legged static or box jump and a single-leg balance, with optimum posture.
- A proper stretching programme must be completed before attempting this exercise, to ensure ideal lumbar alignment and stability.
- The client must exhibit good core strength and stabilisation.
- The client must be properly progressed through stability and strength phases, in order to ensure that there is adequate flexibility, core strength and time for adaptation, thereby reducing chance of injury.

Starting position

The client contracts the abdominals, by pulling the navel upwards and inwards, and stands on one leg in preparation for the movement.

Correct performance

- The client flexes the hip and knee slightly, followed by an explosive extension of the hip and knee to jump forwards and land on the opposite leg. Optimal posture must be maintained throughout the movement.
- The landing is stabilised for 3–4 seconds, while assuming an upright stance. The client then flexes the hip and knee again

and performs another explosive extension, returning to the start position. The movement is performed 6–8 times before swapping legs.

- The above format is used to perform side-to-side hops (frontal plane) and turning hops (transverse plane), where a 90° turn is performed.

Variations

If the client does not possess enough strength or balance, this exercise may be regressed to a multi-planar jump, using two legs.

High-low wood-chop

Muscle group(s): Total body
Phase/modality: Power, strength, stabilisation, balance
Equipment: Cable, exercise band

Purpose

- To integrate the lower extremity into rotational movement patterns.
- To enhance lumbar stabilisation through functional whole body movement.
- To re-educate the torso rotation mechanism and strengthen the oblique musculature.

Prerequisites

- Functional flexibility of the shoulder/arm without compensation in the spine.
- Adequate strength and flexibility in the anterior and lateral abdominals, and lumbar spine.
- Adequate leg strength and flexibility.

Starting position

- Client starts in a standing position, with a shoulder-width stance, facing away from

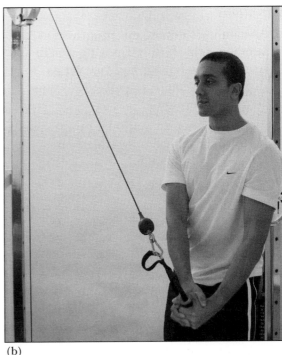

(a)   (b)

Figure 14.42. High-low wood-chop – (a) before, (b) after

the cable machine and holding the handle with both hands above the right shoulder. In this position, the left hand should grip the handle first, with the right hand over the top of the left hand.

❏ Good spinal alignment should be maintained, with a strong abdominal brace, prior to the movement.

Correct performance

❏ Starting from optimal posture, client initiates a rotational movement, from the trunk outwards, towards the left. Do not pull with the shoulders or arms. Client pulls the cable handle downwards and across the body.

❏ Use a slow tempo to start with. Avoid beginning the movement from a forward flexed position.

❏ Do not push so quickly that the shoulders round forwards; generate movement from the core instead of the arms.

❏ Allow the torso and arms to move back to the start position and repeat up to 10 times.

❏ This exercise should be progressed to a functional power movement, by accelerating through the chop downwards and slowly returning to the start. Adding speed in this way requires a high level of core strength and stabilisation, combined with perfect movement technique, and is suitable only for high-performance conditioning programmes (sport-specific).

Variations

❑ As stability is developed, progress to lateral weight shifting (moving weight from right to left leg and vice versa), so that the movement resembles a 'wood-chopping' motion.

❑ The wood-chop may also be progressed by performing the exercise seated on a stability ball. This will increase awareness of the obliques to a greater extent, providing the ball is kept still throughout the movement.

❑ LOW-HIGH WOOD-CHOP – cable is adjusted so that the line of resistance starts low and moves high.

❑ LATERAL WOOD-CHOP – cable is adjusted so that the line of resistance is horizontal.

GLOSSARY

Abduction	Movement away from the midline of the body.
Adduction	Movement towards the midline of the body.
Agonist	A muscle whose action is opposed by another muscle (antagonist).
Antagonist	A muscle that works in opposition to another muscle (agonist).
Anterior	Towards the front of the body.
Atrophy	A decrease in muscle size due to inactivity.
Biomechanics	The mechanics of biological movement, involving forces that arise from or outside of a body.
Bow legs	Outward bowing of legs. Structural bow legs involves actual bowing of the bones; postural bow legs is an apparent bowing resulting from a combination of pronation of the feet, hyperextension of the knees and medial rotation of the hips.
Centre of gravity	The point at which the three midplanes of the body intersect. In ideal postural alignment, it is considered to be slightly anterior to the first/second sacral segment.
Circumduction	Circular movement of a joint about 360 degrees.
Contraction	An increase in muscle tension, with or without change in overall muscle length.
Contralateral	The opposite side of the body.
Distal	Away from the centre of the body or reference point.
Dorsal	Towards the back of the body.
Dorsiflexion	Ankle joint extension.
Dysfunction	Inability to function properly; functional impairment.
Eversion	Turning of the foot outwards away from the body; a combination of pronation and forefoot abduction.

Extension	An increase in the angle on the joint; return from flexion.
Fascia	A fibrous membrane that covers, supports and separates muscles.
Fixation	The application of stabilisation, support or counter-pressure.
Flexion	A reduction in the angle of the joint.
Force-couple	Action of two forces in opposite directions to produce rotation around a joint.
Frontal plane	A vertical plane extending from side to side, dividing the body into an anterior and a posterior portion.
Functional exercise	Exercises designed to prepare an individual for a specific task.
Genu valgum	Knock knees.
Genu varum	Bow legs.
Hyperextension	Movement beyond the normal range of joint motion in extension.
Inferior	Towards the bottom of the body or a position below a reference point.
Inversion	Turning of the foot inwards towards the body: a combination of supination and forefoot adduction.
Ipsilateral	On the same side of the body.
Isometric exercise	An exercise in which a muscle contracts against resistance, but does not change in length.
Knock knees	Knees touch with feet apart.
Kyphosis	An excessive posterior curve, normally found in the thoracic region of the spine.
Lateral	Positioned towards the outside of the body or away from the midline of the body.
Lateral flexion	Side bending.
Lordosis	An excessive anterior curve, usually found in the lumbar region of the spine.
Medial	Towards the centre or closer to the midline of the body.
Mobility	Ability to move freely; often regarded as a combination of flexibility and coordination.
Muscle balance	A balance of strength of opposing muscles acting on a joint, providing ideal alignment for stabilisation and movement.
Muscle imbalance	Unequal strength of opposing muscles, leading to faulty alignment and movement.

Muscular endurance	The ability to perform repetitive muscular contractions against resistance for an extended period of time.
Muscular strength	The ability of a muscle to generate force against resistance.
Neuromuscular control	The interactions of the nervous and muscular systems to create coordinated movement.
Neutral spine	A position or range of movement somewhere between full flexion and full extension of the spine, as defined by the client; it is dependent on existing symptoms, pathology and musculoskeletal restrictions.
Overstretch weakness	Weakness in a multi-joint muscle resulting from repetitive movements or habitual postures that elongate a muscle beyond its normal length.
Pelvic tilt	An anterior (forward), posterior (backward) or lateral (sideways) tilt of the pelvis from a neutral position.
Peripheral	Towards the surface of the body.
Plantar flexion	Ankle joint flexion.
Plumb line	A vertical line of reference that represents the line of gravity; used in postural assessment.
Posterior	Towards the back of the body.
Power	Ability to generate large amounts of force against resistance in a short period of time.
Progression	A gradual increase in the level and intensity of exercise.
Pronation	Rotation of the arm to position the palm downwards; rotation of the foot to position the sole laterally.
Prone	Lying face downwards.
Proprioception	The ability to determine the position of a joint in space.
Proximal	Towards or near the centre of the body or reference point.
Range of motion	The range through which a joint can move.
Resistance	A force that hinders motion.
Rotation	Movement around a longitudinal axis in the transverse plane.
Sagittal plane	A vertical plane extending from front to back, dividing the body into right and left halves.
Scapulohumeral rhythm	The movement of the scapula relative to the movement of the humerus throughout a full range of flexion/abduction.
Scoliosis	Lateral curvature of the spine; may be C-shaped or S-shaped.

Shortness	Tightness; a slight to moderate decrease in muscle length.
Stability	The capacity to provide support.
Strain	The extent of deformation of a tissue under loading.
Stress	Any force that tends to distort a body.
Stretch	To elongate or increase in length.
Subjective	Perceived by the individual; not evident to the examiner.
Superior	Towards the top of the body or a position above a reference point.
Supination	Rotation of the arm to position the palm upwards; rotation of the foot to position the sole medially.
Supine	Lying face upwards.
Sway-back	A faulty postural alignment in which there is posterior displacement of the upper trunk and anterior displacement of the pelvis.
Tension	The effective force generated by a muscle.
Transverse plane	A horizontal plane dividing the body into upper and lower portions.

SUGGESTED READING

Behnke, R.S., 2001. *Kinetic Anatomy*, Champaign, IL: Human Kinetics.

Brooks, Douglas S., 1998. *Program Design for Personal Trainers. Bridging Theory into Application.* Human Kinetics, Champaign, IL.

Brukner, Peter and Khan, Karim, 2002. *Clinical Sports Medicine*, revised 2nd edn. McGraw-Hill.

Chaitow, Leon and DeLany, Judith Walker, 2002. *Clinical Application of Neuromuscular Techniques: The Lower Body*, London: Churchill Livingstone, vol. 2.

Chek, P., 2000. *Movement that Matters*, Encinitas, CA: The C.H.E.K. Institute.

Corning-Creager, Caroline, 1996. *Therapeutic Exercises using Foam Rollers*, Executive Physical Therapy, Inc.

Dick, Frank W., 1997. *Sports Training Principles*, 3rd edn, London: A & C Black.

Feldenkrais, Moshe, 1996. *Mindful Spontaneity: Lessons in the Feldenkrais Method*, North Atlantic Books.

Hamilton, Nancy and Luttgens, Kathryn, 2002. *Kinesiology. Scientific Basis of Human Movement*, international edn, McGraw-Hill.

Hanna, Thomas, 1988. *Somatics: Reawakening the Mind's Control of Movement, Flexibility and Health*, Cambridge, MA: Perseus.

Hoppenfeld, Stanley, 1976. *Physical Examination of the Spine and Extremities*, Upper Saddle River, NJ: Prentice Hall.

Hanna, Thomas, 1993. *The Body of Life – creating new pathways for sensory awareness and fluid movement*, Healing Arts Press.

Kendall, Florence, McCreary, Elizabeth and Provance, Patricia, 1993. *Muscles Testing and Function: 4th edn Posture and Pain*, Philadelphia, PA: Lippincott Williams and Wilkins.

Kingston, Bernard, 2000. *Understanding Joints: A Practical Guide to Their Structure and Function*, Cheltenham, UK: Nelson Thornes.

McGill, Stuart, 2002. *Low Back Disorders. Evidence-Based Prevention and Rehabilitation*, Champaign, IL: Human Kinetics.

Norris, Christopher M., 2000. *Back Stability*, Champaign, IL: Human Kinetics.

Posner-Mayer, J., 1995. *Swiss Ball Applications for Orthopedic and Sports Medicine*, Denver, CO: Ball Dynamics International Inc.

Prentice, William, 1999. *Rehabilitation Techniques*, 3rd edn, McGraw-Hill.

Richardson, Carolyn et al., 2000. *Therapeutic Exercise for Spinal Segmental Stabilization in the Low Back. Scientific Basis and Clinical Approach*, London: Churchill Livingstone.

Sahramann, Shirley, 2002. *Diagnosis and Treatment of Movement Impairment Syndromes*, St Louis, MO. Mosby Inc.

Whittle, Michael, 2001. *Gait Analysis, an introduction*, 3rd edn, Oxford: Butterworth Heinemann.

INDEX

Note: Bold figures indicate definition of terms in glossary.